Changing Lifestyles: Trading in the Rat Race for a Sail around the World

By Kimberly Brown

To view a full list of other publications by Kimberly Brown, please visit the appendix at the end of the book.

For Suzi Harkola. This book wouldn't be here if it wasn't for your patience and kindness. Thank you.

Introduction

This book is a chronological journey, beginning with my husband, Simon, and I deciding that we *might* want to sell up and sail from England around the world. You'll read about our thoughts and emotions, as well as recognition of the challenges and our many adventures on the first part of our journey, which was sailing the Mediterranean and Caribbean and crossing the Atlantic to dock in the States.

A major decision was the impact this journey would have on our three-year-old daughter, Sienna. How would she adapt to sailing around the world on a 56′ sailboat? Saying "no more" to the rat race at the top of our game wasn't easy either. The fact that we had minimal experience with sailboats also makes our story a bit unconventional.

Please read through the blog at https://SailingBritican.com to follow our journey as we continue around the world. Contact and follow us on:

- Twitter: SailingBritican
- Facebook: Facebook.com/SailingBritican
- Google+: Google.com/+SailingBritican
- LinkedIn: http://www.linkedin.com/in/kim-brown-6a578b23
- Pinterest: http://www.pinterest.com/kbrown0149
- YouTube: http://www.youtube.com/c/Sailingbritican

Chapter 1: Saying "screw it" to my life!

Have you ever had a situation when things get so bad that you just can't handle them anymore? You've toyed with making a change for years, but never did anything, and then one day you feel as if you're going to burst if something doesn't change?

Well, I've been living like that for years. Ironically, I've made massive changes to my life, yet they haven't been enough. Let me give you a very quick update on where I was, where I am now and how I'm finally saying "screw it." You'll discover how my decision to sell all my possessions, buy a 56' Oyster yacht and take my hubby and daughter on a sailing trip of a lifetime transpired.

First, I quit my job.

In 2011, I was frustrated, exhausted, bored, unchallenged and seriously lacking fulfillment. Furthermore, my health was declining – mentally and physically. Quitting my job was a bit difficult, as I owned 50 percent of the company I worked for, but that's another story.

I decided to explore ways to live a more enjoyable journey. Up until then I had controlled, forced, cajoled and pushed my way through life. If I wanted something I'd go get it, regardless of whether the journey or the final destination was enjoyable.

Thankfully I woke up and realized that if the journey isn't good then the destination won't be rewarding either. This whole idea of working hard until you're 65 and then you can relax is a total joke. Many people I've met who worked hard and retire either die or lose their sense of purpose, falling into deep depression. And then they wonder why they spent years being miserable!

Not for me. No way. I took a jump off the end of the rat race pier.

I'd love to say that my life became fun, enjoyable and full of great experiences, but it didn't. Just because you change the scenery YOU don't change. I thought that if I removed the thing that made me so miserable, my job, that I'd instantly be happy. Not the case.

It took a while, but I eventually realized that I had to change me. I had to change what I thought about me, my life, the world and my *relationship* with me, my life and the world. What a growth spurt. It was an emotional journey that led to some low lows and some high highs.

After quite some time, I eventually leveled out a bit. I understood more about who I was, what I wanted and how I wanted to go forward through the rest of my life. My main objective was to enjoy the journey – to increase my overall fulfillment of life.

Thankfully, I've made quite a bit of progress, but it seems like the more I learn about me, the more I realize that I'm still not in the right place doing the right things.

Doing the right things for the wrong reasons?

I started my company in 2004 because I wanted to get rich and I also wanted to be a writer. Rather than write a book or take up journalism I instead started my own company. I was told throughout school that I was a good writer but had no clue about grammar or spelling. Starting my own company would allow me to write because I'd be the one who "okays" it. Funny way of thinking, isn't it?

So I started a finance company. Did I mention that I'm not good at math either, and as far as finance is concerned I'm really not interested in it (other than having lots of money). After eight years, I found myself burned out and miserable. On the positive side, the company enabled me to write everything – the website, promotional materials, guides and I even published quite a few books! That led to me writing for many

9

popular magazines. By the time I left I'd been published in over 50 publications including the *NY Times*, *Times* and loads of magazines.

By now, I figured it all out – errrr, not really!

So you'd think that I'd quit my job and then become a writer – yes? No. I'm not a writer …but I do love writing! So once I left my job I started a couple of blogs (for fun) and then offered management consultancy and started a couple more companies. I bombed at the consultancy – couldn't handle it. It was too much like working at my company. As for the companies I started, they were interesting, but there was no real challenge. I've realized that just because you're good at something doesn't mean that you need to do it for the rest of your life.

For the next couple of years I bumbled around doing this and that. For the most part, I really worked on getting myself into a better place. I learned so much about me. And I learned to like who I am.

So, as the title suggests, I finally said "screw it." The pain had become too much for me to bear. I lived a life I thought I was supposed to live based on my past conditioning, and now that I took the time out to figure out who I am, I realized it was time to change.

What about sailing? Where's that fit in?

For fun, I love to sail. I'm not the best sailor in the world and I do get seasick. However, for the past 15 years I've gone on a sailing holiday most years, and every time we've had to return home I've cried. In 2011 we purchased a Moody 34.6' yacht, and I would rather be on that than doing anything else.

My dream has been to sail around the world, but at the time it was only a dream. It's what you tell people when they ask you what you'd do if you won the lottery. It's not something you actually ever do – is it?

This is where the "screw it" comes in. I'm not attached to my house (or the things in it), I think the amount of commercialism in the world is distracting us from what's most important, and I'm craving homemade food from local sources. So…logically, what should I do?

Yep, and here's decision number one: I sold everything I had, bought the biggest yacht I could afford and set sail with Simon and Sienna. And I have been writing a blog that details about my adventures, my doubts, my fears, my successes, my learning lessons and even some practical tips for those who want to say "screw it" too.

Upon my announcement to sell up and sail around the world, the reactions from others covered a wide spectrum. One relative yelled out, "you're going to die," and another jumped up and down with excitement screaming, "can I come too!?"

When hearing our decision, the majority of people took a stern stance, became very serious and questioned me about Sienna's schooling.

My response was that it's very common now days to home-school, so that's what we'll do. My declaration came with such confidence that I avoided any kind of argument.

Otherwise, most friends and family expressed their sadness to see us leave but they were also our biggest supporters. I kept reminding them that our voyage won't be forever, we'll be making periodic visits home, I'll be writing about our adventures and they can join us on a leg of our journey at any time.

An overnight decision that took 10 years.

Let me back up a wee bit and give you some more background to our monumental decision to change the course of our lives.

Previous to our daughter's birth, my husband and I enjoyed a yearly sailing flotilla holiday in the Mediterranean or Caribbean. On any other vacation, Simon and I would be eager to return to our "normal" life, but not when we went sailing! Sailing was different – it was fun, free, fresh and enjoyable. It was a way to switch off yet still be active. Ever since our first flotilla holiday we dreamed of sailing around the world. And going to an annual boat show helped us to dream big.

One year after Sienna was born, and too frightened to take a baby on a sailing vacation, we went to the south coast with a friend and my father-in-law. Simon and I stole a few minutes while Sienna was sleeping and sat in a marina looking at boats – both moored up and some out sailing. A burning fire was gaining momentum in us. Being unsatisfied with a beach vacation I said to Simon, "We're not going to endure another vacation on land! Let's get a boat. It's now or never."

We discussed the idea of getting a boat to practice with for a while and then when we made our millions we could buy an Oyster yacht and sail around the world. And when we did that we were going to name her *Britican* – a combination of British and American. Simon is British, I'm American and our daughter has dual citizenship.

Our first sailboat "baby" – a 34.6′ Moody.

Three months later, and after finding a bargain deal on eBay, Simon flew up to Oban, Scotland, hired a skipper and took possession of a 34.5′ Moody sailboat named *Selene*. Skipper Mike, a recommended contact, and Simon brought *Selene* down to Port Solent, a marina on the south coast of England.

The decision was a good one, as we were out sailing every weekend. Luckily for us, we went out over the winter and the Solent was rather quiet in comparison to the summer months. We were able to make a real mess of things without too many onlookers!

For the first few months of taking *Selene* out, I would have minor panic attacks. My mind would race – will we be able to leave our berth without hitting something? Will we moor up in the lock without hitting someone? What if we take on water? What if we sink? What if we need help? What if we sail somewhere and there's no space for us?

Over time, my panic attacks reduced in size and soon I was able to moor the boat myself. Surprise, surprise.

Unfortunately we had to live in the real world, too.

Enjoying *Selene* on the weekends was great, but at the time I had a job that required my attention, too. And to make matters worse, my employer was me (and my business partner). Some people like to start their own companies for the freedom it provides. Somewhere along the line I messed up because my company was more of a ball and chain rather than a vehicle to enjoy freedom.

After eight years of growing my company, I felt stuck, frustrated, physically weak and nearing a burn out. After considering the path I was on I knew that if I didn't make a change my health was going to force me to alter course. It was the hardest thing I've ever done, but I decided to leave my company.

Not knowing for sure what was going to happen, I made a leap of faith and entered a series of negotiations with my business partner. It felt as if I was going through a divorce and losing everything that identified who I was. In the end, we agreed to a solution where my partner purchased a percentage of my shares through a cash sum and deferred cash over two years.

You would think that my opportunity to sell up and sail away presented itself with the exit from my business, but that's not the case. After leaving my company I was terribly lost. I didn't know who I was or what I wanted. Every day I kept working from 8am until 6pm on various small personal projects, just because I didn't know what else to do.

My main focus was to figure out how to make money while worrying about what to do with my life. I did a serious amount of soul searching and I started to realize that my life was a product of what society deemed to be successful – I made lots of money. It wasn't what I deemed to be successful. To me, success is being happy. I surely wasn't happy!

Looking back, all my decisions were based upon what I should and shouldn't do. Nothing was based on what I wanted to do. For example, in high school I wanted to be an artist/writer yet I was told "you'll never make money doing that – become an accountant."

I don't regret my life path but I wouldn't wish it on anyone either. It's hard looking back and realizing that your ladder was against the wrong building!

After a couple years of consulting and trying to find a purpose in life, I finally came to the conclusion that perhaps it's best for me to do something drastically different. It just wasn't working – consulting was easy but it wasn't enjoyable. Some thoughts included becoming a fisher woman in Fiji, building houses in Africa or, of course, my personal favorite, sailing around the world.

At the same time, we were in the process of selling our house and moving to somewhere on the south coast. We looked for months to find the right house, but nothing seemed right. Our plan was to move closer to the boat so that we could sail even more.

And due to my soul searching, I really started to analyze what I liked and didn't like about my current lifestyle. I realized that I didn't like my eating habits – eating out often, processed food and non-nutritious meals. I was tired of physically crashing in front of the TV at 7pm and using a few glasses of wine to keep me awake until 10pm. Furthermore, I started to question why we had such a big house with so much stuff.

None of the stuff mattered to me – I just had the house because that's what you do when you grow up. You get a bigger and bigger house to fill it with more and more stuff. And then you have to spend your time cleaning it. Nothing made sense to me anymore.

I was tired, frustrated and ready to change in my life.

And then it happened. I said to Simon, "I'm ready for a change. Let's sell our house, use our retirement fund, buy a boat and sail around the world. I don't know how we're going to afford it in the long term, but we'll figure it out."

Both hubby and I pondered the decision for a few days. Although it was overwhelming and scary, it was also exciting – very exciting. Almost instantly, everything started to flow. We found the perfect boat, our house sold immediately, we figured out a way to afford the boat, and life started to be worth living again.

We lined up various courses we needed to take before we took sail, including a radio course, two extensive first aid for boater courses, a week-long engine maintenance and repair course and completion of Simon's Ocean Masters course.

Chapter 2: Health issues and cleaning the closet

At the time, I was 39, Simon 47 and Sienna 3 1/2. I kept thinking, "Are we really healthy right now?" Asking that question and getting a genuine answer – from myself – was quite difficult. Instead of ignoring our health I decided the time had come to really examine it.

As a whole, the family seemed to be okay. There were no chronic problems or immune system issues that I was aware of. We all had a cold here and there but for the most part we were up and running around like everyone else we knew. Hubby had some chest issues – coughing and a touch of asthma. My daughter suffered from eczema occasionally, and I assumed my lack of energy and aches came with my age.

What's odd is that I would have never questioned my health if it weren't for our upcoming adventure. A part of me was so excited to finally set sail that I wanted to ensure that we were all in the best shape we could be. For the first time in my life I wanted to be proactive about my health. Looking back, it sounds crazy that I didn't consider my health to be important, but if you feel okay you don't really question it – do you?

That being said, I was shocked and embarrassed to discover how unhealthy we actually were.

Another thing that ran through my mind was, "Do we need to get ourselves into better shape before we go?" I was having visions of my hubby or daughter being ill and us being forced to visit a dirty medical shack in a Third World country. And I started to panic about cooking. What are we going to eat? We wouldn't have the luxury of ready meals. I had avoided the wholesome mom thing and opted for processed quick foods. On our boat we'd not only have to cook, but we'd be limited by local food choices. I also wondered how my energy levels would cope with such a drastic change in temperature, environment, culture, food...a change in everything, really.

When I was pregnant I remember thinking, if I ever do this again, I'm going to get myself into better shape. Pregnancy was a hard experience for me – I felt physically exhausted, unfit and drained. If only I had prepared for it I could have increased my fitness levels, eaten better foods and worked on ways to maintain my energy. This sailing trip around the world is similar. I know it's coming and I have time to prepare.

But how do you figure out if you're healthy?

At first I thought I'd see a doctor and get a checkup, but I quickly decided against it. The doctor was going to simply look us over – it doesn't take a rocket scientist to know that our hearts are beating, our skin looks healthy and we're functioning to a normal standard. Doctors are great for finding issues and emergencies, but when it comes to being proactive that's usually not how the medical system works.

As fate would have it, a girlfriend mentioned a session she had with a nutritionist, and I instantly knew that was one way forward. Within a week I was able to have the nutritionist, Helen Bowen of Oxford, come to our house.

Helen settled at our dining room table with her computer, Asyra machine (energy system bio-feedback system) and notepad. Previous to her arrival Simon and I filled out a standard question form asking for a medical history, complaints and our typical eating routines. For the first part of the session, Helen went through the questionnaire to get an idea of the lifestyle we led. We had a nice chat and it felt good to openly discuss how I physically felt.

The next step was to hold two metal rods that were hooked up through wires to Helen's computer. I felt a very light buzz when holding the rods, but it was barely noticeable. Helen ran the Asyra tests, each one lasting about one minute. By holding the rods my body was tested for about 25 medical and nutritional conditions, including functioning of 40 major organs, dental profile, toxicity, emotional stressors and environmental sensitivity. The whole gamut of anything health-related you could think of!

I was absolutely flabbergasted by the results. Not only did the machine tell me what foods weakened or stressed my body, but it also noted that I had an issue with my ears (something I forgot to mention to Helen initially) and a chronic candida issue.

Furthermore, Helen asked me what was wrong with my wrists. Still feeling astonished I explained that I was doing the downward dog pose in yoga and I overdid it. I did too many and it stressed my wrists out. I couldn't believe these little rods could look through my body and see everything – even my achy wrists!

I'm not particularly a believer or non-believer of anything. I go with the flow and if something seems to work or I'm benefiting from it, I tend to be open to it. Heck, it doesn't hurt to try new things – if you do the same things you've always done, you'll get the same results.

How did my husband and daughter fare? I was mortified to discover our sugar intake was seriously too high, our protein levels were way too low and we were all heading down a path toward eventual health complications.

Sitting at the table hearing the results for my daughter made me sick. Growing up with a stay-at-home mom who made me homemade food was a blessing that I only now can appreciate. I instantly felt like the worst mother in the world – what was I putting in my precious daughter's body?

I was a workaholic, over-achieving business freak. I never had time to prepare good food – I was always on the run, so when it came to my daughter, she got the best I could buy, but it wasn't homemade.

Sienna's readings had terribly high preservatives, Aspartame, sugar and low levels of protein and good stuff. Hopefully all the love I've poured on her will make up for the lack of nutrition I provided.

We made some drastic changes. The family began to eat way more vegetables, far less bread and pasta (gluten) and we no longer buy anything processed. We added a couple of supplements to our daily routine to also get our bodies back on track. It's been a very hard blow to us but I know that our changes have enabled us to move forward in a dramatically healthier manner. And I've learned to cook!

So, what's the plan?

Our plan was to leave England by the end of April 2014.

Here's the chronology of events:

- go to Palma, Mallorca, an island off the mainland of Spain, to see the boat, an Oyster 56-footer

- instruct a survey

- have the boat moved to Barcelona (and purchase it as she's moving – some sort of tax reason)

- pull her out of the water so she can dry out before we set off – we've been told that boats need to dry out for a month or so every year to prevent osmosis

- complete the sale of our house

- move my father-in-law, Keith, into his 2-bed flat. (Keith lived in an apartment attached to the house we were selling)

- fly over to North Carolina to see my family for the holidays

- cram in all of our courses

- get my British citizenship to make sailing around the EU easier

- find a pre-school to put our daughter in while we do the courses

- sell our current boat and car

Clearing out my closet – in more ways than one!

From the overwhelming amount of tasks that needed to be performed, I have a few that stand out as major stressors. The ones that niggled at me strongest were getting my British passport (taking the "Life in the UK Test," filling out a huge form and paying loads of money), sorting out my taxes and clearing out my closet.

Although I lived in the UK for over 15 years I never felt the need to become a British citizen – my passport had a stamp that allowed me to work and come and go as I pleased. However, flying and sailing around the EU using an American passport could cause visa fees, more paperwork and more headaches. Getting my British passport simply made things easier. Furthermore, when I travel in and out of the UK I can finally get in the fast lane through border patrol!

And my taxes are always an annoyance. Throughout the year I stuff receipts into a big box and then feel horrified when I have to go through all of them and figure out my expenses for the year.

Then, my closet – the largest stressor of them all. I must have had over 150 pairs of shoes alone!

Face your stressors right in the eye and tackle them first!

Many people procrastinate when it comes to doing things they don't like. I suppose it can be said that I've procrastinated for 15 years to get my British passport, but I like to think I simply didn't need it. As for my taxes, if my life was carrying on as normal I'd wait until the very last week to send them over to my accountant.

The closet?! Well… that's just a beast that I pretended didn't exist.

That being said, our plans to sell up and sail forced me to reprioritize everything in my life, and I mean everything. I had to do things that I really didn't want to do.

In a strange way it felt liberating. Rather than having something haunting me over my shoulder I looked right into my stressors' eyes and said, "Let's get you sorted." Instead of living my normal routine and its related stressors, I actually had to deal with them rather than live with them.

Switching lifestyles helped me clear out my closet in more ways than one. The process forced me to look at my life, with all its stuff, with different eyes. Things that continuously haunted me are finally being dealt with.

Chapter 3: Getting the boat of our dreams

A reoccurring pattern seems to happen in our large purchase decisions. Invariably we always go after something that is slightly out of our reach. In the past we've gone after houses that were a wee bit too much – we'd have to pull out all the stops to get it, but when we wanted it, we usually found the money. Oddly, we've never found something and thought, "Yeah, we can easily buy that," and then we buy it.

With our sell up and sail plans, our negotiations on a 56' yacht were almost at breaking point. The price had gone back and forth five times and, although we were getting an extremely incredible deal, it was still too much. We could easily buy the boat, but if we paid the heavily negotiated price we'd have very little to live.

However…and this is pivotal…we knew that if we sold our current boat quickly, we'd be good to go. The question was, how quickly could we sell our boat? Some boats sell in months and others take years.

Part of me wanted to say "screw it – let's buy the boat and pray that our boat sells quickly," and another voice said, "screw it – forget this great deal…there's something better out there."

Who needs the exact dream boat anyway? Why stretch ourselves to breaking point when it's going to cause us financial worry? Why get an amazing deal if the journey won't be as amazing. Negotiations on our dream yacht just weren't working. It was impossible for us to buy the 56' Oyster yacht we wanted AND have enough money to sail around the world with her.

It was time to consider another boat. And then everything changed.

Our "solve-every-problem" broker asked us about having the option of making a final deferred payment. In short, we could pay for 90 percent of the boat and defer about 10 percent to give us breathing space. We'd still be able to take possession of the boat – we'd just owe the previous owner a final sum within a set time frame.

Surely our current boat would sell within a year. And the payment for that boat would clear our final debt with the seller of the new boat. And even if we didn't sell the boat, if all else fails we'd have some savings. We had the money.

My shoulders relaxed a bit but my jaw tightened. The discomfort I felt in my mouth alone would be enough to send some people to the loony bin. Every tooth in my mouth was untouchable – I couldn't eat. I couldn't chew. My whole jaw was involuntarily wound up tight. I couldn't even talk normally.

I'm prone to stress but it's always manifested in my shoulders – this must be a different kind of stress!

Meditation, EFT and wine.

Desperate for relief, I did a stress releasing guided meditation to unearth why I was so wound up. I kept drawing a blank when the audio woman calmly intoned, "Let any beliefs, images, ideas come to mind when you focus on the pain." And throughout the day I'd watch my thoughts wondering what was causing this tension, but I'd see nothing. It's as if I had this underlying switch – the freak-out switch – and once it was turned on, it was on.

After the meditation I tried Emotional Freedom Technique (EFT). It's a way to short-circuit your nervous system. Someone mentioned it so I looked up how to do it on YouTube. While thinking of the issue, you tap on various points on your body to shock your body into removing the stress, pain or issue. I must admit that I was surprised to feel some relief, but it wasn't long until the pain resumed to full strength.

After a bit of wine, my ultimate medicine of choice, I felt a bit more ease in my jaw. I suppose the alcohol got in there and relaxed some of the muscles a bit.

I don't want to sound ungrateful and complain that I'm suffering stress because I decided to sell everything I own and sail around the world. On the other hand, I was in pain – physical pain. I saw no logical way of alleviating my body's reaction to me smashing all my comfort zones. It's like I'd thrown my body into a raging river, carried along for a ride that I couldn't get off of.

I wanted to focus on the exciting adventures ahead – soaking up the warm sun rays, swimming in the blue waters and enjoying local fresh food. I wanted to visualize new friends, exciting new places to visit and the closeness that our family will experience. I wanted to play out in my mind the friends who would visit, the laughs we'd enjoy and the memories we'd make. But none of that came through with my present body state. My whole body was a bag of nerves, vibrating all sanity away from me.

I can totally understand why people stay in their comfort zones! I felt a similar way when I started my company – for months I was physically unwell. My shoulders were tight, my breath shallow, my tummy in knots and my mental outlook shadowed with greyness.

I knew that I must find a way to live the dream and enjoy living it. I searched to find a way to break out of my comfort zone and get my body to agree to dance or flow through life rather than turn into a bag of nerves! I don't want to paddle upstream – I want to be comfortable flowing down the raging river. I so hope that my heart is able to weather this ride.

Everything was going well...

Before leaving England for our sell up and sail around the world adventure, we needed to make sure my father-in-law, Keith, had a place to live and we would have a place to crash. My husband and I were hoping we could kill two birds with one stone – get a home for Keith and a place where we could live until we were ready to set sail. We found the perfect place, and our plan was progressing on schedule.

Then, the bad news. The woman who agreed to sell us the flat in Gosport had decided to sell it to someone else.

In England, until the deal is done and money changes hands, sales are not guaranteed.

We had agreed to purchase the flat in that specific location because Keith wanted to live near the sea, our daughter would benefit from a good pre-school with the availability we needed. Furthermore, the flat was in close proximity to the training school that hubby and I needed to attend for a few weeks.

Bizarrely, upon hearing the news, I shrugged it off and thought, "So be it." I knew that Simon would simply start looking for another property. There must be something better out there!

An injection of PMA never hurts! (Positive Mental Attitude).

It seems as if there's a tipping point for my nerves to go haywire and affect me physically – shoulders, jaw, bad digestion, insomnia. And then there's a tipping point for the stress to just disappear. Perhaps it all becomes so much that it's laughable rather than serious.

On a daily basis all our plans went from one extreme, like not getting the boat of our dreams or having a base to move to, to another extreme like getting the boat and losing the base. I think I'm starting to learn the Buddhist concept of non-attachment. (I think that's what it's called.) If you wait a little while things will surely change, so don't get too excited and don't get too down in the dumps. If you're not happy just wait a bit – things will change.

Living the dream is hard work.

My dream was to always own a successful company. I did that by the age of 35 or so and when it happened I felt a bit lost. I got my dream and I felt as if there was nothing left to do. Furthermore, I was actually a bit disappointed by the reality of my dream. I thought loads of money would solve all my problems. In actuality, I think it made my life more difficult, but, again, that's another story.

Thinking of the journey ahead created excitement and fear. I was overwhelmed by it all, but I felt that the person I will become by doing it will be transformational. I was essentially exchanging one life for another.

Every so often I wondered, "Am I doing the right thing?" I didn't know, and as the adventure continues, there are still question marks. Will I miss the socialization with my friends and family? Will the boat sink? Will something serious happen to one of us? These are questions that stop most of us from living the dream.

On the other hand, what if it's the adventure of a lifetime? What if my family and I truly blossom into a life that's amazing? What if we enjoy new adventures, make new friends and experience magical moments?

Overall, giving away my stuff wasn't too hard. I still have doubts and think, "Oh-my-God, what are we doing?" I wondered if I would miss all the rooms in my house. I wondered if would miss my big closet and comfy blue sofa.

Only time would tell.

Chapter 4: Sea trials and the survey

For over 10 years we'd wanted an Oyster yacht and for over 60 days we've wanted a specific Oyster yacht. The time had come to meet our dream in person.

We flew from Stansted Airport in England to Palma, Mallorca, a Spanish island located off the East coast of Spain, where we were greeted by an Oyster broker representative. We'd been told that we can either go right to the boat or settle in at the hotel. Hubby's response when I asked his thought was, "We should go right to the boat – shouldn't we?"

I'd never seen him like this before. We've done all sorts of things and gone all over the world, but he never really gets excited and nerves are not in his character. It was actually nice to see him come alive – even though his aliveness was a tad bit uncomfortable for him.

Simon hadn't slept well in months. Night after night he awoke around 2am, and with a racing mind he couldn't get back to sleep. Neither of us was sleeping well. Aside from the thousands of tiny details to wrap up, there was the largeness of it all that wanted to swallow us up.

Part of me felt like we were two common people going out to buy a very uncommon thing. I felt a bit out of my comfort zone. Going from a tiny 35′ yacht to a 56′ yacht is quite a leap. I thought to myself, "look at little ol' us going and buying this big boat!"

"Future proofing" helps me set expectations and results. In other words, I think about the outcome I want to have. For example, for my last trip home to Rochester, New York, I wanted to have the best trip ever…to have quality time with my family and friends…enjoy the food and enable Sienna to get to know her family more. I often imagined how I'd feel when I returned and what I'd say to my friends about the trip.

Doing this future proof allows me to tell my mind/body what I want, and it's never let me down. I don't dictate how things go; I simply outline how I want to feel when it's over.

To future proof the next three days of the journey, I envisioned coming home and telling friends and family that the boat is more than we expected. "It looks great, smells great and feels like it should be in our command. Not only was the sea trial and survey a success but hubby and I had an absolute blast. We had no worries about leaving Sienna with my father-in-law – she was an angel. The flights were great, the weather was sunny and warm and both hubby and I managed to chill out for a few days and really enjoy our time together. We also hit another milestone toward our sell up and sail away plans – we officially agreed to buy the boat."

The night before we left, I wanted to feel excited, but my sleep was not good. I got stuck in a dream loop – where you keep dreaming the same thing over and over. The dream was all about making sure that I finished the chicken soup! Earlier I had boiled down a chicken carcass to make broth and finished it around 10am. Apparently, my mind wanted to carry on and turn the broth into the finished soup!

Around 2am I woke with an upset stomach and proceeded to get sick three times. I finally drifted off around 4am and woke at 6am. For some odd reason, the only thing that could take my mind off my sick tummy was recalling all the guys I dated in the past. Is that random or what?

I've never been ill like that unless it was too much drink or bad food. I didn't drink and everyone else was fine – we all ate the same food. Perhaps it was nerves.

Anyway, I felt good enough to get in the car and thought that nothing would stop me from checking out the boat. We left a grey drizzly

England and soon I was looking out at beautiful blue sky on the Spanish island of Mallorca. How exciting.

Otherwise, I was tired, perhaps a tiny bit nervous. I wanted to be full of energy and excited to see the boat but I was actually feeling like a long sleep would be better. Simon seemed quiet. He didn't sleep very well either. It's hard to explain how this all felt. We were going 47 million miles an hour and not thinking too much about what we're doing for fear that the stress will eat us up. Saying that, I envisioned us sitting at a bar laughing, smiling, and saying, "Oh-my-gosh...this is all really happening!"

Sea trials on the Oyster 56'

We arrived in Palma late afternoon. The broker from Oyster picked us up at the airport and took is directly to the boat.

During the car journey I was quiet and Simon tried to make small chitchat. Thankfully the transit was quick. Upon entering the marina, Simon nudged me and whispered, "There she is!" Sim could pick an Oyster out from thousands of different makes. His brain was hardwired to spot them after so many years of admiration.

The broker showed us around and then left us to do our own thing. I walked around the deck first and then went down below. At first I was afraid to touch anything but then I started opening cupboards and looking under floorboards. We would yell up to the broker, "Hey Jamie – are these tools staying with the boat?" and he'd respond, "Everything you see is everything you get."

I was surprised to see all the cutlery, dishes, bedding, tools, spares and DVD's that the owner was leaving. I assumed we'd be buying just the boat. Simon and I kept looking at each other. We just didn't know what to do with ourselves.

That's when I realized I should have researched more about how to buy a yacht.

Neither Simon nor I knew what to look for. We didn't know what to ask. We were completely stunned. Before we knew it, the time had come to leave the boat and check into the hotel. Sim and I found our room, then we headed up to the top floor to have a drink. We needed to process the day's events! Overlooking the majestic Palma Cathedral, we sat across from each other, grinning goofily.

That evening, we went to dinner, snuck into the marina and sat by the boat staring at her in the moonlight with absolute admiration. Could it be? Could it be possible that we might actually call her ours?

I'm not sure if we slept that night. In the morning we woke early, went out to find breakfast and sat by the marina anticipating our next step – actually sailing the Oyster!

Time to slip the lines!

The moment finally arrived for us to take the boat out. Hubby seemed a bit quiet and I tried to make myself look helpful. The owners greeted us kindly and told us to make ourselves comfortable. We couldn't help but feel like we were looking at a house for sale while the owners were there – there's that awkward feeling.

I felt quite at home within a few moments. The owner, Phil, put Simon at the helm and had him take the boat out. We slipped the lines and off we went. Not long after I was actually helming her while the guys put up the mainsail.

Finally the engine was turned off and we were gliding gracefully through the water. The grin on my face couldn't have been any larger. After my helming stint, I went around the boat taking pictures and videos of us sailing.

I then settled in and started talking to Susie, the boat owner's girlfriend. We had a great chat. I asked her about anchoring and whether she was nervous while sleeping under anchor, and we chatted about finding food at the various harbors. I eventually started to discuss our dreams and plans and the reasons for our big adventure.

I just couldn't stop talking and asking questions – I was so excited. Ironically, Simon was quiet and looked like he was hit by a stun gun. No – he looked like a deer caught in the high beams of a car.

We sailed around for a couple hours and then went back into Palma harbor. The whole voyage was over in a blink of an eye. We were just so excited to finally be sailing the boat. Overall, it felt natural and normal. Every once in a while I would think, "Oh-my-gosh – I'm going to be living on here. Yikes." And then I'd bring myself back into the moment and listen to the waves.

Susie mentioned that we're getting the deal of the century and she wasn't wrong. This same boat (but older) is selling for LOADS more. I explained to her that we didn't haggle the price down because we wanted a deal...we had to haggle it down to afford it! Furthermore, we were selling all our stuff to pay for the boat. I think it comforted her to know that we truly are on an adventure of a lifetime. We're not some rich people looking for a little toy to play with.

We moored up and before we knew it Simon and I were sitting at a lovely restaurant along the marina looking shell-shocked. Simon couldn't really talk or handle a conversation. He just didn't know what to do with himself. We had a couple of beers and then walked along the harbor to take in the breathtakingly beautiful sites of Palma.

The Marine Survey

The buzz of seeing and sailing the 56′ Oyster yacht was still lingering when we met our surveyor, a dower Scotsman, and boarded the Oyster once again. The only time-sensitive task was to have the boat craned out at another marina at a set time. We had hired a surveyor to make sure that we were buying a boat that was sea worthy, solid and ready for a family interested in sailing around the world. Similar to when you buy a house, getting a survey provides the added benefit of having an expert check her out before you formally commit to buy. After a general chit chat the survey began and we helped our broker prepare the boat to slip lines.

We arrived at the crane area and easily navigated into the hoisting. The boat was lifted up a bit, we were let off and then she was lifted way up to clear the keel. The survey was to take place while the boat remained in the hoist. We did it this way to save a substantial amount of money. Once the boat was set off to the side, we walked under her, pretended to know what we were looking at and then decided to get out of the way. Hubby and I headed to a nearby café.

Back at the boat, we used the ladder and climbed up to spend more time on her. I felt exhausted so I laid down in the aft cabin and thought, "This will soon be my new bedroom! It's utter bliss! I wish it was here now…I wish it was time to set sail now!" I rested on the bed dreaming of all the adventures yet to come.

Hubby went around checking all the cupboards and lockers again. He excitedly came back to me and announced that the owner was leaving fishing poles on the boat.

My mind drifted to thoughts of fresh fish, fresh vegetables and fresh fruit – sounded like more bliss to me.

The boat was lowered back into the water and a few more tests were conducted. By this time the surveyor broke off the handle on one seacock, found a small leak in the front toilet system, a leak on the hot water line, and some carbon in the engine. Apparently, none of these things were deal breakers.

We slowly motored back to the berth and knew that our time with the boat was coming to an end. But there was no doubt about it; we'd be back on her as soon as we possibly could.

The boat was moored and our surveyor explained he had a few more hours to go. Our broker gave us the indication that he was heading out so we felt it best to make our way.

After spending an emotionally amazing weekend doing our sea trials on the Oyster 56' and getting it lifted out for a marine survey, Simon and I few home ready to sleep for a week!

The next morning I was greeted by a thump, thump, thump (Sienna slowing making it to our bedroom) and then the door pushed open with a loud, "Mummmmmmmmmmy!" She jumped into bed and said "I've missed you so much." My heart melted – and I was happy to be home.

"Home." Yikes…I was happy to be home. This won't be my home for much longer. My car won't be my car very soon nor will my things be my things. If I'm unwell or feeling blue I can't go "home."

Will the boat become a home? Will I always feel like being on it? After a long day of adventure will I want to return to my boat or will I yearn for a bricks and mortar building? Will I yearn for the home I have now?

I wonder what "home" really means. Is it a place where you are surrounded by loved ones and feel comfortable, or is it a structure? Or perhaps both? I feel a bit worried today but I also know that I'm going to push on and keep making our plans happen. It was too late to turn back now.

[See Appendix A, 'V1. Buying the boat' for videos covering our boat buying experience]

Chapter 5: Saying goodbye to my old routines and old lifestyle

My old routine was to get up, walk to the coffee shop, write, do emails and create my to-do list. I savored my coffee as if it was life sustaining energy juice. The coffee shop was my temple – I loved this time of day as I let my creativity go and worked on things I enjoyed. I would then grab some food for the day – something for breakfast like an egg sandwich and perhaps a salad or ready meal for lunch.

Once I was home I'd sit diligently at my computer and work. I'd do this and that. My body would get tight and my hands cold from sitting so long. I'd become irritated because hubby would interrupt me or the doorbell would ring and no one else could be bothered to answer it. I updated a website, hired a new graphic designer, updated my action list and discussed projects with my business partner. Ho-hum is how I felt. I couldn't understand why my enjoyment of the coffee shop never leaked over into work time.

I'd put in my 8-5 computer time while munching on my store-bought convenience food. Every so often, I'd take the train to London or drive to a nearby venue for a meeting, but for the most part, I spent my days in my computer room overlooking an unexciting road. I suppose I felt as if I was filling time rather than enjoying time.

At 5pm I'd reluctantly stop work to start my playtime with my daughter. I always felt as if I should work until I couldn't work anymore. Having a child forced me to stop that practice. At this point in the day, however, I was tired and really didn't want to play, but I dragged myself from sofa to floor to sofa again. I'd say to Sienna, "Let's play sleep time. We can pretend to sleep and see how long we can pretend."

We owned a hot tub and that's a good half hour time eater. When I was desperate, which was every night, I'd suggest that the family go for a soak. It was great to sit in the bubbles, but relaxation wasn't my main aim. I was simply so tired that I needed some sort of activity that allowed me to sit and my daughter to think I was playing with her.

Such a sad state of existence.

By 7pm I'd be so tired that I'd have to get my first glass of wine. This allowed me to wake up a bit. I'd sit from 7 to 7:30pm watching cartoons with Sienna while I sipped my wine and replied to emails on my iPhone. Simon would cook dinner – usually one that required removing the packaging and placing it in the oven. At least once a week he made something from scratch, but it was best to avoid him during the process.

At 7:30 I'd painfully force myself off the couch and into the bathroom to brush Sienna's teeth and get her to do her business. Then I'd pray that her book choice was a pre-recorded book (thanks to my grandparents and parents) or one of those pop-up jobbies that looks good but only has three words per page.

By 8pm I was on my second glass of wine while eating dinner in front of the TV. I'm not sure if I contemplated what I was eating. I knew I had to eat, and whatever it was that was in front of me was good enough.

Making it until 9pm before lying down in bed was the goal. Usually, we were in bed at 8:30 watching "Pawn Stars," "Storage Wars" or some sort of documentary about alien invasions. All I could think was, I'm so, so tired. I'm so exhausted.

My dread was waking up the next morning at the calls of "Mummmy...mummmmmmy...is it morning time yet?" Of course, I wouldn't fall off to sleep until 11pm and sleep would be broken.

Groundhog Day all over again.

Looking back at my old routine makes me cringe. I suppose it wasn't that bad all the time, but it wasn't that good either. Hubby and I did go out for meals often and we met with friends. I enjoyed my writing…and of course, my time with my daughter when I felt good. And when the sun came out we rushed down to the boat and went out sailing for as long as we could. I loved our sailing trips. They seemed to bring a bit of pleasure into an otherwise dull existence.

Never again will I buy a big house. I've realized that absolute waste of it. We're taught to get a high paying job, work like crazy so we can buy a big house; yet with the big house we spend more of our money filling it with crap. Absolute crap. Every cupboard, closet and storage space has stuff we don't ever use.

Saying goodbye to my old routines was the best thing that I'd done in a long time. I visualized my new routine: "Today we all slept until 8am and I had the best sleep ever. The rocking of the boat and the waves hitting the hull sends us to dreamland in the best way possible. After eating a healthy and yummy meal of porridge and fresh local fruit, we set sail for a new port. There's a Roman ruin, a market and several fish shops where we're going! The sun is shining, we're all full of smiles and looking forward to spotting more dolphins than we did yesterday. And who knows what adventure or new people we'll meet at our next port of call."

Our lives have truly become an open book – one that we're writing ourselves day by day. Aside from being interesting, it's also a bit uncomfortable. Dealing with uncertainty is something we're continuing to learn to live with. Or perhaps it's more accurate to say that we're learning to cope with it.

In my heart I know that we're going to get the boat and everything is going to take place. In my head, however, I'm still allowing disempowering thoughts to seep in, like "What if this all falls apart?" and "What if things don't work out?"

And because the what-ifs have seeped in, they were extending to other areas of my life, even extending our sell up and sail plans. I've heard myself think, "What if I don't like sailing around the world?" and "What if I'm not happy on our boat?" and down the spiral goes.

When I focused on the trip, I felt different. My shoulders seemed to ease, a smile came across my face and I felt excitement boil up.

It just seems that the world I was in is so different than the world I would be in soon. I wonder if this whole transition is so stressful to help me better enjoy my new life? If you experience one extreme you're more apt to experience the opposite – yes? I'm not sure.

What you focus on creates how you feel.

The one lesson I am truly bedding into my body and soul, however, is that what you focus on creates how you feel. If you focus on all the scary "what ifs" you'll most definitely feel stressed. If, however, you consciously choose to focus on the exciting opportunities, your whole mind/body can change for the better.

The key is to make sure you're conscious of what you're focusing on, and if it's not productive, decide to change your focus. Sounds easy, but it isn't if you're not watching your thoughts or noticing your feelings of stress.

The easiest way to "get it" is to realize that if you don't feel well, your focus is going in the wrong direction. Decide to change your focus for the better and your mind/body will fall in line.

In my case, I just had to keep reminding myself of this quite often! Heck – if nothing else I'd get much better at falling in a rut only to quickly realize it and get myself out.

Chapter 6: "A boat is no place for a child!" Really?! I don't think so.

By far, the biggest question we get asked when we tell people we're sailing around the world is, "But what about your daughter - is she coming with you?" My husband often replies to that question with, "You're welcome to keep her if you want, but considering she is our child, yes, she's coming with us!" We've heard often, "A boat is no place for a child!"

People are funny. I assumed that the reaction we'd get would be more about our safety or questions as to how the heck we're paying for this epic trip. I thought people would want to know how we're doing what we're doing, but the fact is, since we decided to sell our possessions and buy a 56' yacht, the majority of questions focus around our 3-year-old daughter, Sienna Maddison Brown.

Education and socialization are the biggies. How will Sienna get an education? What will she do about learning social skills? After that, safety is often brought up. People ask, "Is it safe for you to sail to certain locations with your daughter? Will she wear a life jacket? Can she swim?" It's funny that few people express concern over my and my hubby's safety!

And then we get a few questions regarding health risks such as, "What happens if Sienna gets sick? What will you do if she needs medical attention? What if she gets malaria?"

For the most part I think people are genuinely interested, but I can't help but feel that sometimes the questions are asked with a tone of condemnation. Friends and family can't say, or don't have the courage to say, "Are you crazy - how irresponsible can you get?" Of course, I could be way off the mark on this, but I sometimes feel judged when people shout at me, "But what about your child?"

I think we're doing the best thing imaginable for our daughter.

Not only will we help to educate her through homeschooling, but our family will all be together on an adventure that will enable us to see a massive amount of the amazing world we live in!

I must admit that that the whole concept of homeschooling freaked me out at first. I was all set up to send Sienna through the UK schooling system. One month before we decided to sell up and sail away, I was contemplating what school to register her for.

After Simon and I decided to go for our dream and the dust settled a bit, I started to question the whole homeschooling side of things. My initial reaction was, "I'm not a teacher! I have no clue about teaching! I can't teach my daughter!" I immediately purchased a few homeschooling books.

The books helped!

In fact, by the time I read them I was convinced that homeschooling has just as many, if not more, benefits to the standard education system. I also grew in confidence about ways to teach. There are two extremes. Some parents teach just like teachers in a school. They have timetables, workbooks, etc. and follow the school curriculum to the exact syllabus. The other extreme are parents that go with the flow and find teaching lessons in association to what the child is currently interested in.

For example, if your child is into a doll's house right now, you can create learning opportunities around the doll's house. You think about, English, math, science, history and work it into playing. If I wanted to teach Sienna about colors, we could name the colors in the house. If I wanted to teach her history, we could put on a historical play with the dolls.

I'm not sure what approach we'll take - we'll probably use both structured and unstructured learning.

The key thing is that after a bit of education I now feel completely confident in my abilities to teach my daughter.

And as for the Education Board, when we called up to tell them what we were doing, they said just register Sienna in school when we return to the UK. My husband was shocked. They didn't want to know our names, what we were planning on teaching - nothing. Since Sienna isn't in the system yet, there's no need to tell the system what she's doing. Interesting, eh?

Socialization is the other big issue that most people mention.

And I must admit that it was a concern of mine too. How will a 3-year-old get on in the world of socializing when she's stuck with mom and dad on a boat? Well...from what I've read, children who spend more time with adults (e.g. homeschooled kids) actually tend to have more advanced social skills. Rather than learning both the good and bad traits from their school peers, homeschooled children mature a bit quicker. Let's face it, Sienna is less likely to be a bully, be bullied, act immature (for her age) or be mean. She won't learn anti-social behaviors because Simon and I are not anti-social.

And, just because we're going to live on a boat doesn't mean that we're isolated. In fact, we'll have more of a social life than most! We'll meet other boaters during our travels, in addition to thousands of locals. We'll go to playgrounds, visit attractions and we'll be out and about all the time. Also, there are activity clubs for kids at the major marinas and there's a massive international homeschooling network providing several opportunities for us to introduce Sienna to other children. (It's actually a great way for hubby and me to make new friends, too!)

And what about the risks? What about pirates, being so close to water all the time, storms, tidal waves, human-sized squid, killer sharks, back flipping boat smashing whales, the Bermuda Triangle, capsizing possibilities, foreign bacteria, health issues, blood sucking leaches, jelly fish stings or collisions?

Hmmmmm, yes, those are risks, but compare them to "normal" day-to-day living.

I bet that doing the daily school run is a higher risk than all the risks associated to sailing. In other words, I bet that there are more fatalities caused by car crashes than all the fatalities caused by living on a boat.

Furthermore, it's not like we simply decided to sail around the world and haven't prepared for it. Both Simon and I have taken engine, First Aid, medical, and several sailing courses. We'll never be able to prepare for everything, but we've definitely taken the risks associated to sailing very seriously.

And as for the pirates, we'll never go anywhere near them!

Regarding the medical side of things, we've purchased thousands of dollars worth of medical equipment and drugs and have learned how to use the equipment! On board, we have observational equipment including blood pressure apparatus, stethoscope, thermometer, pulse taker, pee strips, pen light, and ear/nose/mouth instruments. We also are carrying a variety of drugs that will help in an emergency. For example, we have the antibiotic that is needed to combat meningitis and the drug that prevents secondary drowning. We also have the amazing substance created during the Gulf War that forces blood to clot (for massive artery bleeds).

And after much debate, we also purchased a heart defibrillator.

So, is a boat no place for a child? No way!

Chapter 7: Our very first voyages

Originally, we planned to sail 17 hours to nearby Barcelona, Spain but due to a change in our tax situation we had to sail out of the European Union. The closest non-EU country was Gibraltar, located three to four days away.

What if our skipper couldn't extend his help for the extra days? What if Simon and I had to sail the boat by ourselves? What if we couldn't find another skipper? For insurance purposes we needed a certified skipper!

I then told myself to chill out and stop thinking about it. Fortunately, I had other things to hold my attention. The move alone took up much of my mental capacity. And looking after Sienna also distracted my focus. I decided that I must just go with the flow.

To my delight, our skipper came back to us within two days letting us know that he could get us to Gibraltar. What a relief.

My worries then turned to provisioning the boat. It was my job to get to Palma, find a grocery store and buy enough food for the trip. It probably sounds like a small task, and in light of other things, it was. I suppose I was scared because I don't know what we would want, I'm not sure if we'd be able to actually prepare food or it's more of a heat up beans type of thing. I hope our water maker works. Hmmmm, I would need to get some water, too, just in case.

So, there goes my gluten free, non-processed food diet! In actuality, it's been impossible to follow it anyway. But I know we'll get back to our healthy eating as soon our lives slow down a little bit. Most of our meals have been at restaurants or from take-out, but whenever possible we were choosing the best of a bad bunch.

How did I feel about this sailing adventure?

I started really questioning myself as to why I was so afraid yet so excited to sail around the world.

One of my many weaknesses, aside from a lack of patience, is my uncontrollable need to try and control everything. Yes, I am a control freak. Although I love the concept of going with the flow, I don't subscribe to its true meaning. Rather, I work to control the size, width, depth, length, terrain and tide of the flow – once I feel that there's some level of control, I jump in and go with the flow.

I couldn't just jump into an unknown river and float along. But that is precisely what I was doing with this sell up and sail away adventure. And I wasn't just jumping into a river, I was jumping into an ocean that has the power to send me lovingly into a sunset or alternatively, spinning and crashing into a thousand pieces.

Rather than take calculated risks, stay safe, remain in the job, keep the same lifestyle, save pennies for a rainy day, don't rock the boat, wait for the right moment or live with the devil I do know, I was throwing that all away, and it's a huge risk.

I won't be as safe as I'm accustomed to, I had quit my job, I was completely changing my lifestyle, spending all my pennies, rocking the boat. There is never a right moment so now was the time.

What do I have to lose?

My life. But I suppose if that goes I won't really care too much. I could lose a family member. That would be devastating, but I could just as well lose a family member living my normal life. In fact, I bet it's riskier to live on land and drive every day than it is to live on a boat and sail every day.

I could lose my dignity. The whole adventure could turn out to be a dud and I have to crawl back to England, find a job and feel like a loser for the rest of my life. Somehow I don't think that will happen.

I could lose my attempted control over life…hmmmmm. Now that's a doozy. Perhaps I need to ask a better question so as to change my spiraling thought-train of doom.

What did I have to gain?

You see, that's the question that I don't have an answer to – no control. That is what I'm here to find out. What will I gain? Will I gain a better attitude to life? Will I gain more patience? Will I find more peace? Will I gain more of an understanding as to what life really is about?

When you meet a new lover, you know what your potential gains are. When you get a new job, again, you can speculate your gains. When you live the "normal" life that society advocates - school, university, marriage, babies, job, retirement, death, you generally know where you're heading and what to expect.

But what about a drastic change of lifestyle? Yes, I can speculate that I'll change, but I don't know what I'm going to change to. I don't know what I don't know…and I'm diving off a cliff here. This isn't a slow approach. One day I live in a house on land, surrounded by convenience, TV, technology, a very safe savings account and friends/family. The next day, I will live on a boat, surrounded by the sea with very little convenience, no TV, little technology, draining down my life savings at a very far distance from my social network.

I can't control my environment. Perhaps that's the issue? And that's why I mentioned that time might play a huge factor in all this.

But I didn't want to control anything anymore!

And that's why I think I'm doing what I'm doing. I don't want to have this need to control anything anymore. I truly want to go with the flow. I want to stop thinking, analyzing and speculating; I want to be in the moment as much as possible. I don't want to worry. I don't want to fill my head up with all the things that could be wrong. I just don't want to fill my head up with anything other than what's in front of me – for the most part.

As a routine, I always write about my trips/adventures before I take them. It's a way for me to get my mind/body to focus on what I want to happen, so here's what I wrote regarding our adventure:

Pre-trip preparation visualization:

> "Our flights from Stansted to Palma are fantastic. Sienna and I have a great time making crafts, coloring and enjoying the flight. Meeting our skipper, Richard, face-to-face for the first time is great. I know instantly that I'll easily get on with him. Sim is like a kid whose had all his Christmases come at once – he's buzzing with excitement.

> "We go straight to the boat after our arrival in Palma. Everyone is excited and eager to unpack and get situated. Due to the limited time we have with our skipper, we'll be eager to get going as soon as possible. Sienna and I will easily find a grocery store in Palma and get all the stuff we need for the trip.

> "After all the paperwork, checks and hand-over essentials are taken care of, we need to sail for 12 miles off the coast, instigate the sale transaction and then sail on until we hit Gibraltar.

"The actual journey from Palma to Gibraltar is amazing. Absolutely amazing. Sienna is a perfect angel helping out where she can and playing on her own when needed. We quickly get into a routine and enjoy each other's company. The sail is comfortable and easy-going. We're flying – over 9 knots yet it's a smooth sail. Furthermore, the food I purchased is perfect – it's healthy, tastes great and is a joy to prepare. I actually feel GREAT the whole way.

"We get to Gibraltar in record time and when I see the port I'm so excited to get moored up and check off the next milestone on the list of our adventure. We did it! We purchased our dreamboat and we successfully sailed it on her first journey. And she's perfect…she's in excellent condition and we know that we found the perfect boat to sail around the world. I'm so happy, proud, excited and in love with life."

My first trip on our new yacht - dolphins included!

Leaving the mooring at Palma was easy enough. Before departure, Sim, Sienna and I took a taxi to a grocery store. The store was huge! We purchased food for several days in addition to garbage bags, dishtowels, sponges and a necessary pair of slippers for me! If my feet get cold, I get cold and we're not having that.

We discovered that our broker was not needed to complete the transaction. Originally, we were going to sail to mainland Spain and that would have required the transaction to be completed 12 miles off the coast. Due to our change of destination – Gibraltar – we could complete the transaction once we arrived.

For the course of our travels, the current owner will need to cover us under his insurance and then once we're in the Gibraltar, money will switch hands, and the boat will become officially ours. Our insurance will then kick in.

Once the boat was full of groceries and we figured out how to turn everything on and off, we slipped our lines to first find fuel. Since we left this port during our sea trial a month ago, I wasn't too nervous about heading out as I knew the area a bit. Simon handled the boat perfectly and Richard, our hired skipper, kept quiet just making sure everything was going well.

Simon came parallel with the dock and then used the engine and bow thrusters to push us in. I was so proud of him. Richard threw a line to the petrol attendant and I threw another line from the bow. Three hundred Euros worth of petrol later, we once again slipped our lines and left Palma for good. Instead of filling up the tank we put enough fuel in to make it to Gibraltar, a tax-free haven where the petrol was far cheaper.

The winds were good so we decided to put the main sail up as soon as we left the port. Richard went to raise the main and discovered a problem. The winch wouldn't move the sheet – it was jammed. Simon and Richard tried to locate the problem and, using binoculars, it looked as if the main halyard was jammed at the top of the mast!

Simon's face was full of anger, fear and anguish. I could see that his mind was racing and he dreaded the idea of motoring the entire way to Gibraltar.

For some reason, I said, "Don't worry – it's fine. Richard will fix it." I have no idea why I said it. Something in me knew that our travels weren't going to be spoiled by broken rigging.

A few minutes later, Simon started hoisting Richard up to the top of the 85' mast! Holy smokes, that's high! I'm not sure I could do that. Sure enough, once Richard got to the top he was able to free the halyard.

The rest was smooth sailing. Sienna, Richard and I sat in the cockpit enjoying the sunshine, light winds and smell of the Mediterranean. I kept thinking, "I can't believe it's all coming together."

Simon then came up from below deck and said, "Happy hour?" We all celebrated our departure with one drink. After a few sips, something remarkable happened.

"Did you just see that? Something big just jumped out of the sea!" Those were the words I spoke to Richard as he walked from the cockpit back toward the aft seats. I then started to doubt myself and said, "Oh – it must have been a big wave…but I swear I saw something."

"Dolphins ahead, starboard side," Richard yelled out with his Dutch accent.

Oh-my-gosh. Sienna and I were beside ourselves. There must have been 30 to 40 of them. Some came close to the boat and others remained further away. They would come up two at a time or individually. Some would just break the surface and others would jump out of the water to make eye-level contact.

For over a half hour all you could hear was, "There's one. There's another one. Look at that one!" Sienna and I walked to the front of the boat and saw loads of them crossing our bow.

We seemed to be just as interested in them as they were in us. I looked around me and noticed that there was no land as far as the eye could see, nor were there any other boats or ships. I have no idea how much sea I could see but I couldn't help but feel special that the dolphins found us. I felt honored and privileged.

Over our three-day journey from Palma, Mallorca to Gibraltar we were graced with dolphin visits four different times. They seemed to greet us night and day, and each time I was just as excited and honored.

Sea sickness hits.

Having taken Sturgeon, a motion sickness pill, I at first felt untouched by the increasingly turbulent moves of the boat. Sadly it was short lived. Being below deck while chopping food didn't bode well. I was feeling rough.

Halfway through my spaghetti with meat sauce preparation, I had to call Simon down to finish up. I then spent the rest of the evening in the cockpit feeling kind of okay. I didn't feel like I was going to puke, but I didn't feel good either. Eating seemed to make me feel okay. So I simply sat in the cockpit keeping an eye on the ASI and radar – both devices helping to keep an eye on other sea-bound vessels.

By this point we were motor-sailing.

Unfortunately we were sailing right into the wind – a direction that makes our sails useless for propulsion but necessary for stability. That's something I learned – having the main sail up even if you're not using it to sail helps to keep the boat more stable. And I'm all for stability!

On one hand I felt a bit green, yet when I looked out at the reflection of the moon on the sea, absence of land/lights I felt this amazing sense of awe. I fell in love with the experience (again). I suppose that's what brings people back to sailing. I get so sick sometimes, but there's something about sailing that lures me in like a drug.

That evening, I slept in the aft cabin with Sienna. Actually, I didn't sleep. Imagine drifting off to sleep and then jerking into wakefulness because your muscles are needed to keep you on the bed! The boat was going up and down and rolling left and right. Furthermore, the engine was on and there were all sorts of weird noises. And when Simon or Richard adjusted a sail it sounded like a band saw was slicing through the ceiling.

In addition to keeping myself on the bed, I had to keep pulling Sienna close to me. At one point she rolled a few times and ended up side down on the seats next to the bed. Did she wake up? Of course not!

All in all, I wasn't feeling great, but again, I wasn't feeling like I was going to puke. The Sturgeon was doing something. It was keeping me away from the "I want to die" zone so I was thankful for that. Twelve hours after my last pill, I quickly took another knowing that I had to keep myself in the best shape that I could.

On day two of our three-day sail, we were all on deck around 6am sitting in the darkness. Eventually around 7am the sun peeked out and I enjoyed the feeling of its beautiful rays on my back. I made us all some eggs, ham and coffee.

Once again, I didn't feel well, but I didn't feel bad either. I felt very tired and all I could think about was the next meal. I just wanted to either sleep or eat. By lunchtime Simon had to fix the sandwiches. Afterwards, I headed down into the aft cabin and took a nap. Thankfully, Sienna was an angel. She sat with me and we read a book or watched a movie, and when I felt ill she'd leave me to myself. I managed to sleep.

After sleeping in the aft bed the last couple days I was accustomed to a particular arrangement. Not wanting to disturb Simon who was sleeping in our bed I decided to try out another bed. Let me state that the midship upper bunk was a whole new experience. Once I got in, I used the lay-cloth, a cloth that comes from under the bed and raises up to tie onto fixtures high on the wall, to tie myself in. It was a bit claustrophobic. And the best way for me to describe it was like a hill on a roller coaster. The winds and waves started to increase and the boat was going up and down. While resting flat on the bunk bed, I kept losing my stomach – like you do on that first hill down a roller coast.

I thought, "There's no freaking way I will ever sleep in this bed." Luckily, Simon got up and had me move to the aft bed to keep Sienna in one place. I moved back to the aft cabin and I learned that the starfish sleeping position was the only thing I could do to keep myself in the bed. I also realized that by putting Sienna above me, I acted like a break-wall. Thankfully, I was able to sleep more on night number two of our three-day journey.

Problem solving and investigations.

As the journey progressed, issues would pop up and we'd all go to work to solve them. These included figuring out where and how to slip our lines, manage the bow thruster, get diesel, de-lodging the main sheet from the top of the mast, finding the diesel dip stick, fixing a busted reefing line, grading the seriousness of an engine leak and short-term fixes, determining the result of switching on/off various circuit breakers, starting up the generator, working the shower, getting fresh water rather than salt water into the toilets, turning the oven on – that one took a quite a while to figure out; inside a cupboard was another switch that we missed!

And in between the issues, there was usually a bit of time for investigations. Below deck, I'd inquire, "What's under that floor board? What does that switch do? What does that button do?" and above deck we'd play with the various sails – changing cart positions, reefing the main, putting sails up and pulling them down. We played with the AIS to determine where vessels in our area were and the ships' details. I'd open the various lockers and inspect cleaning agents, hoses, spare parts and on the list goes. The previous owner left us all sorts of goodies.

On the third morning we realized that we didn't have enough diesel to get us to Gibraltar. The wind was consistently not in our favor so we had to motor-sail against the wind achieving slow progress.

Simon and the skipper decided to find a port on the south coast of Spain to re-fuel. Around 7:30 am we sailed into Fuengirola. All the fishing boats were still out, with many making their way back into the marina. The sun was lighting up the hills in the background and everything glistened.

The sign on the diesel door stated that it opened at 8am, but no one came. Our skipper, Richard, found a number and called someone. He was told that an attendant would open up eventually. Around 8:20am the boat was fueled and we set sail once again.

Before leaving we tried to get a weather forecast. Our reports were conflicting. The day before, we discovered a storm was coming, so Richard and Simon were working hard to get to Gibraltar before it hit. The recent report was that the day called for sun and light winds. Looking at the scenery, I decided the day was going to be wonderful.

Boy, was I wrong about the weather. I can't be certain when the winds started, but it wasn't long after we left Fuengirola. The boat was going up and down, crashing, swaying, banging. All I could do was rest in the aft cabin. Looking out through the galley to the mid deck windows I would see sky and then water, sky and then water. We must have been going up 120 degrees and then back down.

Things were crashing, water was coming in. I almost wanted to die. As long as I kept my head down, I felt as if I'd survive. Going to the bathroom was an agonizing event. I'd think about it for a half an hour and then I'd scrunch myself down to the bottom of the bed, roll my body off – keeping my head on the bed. I'd sit there for a few moments and then with all my strength I'd force myself to get up and sit down on the toilet. Holding on for dear life, I'd have one foot propped on the side to stabilize me and I'd do my business. Once I was done, I'd leap back into bed.

Sienna was great. She could see that I wasn't well. She played a bit with Simon or amused herself next to me. Staying on the bed was quite a feat. And keeping Sienna on the bed wasn't easy either. I put her on the higher side, so she would slide into my back and then I'd lodge my leg into the sofa next to the bed.

At one point Simon came down to say that we're in a Force 7 – I'm not sure how fast the winds are with a Force 7 but I can tell you it isn't nice. After he went back up, my mind wandered and I'd think, "What if they got swept away? I'd be none the wiser."

Both Simon and Richard had life jackets and safety lines on but I had this tiny fear that I'd finally get up, go to the cockpit and find it empty with auto-helm taking us to Gibraltar. I pushed my fears away. All I could think was, "God, please get us there quickly. I don't think I can take much more of this."

Then things got worse. Simon came down and said, "We've hit a stable Force 10 now. It's a terrible storm but we're okay. The boat is handling very well. Richard says that she was made for wind!"

In my misery, I couldn't help feel a tad bit excited for Simon. I could tell that he was in his glory. I don't think he enjoys storms but in a weird man/ego way this storm is allowing him to say that his new boat can handle anything. Does that make sense?

The countdown then began. "Kim – we'll be there in three hours." I thought, "Three hours is the time it takes me to drive from my hometown to my summer cottage. Three hours is a long time. That drive was long and boring. What am I going to do for three hours?"

Well, I wasn't going to do anything but keep my head down. Eventually, it was two hours and then it was one.

Before I got up Simon yelled down to me to poke my head up. He said that water was shooting 50′ to 60′ in the air near the Rock of Gibraltar. I thought to myself, "Even if Jesus was outside walking on water, there was no way I was getting my head off the pillow."

Eventually, I forced my body up. I put on my waterproofs and went up into the cockpit.

As we sailed along the Rock of Gibraltar I was in absolute awe.

Wind and water were spraying up all over the place. Everything was wet and cold, yet before me was this most amazing rock structure. And when I braved the elements and poked my head out from behind the spray hood I could see loads of ships – I must have counted 10 before my head started to tingle with spiky rain.

It was dark, perhaps 7pm, as we rounded the Rock and started to head for the marina. Simon called the marina on the VHF radio and requested a spot to berth that would be easy considering the weather. The marina told us to moor up along the wall after pontoon B.

Being up on deck I felt much better, and knowing I was going to be able to get off made me want almost want to jump for joy. But there were also some nerves – where is the marina entrance? I can't see it. Where is pontoon B?

Richard took us into the marina. It looked as if we were motoring right into rocks. Only one boat could go in or out at one time – the entrance was so narrow. Once we entered the marina, the winds stopped and things were calm. After a bit of practicing, Richard lined the boat up to moor.

As he backed her in, the dinghy that was hanging on the davits hit the wall and it popped. When I saw that, I had to stop myself from crying. I was at the end of my rope and I felt as if I was going to break. We secured the boat and I took some time to compose myself. Not really.

I spiraled. I yelled at Simon that the toilets were full of black water, there were leaks on the boat and our skipper had just destroyed our dinghy. At a time when we should be celebrating I was unloading on Simon. After a few minutes, the smoke cleared and I changed my attitude.

Getting on and off the boat.

The leap from the yacht to the mooring pontoon was quite a large one. Furthermore, anyone trying to get on had to step in our dinghy first (hanging off the back of the boat) which was very unstable. So, we decided to put the passerelle out. I'm sure it should be a five-minute job but it took two hours and provided great entertainment for the onlookers drinking at the local restaurants.

Back to the passerelle, or gang plank, as I call it. We had to loosen the ropes (warps) on the back of the boat and winch the front of the boat forward. We also had to put the dinghy in the water. We saw a plug that needed to be inserted to prevent the dinghy from filling from water, but we missed another plug.

So...while the dinghy was sinking, we looked like a bunch of morons trying to get the gang plank to land on the pontoon. When we first attached and dropped it, the silly thing reached over to the adjacent boat making a bridge. That would have been fine if we wanted to visit our neighbors, but the other boaters might have been annoyed at having to climb across the passerelle to get to their boats.

Needless to say, we finally got the passerelle sorted and we all joyfully walked, rather than leapt, off the back of the boat. While passing by another boat we noticed that they used a ladder and just tied it onto the boat and hooked a fender under the area that hit the jetty. That looked far easier than our passerelle!

After all was said and done, my reaction was, "Who wants to get a glass of wine now?" I felt as if we did a day's work and needed some kind of reward.

My phone rang and a guy named Ross said he was calling from BBC Radio 5 and requested an interview. He said he'd patch me into the live show so I could hear it as it was being broadcast. Once he patched me in I could hear the radio over my phone and then I heard Ross say, "Can you hear the live broadcast?" I said "yes" and then left the line. After a couple of minutes, I heard one of the broadcasters introduce our story and us.

I was shaking uncontrollably and kept saying to myself, "Stay calm, stay calm." The questions they asked were fairly straightforward and I felt that I responded to them in the best way that I could. They asked about homeschooling, and they mentioned safety. One of the broadcasters asked me to tell them something I hadn't yet mentioned so I explained my mom's fear of us being attacked by a giant killer squid. Everyone seemed to find that funny.

And when they asked how we're going to keep Sienna safe I responded that we just keep her tied down. Now of course I don't mean that literally, but I'm a parent and my daughter's safety is paramount.

Just after the interview finished I had emails from BBC Radio 3 and "The Sunday Times" in my inbox. I couldn't help but wonder why my life had changed so much and in such an interesting fashion. I was so pumped up to sail around the world. I had no clue that the media would want to talk to little ol' me!

Some of the press that I received wasn't very nice. The article in the "Daily Mail" definitely didn't paint me in a good light. They indicated that I was being irresponsible and putting my daughter at risk. Sadly, I think that even if you were perfect, the "Daily Mail" would find a way to paint a negative slant on a positive story. But some people like to read that kind of stuff and that's what's so cool about the world we live in – we all have the ability to choose what we want to fill our minds with and what we don't.

While in Gibraltar I went through a whole range of emotions, some good and some terrible. Overall, I was feeling amazed, scared, overwhelmed and useless.

On the positive side…

While I was typing in my journal along the quayside I looked up, felt the sun, stared at *Britican* and felt elation. I felt as if I was truly thriving. There in front of me was my new floating palace. The sun warmed my body and I could see my family having fun investigating new areas on the boat. I felt as if all the pieces of the puzzle were falling into place.

We were greeted by Gibraltar's meteorologist Steph and her husband Steve. Before leaving on our great adventure I met Steph over Twitter and it was so very nice to put a face to a name. It's so interesting to discover how people end up where they are – where they live and the profession they've chosen. Steph took us up to the top of Gibraltar, introduced us to the cheeky monkeys, showed us some absolutely awesome caves and drove us around the various areas of Gibraltar. After all the hard work we'd been doing, it was a wonderful break. I added the experience to my top 10 life experiences ever.

And speaking about Twitter, another Twitter friend put a Gibraltar pilot book in the back of our tender while we were out. It's a great way to connect with others.

On the negative side...

Last night I found myself using a screwdriver to take apart wooden panels located behind our seating area. Luckily, while Simon and I were finding all the seacocks, we came across a rather serious leak. Seacocks are levers that open and close inlets and outlets in the hull, areas where water can come into the boat. On a monthly basis you need to keep these greased up and moving easily. Our boat has 23 of these little babies and it took us hours to find them all! We had floorboards pulled up all over the place.

One of the bolts that held our rigging down caused a leak. The bolt goes through the top of the boat into a cupboard area behind our table area. The rigging is attached to the mast and is under serious tension so it's not a job that we can fix. We need a professional. Fingers crossed that someone could fix it the day after we were planning on leaving Gibraltar.

The leak wasn't very manageable! The water was pouring into the boat. We did our best to cover the bolt from the top and stuff towels into the leaking area. Both Simon and my cousin, Loryn, (who had joined us from the States for the voyage) woke up during the night to change the soaking towels. I wasn't too worried about water getting into the boat as the bilge pump would push it out. I was more worried about the water ruining the beautiful woodwork.

Aside from the leak, we had issues with our batteries and discovered an internal leak from our aft head (back bathroom). Simon and I had no clue about anything and overall felt a bit useless.

We don't have a master resource that we can call upon to say, "What do you do if this happens?" Yes, we have access to Google, but we didn't even know what question to ask!

After buying a hydrometer (recommended by a guy we called) and testing our battery acid, we discovered that our batteries were all in excellent shape. Somehow the digital reporting device was wrong and needed to be reset. I had no idea that you could use a baster type device to suck up battery acid or that we could buy an inexpensive tester.

I knew that we would get everything sorted out, that it's part of the adventure.

Before we flew down from England, I created a daily, weekly and monthly checklist. The daily checks include things for the generator and engine in addition to things like making sure the freezer and fridge water flows are working fine. On my list I have "Check Racors."

Well...I've found the Racors (a filter for the water system) but I didn't know what they were or what I needed to do with them. The learning curve was so steep; I felt so vulnerable.

During the one-week lead up to our departure to Malta from Gibraltar, Simon, Loryn and I worked tirelessly to prepare the boat for a seven-day non-stop sail. Our activities included buying groceries and cooking meals to freeze, checking all our systems (generator and engine), cleaning and stowing away the few possessions we sent down on a pallet from England. We also did a few loads of laundry and tried our best to organize our living space.

Loryn volunteered to be hoisted mid-way up the mast to sew up a sail protector on one of our spreaders. I was quietly pleased that she was up for the task. I'm not sure if I'd be able to control my fear of heights!

Additionally, every evening I spent a few hours answering emails, updating my website, posting on Facebook and Twitter while Simon and Loryn connected with friends and family on Skype or email. Two days before departure, we were greeted with our guests Skipper Mike, the skipper who helped us move our first boat, *Selene*, down to the South of England, and friend Ene, who joined us for the trip to Malta.

The combination of stress, fear and anticipation contrasted with a day out seeing beautiful sites, spending time with friends/family and chilling out was noticeable.

The day after our tour of Gibraltar, we prepared to slip lines. Several marina residents congregated to wish us fair winds as we left the jetty.

With all of us wearing our Sailing Britican polo shirts, we waved to the people on shore and slowly pulled out of the marina. I felt very anxious and excited. We all felt as if the adventure had truly begun.

Once we entered the main waters we put on heavier clothing. Although the sun was shining, it was cold on the open sea in April. We navigated out past the Rock, with both Spain and Africa within our sights, and weaved between the several tankers spotted all over the Straight. With the wind on our nose we had to use our engine, but reports indicated a change in wind the following day. We knew that it was only a matter of time before our sails would be propelling us forward on our journey.

Dolphins!

Not long after we passed most of the tankers we were greeted by a pod of about 50 dolphins. I think they were common Atlantic dolphins. I grabbed my camera and took a video of them swimming under the bow of the boat. There must have been 10 or more just around the bow with several others all around the boat. In my usual fashion, I became super excited and squealed with delight in my high-pitched voice. I don't think I'll ever tire from seeing dolphins – they are so amazingly beautiful.

While admiring them I noticed that some of them turned their heads and looked at me with one of their eyes. I truly felt as if they were just as curious about me as I was them.

Simon walked Sienna down to the bow of the boat so that she could get a better view of the dolphins. She smiled and said, "Wow – they are amazing!"

A night watch system was instigated.

From 7pm to 10pm, Simon and Ene were on watch. From 10pm to 1am, Mike and Loryn took over and then from 1am to 4am it was Simon and Ene with a final switch at 4am back to Mike and Loryn.

Since my main priority was Sienna, I had watch over her! I'm not sure who had the better deal, as Sienna can be a light sleeper. Throughout the night she would get up either crying or giggling. She was often still sleeping so I'd just have to get her to lie back down. The worst was when she woke up at 5am saying, "I'm hungry!" With so much change, her sleep was unsettled, but I was sure she'd get into the swing of things.

Sleeping was impossible!

The first night's sleep while under engine was torturous. No matter what I did, I couldn't get into a position that was comfortable. My body was rocking back and forth and the only way to stabilize myself was to either lie on my stomach or my back. I couldn't help but go on my side only to realize that it was impossible to stabilize. Making matters worse was having Sienna roll into me. I kept pushing her up to the higher side of the boat using my back as stability for her so she could sleep.

Every time I drifted off I'd be awakened by a sudden shift in my body. Additionally, the noises were abrupt and loud. There was the murmur of the engine, the spray of the waves, the wind and various creaks and what sounded like droplets of water. Around 5am I finally fell asleep and woke around 8am feeling like a zombie.

After waking I got out of bed, made some coffee and some oatmeal for everyone. I poked my head up on deck to survey the view. Africa was gone but I could still see a bit of the southern tip of Spain. I felt fine as far as my seasickness was concerned so I was pleased that the medicine I was using seemed to be working.

Finally – time to get our sail out!

We put up our genoa (front sail) and that's all we needed to hit 7 to 10 knots. We all yelled, "Hurray – we're sailing!"

Throughout the day I'd sit on deck talking to everyone and then I'd spend some time playing with Sienna – we'd play some educational games on the iPad, watch a movie or attempt to color in a coloring book. Simon and Mike spotted a pilot whale – about 10 feet in length.

As the day wore on the seas increased in size and the wind started to howl.

Eventually the boat sunk between the rolling waves. When looking toward the back of the boat the waves were higher than the dinghy held up on davits. When the waves rolled under us we'd quickly surf downwards. Skipper Mike estimated that the waves were 30 feet in height. With the increasing waves and blowing gusts, both Sienna and I started to feel green.

Sienna couldn't hold down any food and I wasn't able to move around. I was unfortunately restricted to the bed with my head down. The whole boat was rolling, pitching, surfing and it got worse throughout the day. Things started to fall into the main living area, stuff started to fall on Sienna and me from the couch, jars were rattling in the cupboards and dishes were clanking. It was a cacophony of irritating sounds.

The noises increased. The boat was banging, crashing, lashing and bashing. Helming the boat was a constant fight, with anticipation as our only guide. I'd turn the wheel to the left, hold it strong, and then as we surfed down a wave, turn it to the right... hold... anticipate when the boat was going to swing back and then adjust accordingly. We had autopilot but it took a lot of juice from the batteries so we tried our best to use people power.

Throughout the night, fears started to creep in. What if we hit something – like a whale? What if one of these waves tips us too far over? What if....we die!! As soon as the fears popped up I'd tell myself to think about something else. At one point I forced myself to take a mental tour of the Seneca Park Zoo in my hometown of Rochester. I just needed to get my mind off the situation.

I'm not sure if anyone slept for more than a couple hours – we were in a full-blown storm.

It had now been two days with Sienna feeling unwell. I was starting to get worried. Her spirits were fine – she acted fine apart from puking within a half an hour of eating. Luckily she was still drinking fluids. Regardless, I asked Simon if he would consider making a stop. I was feeling more and more green, so a break from the rolling and crashing and bashing was of interest for me, too.

Mike and Simon surveyed the map and came up with two options. We could go to Ibiza, which would take 25 hours, or go to Algeria which would take eight hours. My first question was, "How safe is Algeria for us to stop - isn't that North Africa?" After a bit of discussion we slightly altered our course to Algeria and once we got closer we decided to survey the situation.

While Sienna and I were in bed, Skipper Mike took the opportunity to teach Ene and Loryn how to do a traditional Scottish dance on the aft deck. What are the chances of sailing through a storm in the Med and learning how to dance?!

As a last ditch effort to help Sienna and me feel better, I asked Sienna to listen to an app I downloaded from the App Store called Nevasic. The app was designed to help people reduce or eliminate motion sickness or morning sickness in pregnancy. It's an audio offering that lasts for 20 minutes. It just sounds like a variety of music clips.

Sienna stopped puking after she listened to it! I couldn't believe it. I wish I could say that it did the same for me, but due to the medication I was already taking I'm not sure if it had an effect. Regardless, I wasn't puking. I just didn't feel well. For the most part, I had to put my head down and then I was okay.

Forget stopping, we can make it to Malta!

I told Mike and Simon to keep going. Since Sienna was eating I felt much better, and as far as I was concerned, I'd have to somehow make peace with this seasickness. So, we carried on.

Two hours outside of Algiers, Algeria, Loryn came down to my bedroom and announced that we were going to Algeria now. The gusts of wind were up to 60 knots, the genoa was ripping and the overall strength of the crew wouldn't be able to keep going. The storm was relentless. We all needed to sleep and to feel stable.

As we approached Algiers, Mike radioed the harbormaster three times and received no answer. He also called a marina. Up on deck we all looked at each other and thought perhaps they wouldn't respond to us. We made it to the opening of the port and a man from the marina got on the radio in response to our calls.

Mike explained that we were in need of safe refuge. The storm was too much for us and we had a little one on board who was a bit seasick. The marina attendant then asked us the size, length, weight and all the particulars of the boat.

He then came back on the radio and said, "Algiers welcomes you."

Our instructions were to go to Customs and Immigration first. We entered the port and pulled up to a concrete wall next to a lighthouse. We were greeted by a man dressed in navy with Immigration Police badges on his very handsome uniform. Behind him were two men carrying semi-automatic rifles.

Thankfully, when we tied ourselves off we received lots of smiles and nice greetings. As soon as the officials saw Sienna's smile, they immediately gave her kisses and cuddles. Sienna was happy to get showered with a bit of love.

Once on our boat, the immigration officer had us fill out a one-pager full of our details – name, passport number, etc. Luckily he spoke enough English for us to figure things out. If only we spoke French we would have able to have a conversation! Mike had a bit of knowledge of French. The official then said we needed to wait for someone else to come to give us clearance.

The official looked at Simon and said, "You have made a very big mistake!"

And Simon sank in his seat. We failed to fly an Algerian courtesy flag. Whenever you enter a new country, you need to fly a small flag off the side of the mast shrouds. We have over 50 flags, but never in our wildest imagination did we think we'd need an Algerian one.

Simon groveled a bit and the official said, "You can go to court for that." Afterwards, however, the official lightened up and said. "Don't worry." He asked if we had any pets, drugs or alcohol and he then took all our passports to take photos.

Whenever you watch documentaries about people going to Africa they are inevitably held up doing paperwork for hours.

Contrary to our thoughts, the second official arrived, and both came aboard to do paperwork for the boat. They sat down in our saloon and had a great time teasing Sienna. They took turns holding her and pinching her cheeks. Thankfully, Sienna kept in good spirits and played along with everyone.

Within a half an hour our passports were returned, we were through customs and directed to moor up on a ferry mooring. As we approached a concrete jetty, there were two more immigration police. They helped us tie *Britican* down and then entered the boat for us to fill out a two-pager on the boat. They were very pleasant and one of the officials announced, "You are welcome in our country and it is free for you to stay here."

Wow. I couldn't believe how generous and kind everyone was being to us. Part of me thought, is there a catch? Well, only time would tell.

The official then explained that we needed a pass if we wanted to leave the boat. I asked if it was safe for us to walk around the town and he responded, "You are very safe here."

We all sat around the saloon after the officials left thinking how fortunate we were to be greeted in such a welcoming way. I took time to look around and noted that there was not one sailboat as far as the eye could see. We were surrounded by fishing boats and tankers. Right outside our mooring was a huge warehouse that looked like a processing area for imports. It was a bit eerie.

Not long after our chitchat we all went to bed and slept like logs. I woke in the morning and noticed a policeman near the warehouse. After mentioning him, Ene remarked that she saw him last night. I think he's our protector. Either that or he was our watcher!

Simon took him a coffee and he seemed very grateful. Not long after sipping our coffee a police van drove up and we had two more visitors. They greeted us kindly and gave us a bit of information. They said that we could get a pass to enter the city, however nothing was open as it was Friday, their day of worship. They said that if we need anything to ask the man outside and he will send for it. He even mentioned someone going to the chandlery for us.

We were in Africa with a bodyguard outside our boat and various people visiting us every few hours. The officials simply couldn't do enough for us. Thus far, every generalization I've ever heard about African states has failed to materialize. At one point our police friend asked if I was European. Reluctantly, I said "No, I'm American," thinking that perhaps I should have lied. His response was, "Oh – Americans are good people!"

After a lovely meal we all went for a walk. We were restricted to the length of the ferry pier with a guard in front of the boat and at the end of the pier.

We felt as if we were quarantined and being watched at all times. All the immigration, customs and police officers were so nice to us and I believe the government, rather than the officials, restricted us from leaving the boat.

Overall, I felt as if I needed to sleep with one eye open at all times, but that's because of my fears rather than the treatment we received. I looked forward to getting to Malta and cruise around Europe where I felt more comfortable.

Before leaving Algeria, Skipper Mike felt it was important to fly the Algerian flag. He went to the police office at the end the pier and inquired about buying a flag. The policeman turned around, stood on a chair and ripped the Algerian flag bunting off his wall. He then cut one of the flags off and gave it to Mike.

We were very proud to hoist the Algerian flag.

While waiting for our departure clearance, an Algerian policeman joined Sienna to point out the animals native to Algeria using one of her animal apps. He then gave us a brief outline of Algerian history, rule under France, independence and telling us about the desert. Over 70 percent of Algeria is desert. For all those nay-sayers about Sienna's education, I want to ask them what could be better than an opportunity for her to learn about native African animals by a true African!

Even though we were treated very well in Algeria I couldn't help but worry a bit. Algeria doesn't have a positive record from sailors who have had to stop there in the past. Part of me wondered if they'd let us leave or if they'd come up with a way to request money. I was also worried that we'd leave and a random boat might come out and rob us. I was afraid they'd want to take Sienna. I once again told myself to focus on the end result. Focus on enjoying a glass of wine in Malta! Contrary to my fears, they wished us well and we enjoyed an easy departure.

Our fears about Algeria changed to fears about our lack of water.

We only had one tank of water and when it was gone, it was gone. We used the water for cooking and washing dishes. And then we had bottled water to drink. All of us girls had hair that looked terribly greasy. Moreover, our heads itched. It was so gross we decided to put French braids in our hair. At least that way it didn't looks so ghastly!

As for personal hygiene, we used wet wipes to clean under our arms, and of course we did our normal brushing of our teeth and so forth. Thankfully, no one really smelled too bad.

As we were sitting up on deck, Mike came up and announced, "Girls – we're making water! That means you all can now take showers." Never did a shower feel better than the one we had on *Britican*.

But our enthusiasm was short lived. Not long after getting the watermaker to work, our main sail got stuck three-fourths of the way up. It was totally jammed – couldn't go up or down.

The seas were calmer than when we were in the storm but there was still a very noticeable swell. Simon was hoisted half way up the mast and just couldn't hang on. The mast was swaying so drastically that we had to pull him down and come up with another plan.

Tunisia – here we come!

After a lot of thought, Skipper Mike decided to enter the Tunisia port, another African country, so that we'd have enough shelter from the swell and waves to get Simon to the top of the mast.

Based on our experience of Algeria, I quickly got to work at creating a courtesy flag. Luckily, I had a children's atlas for Sienna and could easily find the Tunisian flag. I spent a good hour drawing, cutting and gluing a flag out of construction paper. Once I was finished I lined the edge with Scotch tape and a bit of duct tape where I planned to put the holes.

As we entered the port, Loryn and I went up front to prepare the anchor. I saw something huge come out of the water near us. I pointed it out to Loryn and we kept looking. After a couple seconds, we saw bottlenose dolphins all around us, and they were huge! I'm not kidding when I say that one of them was at least 10 feet long. Trying to be serious and get the anchor out, we couldn't help but keep an eye on the dolphins.

After a bit of messing around, we got the anchor out. Mike was in communication with the Tunisia port control so they knew why we were there. Simon was then hoisted up to the very top of the 85-foot mast. What a brave soul!

He took pictures of the problem, alleviated the jam and the main sail came down. Sim was a bit battered and bruised but he got the job done. The problem was a broken pulley wheel causing the main halyard to pop out and jam between the two pulleys as the top of the mast.

By day five or so, Loryn admitted that she thought the storm conditions were normal. Apparently, none of us acted strangely or panicked so Loryn assumed that the high winds, huge waves and rocky conditions were standard sailing experience. She questioned to herself, why do Kim and Simon love sailing so much – this is ridiculous!

We all laughed when we discovered Loryn's thoughts and explained that we'd never sail in the current conditions on purpose. The forecast called for a storm force of 5 to 6, but when we got out there it was more like 7 to 8. Thankfully we were sailing with the waves rather than against. Once we explained to Loryn that the sailing conditions were not normal and we didn't envision sailing in these types of winds, I think she felt much better!

Around 10:30pm we directed the boat toward the Valletta port entrance in Malta. The marina was closed; however we were instructed to anchor right outside and moor up in the morning. Loryn and I dropped anchor and then we all sat in the saloon talking about the highlights of our trip. There were loads of laughs accompanied by a strong closeness. We were a unit – all of us became a family. There was also a tiny sense of sadness. We knew that our time together was about to end.

Overall, I know that we have a huge learning curve and part of me feels overwhelmed…but another part of me knows that there are loads of people out there to help us on our way. I have to express my absolute gratitude for having Skipper Mike, my cousin, Loryn and good friend, Ene with us. Boy, did we need a lot of extra hands. We couldn't have picked a better crew.

Our adventure from Gibraltar to Malta was crazy – dolphins, storms, stops in Africa (Algeria and Tunisia), sea sickness, Scottish dancing lessons and more…

What a whirlwind!

After 16 years of life in England and 23 years growing up in the States (on land), I was living on a floating palace. What a change.

Part of me kept asking, what the heck happened? How did we get here? The other part of me remembered the stress, all the organizing we had to do, the many lists of to-do's and the constant juggling act that enabled us to sell up and sail away.

I felt a bit numb. I just couldn't believe that it happened and was happening. We were finally living our dream.

The marina was well protected so we barely moved at all, making it so comfortable to sleep in. Later that morning, two reporters from the "Malta Times" came aboard to meet and interview us. My cousin and I were able to chat to them about Malta history, places to visit and a variety of interesting facts. Simon was entertaining Sienna in the back cabin and we girls got some great information. The reporters were both Maltese so it was fantastic to hear the enthusiasm and energy they had while discussing their own country.

While getting photographed, one of the lovely reporters asked me if we had any sort of routine yet. My response was a definite no. "Every day is totally different – we're just going with the flow. Some days we clean, do laundry, connect with family back home and other days we hop on a bus and find an ancient city or enjoy the local cuisine for lunch or dinner."

[See Appendix A, 'V2. Gibraltar to Malta' for videos covering some of our trip]

Chapter 8: Sailing from Malta to Sicily

The night before our sailing from Malta to Sicily trip, we put our mended headsail back on. We waited until the wind died down and the three of us attached it and hoisted it up along its track. It was very dark but the moonlight helped us to get the task done. Once it was up, we furled it (wound it up) and spent the rest of the evening preparing the boat to leave.

Our sailing trip from Malta to Sicily was calculated to take about nine hours.

We wanted to leave with the rising sun. To prepare, we put everything away, did the engine and generator checks and exercised all our stopcocks.

We woke early to prepare to slip lines. At 6am we left Malta in flat calm waters with an amazingly beautiful sunrise. Leaving the mooring was easy. I dropped the lazy lines, Loryn slipped the aft warps (ropes), and Simon calmly took us out. I couldn't help but be a bit nervous – it was the first time that Simon and I took our Oyster out for the first time alone. Thankfully we had Loryn's help.

Once we got out of the marina, Loryn yelled out, "I love sailing." That made me happy. I was wondering if the trip from Gibraltar to Malta scared her. Luckily, she was able to experience a very easygoing sail across to Marzamemi, Sicily. The weather report called for 10 knots of winds across our beam (light winds flowing across the center of the boat).

Once we were far enough away from land, Loryn and I hoisted the main sail. It went up perfectly.

While getting things all sorted on the boat I started to feel seasick. I'm not sure why, as the sea was very calm. There was a tiny swell, but nothing major. Perhaps I was so nervous that it caused me to feel sick. Within a half hour of getting the mast up, I was puking over the side. I puked once and then 20 minutes later I puked again. Feeling rough, I decided to put one of those seasick patches behind my ear. I knew that if I took a tablet it wouldn't stay down, so the patch was my only solution.

Thankfully, the patch stopped my puking response and I spent the rest of the trip sleeping on our aft deck double bed-sized cushion. It was quite cool but under a blanket I felt very comfortable. The sun was out, the smell of the Mediterranean was strong and although I didn't feel 100 percent, I was still happy to be out on the sea.

I woke to something walking on my back. I wasn't sure what it was, but it did alarm me. To my surprise, I had a carrier pigeon checking me out – he walked from my foot to my head! When I raised my head, Simon yelled out, "We've had these two pigeons with us for the last couple hours! They're tagged so maybe they're carrier or racing pigeons." The pigeons both had coded rings around both their legs. We named them Lavern and Shirley and they stayed with us all the way to the marina. In fact, they stayed with us for hours after we moored up.

And that's when the winds decided freak out on us.

Unbelievably, when we had Marzamemi in our sights, out of nowhere the wind went from 16 knots of wind to 45. What the heck?! Simon quickly pulled in the headsail and then turned the boat into wind so Loryn and I could lower the mainsail. Everything came down quickly and then we started shooting our cushions down below. It was really blowing a gale.

A huge wave hit Loryn while in the cockpit and her entire backside was soaked. Both Simon and I thought, what are the chances of this kind of weather again? Simon used the VHF radio to call the marina. The attendant at the marina didn't speak English so it was difficult to determine if he knew we were coming in.

Simon used his mobile phone to call the attendant he spoke to before leaving Malta, as he spoke English. His contact said, "Don't worry, I'll let them know you're coming in. A tender will greet you outside the marina. Just follow him in."

Sure enough, a tender did greet us. Three people lined the jetty ready to help us dock in the gale winds. The marina was sheltered but it was still very blowy. Loryn prepared to throw the back warps (ropes) and I put gloves on to grab the lazy lines. Simon slowly backed us in doing an excellent job. Luckily there was only one boat to moor next to rather than fit between two.

As we got closer, Loryn shot the port (left) side line and then I heard her yell out, "Oh no!" She forgot to tie the rope to the boat so the attendant had a line leading to the water. Working fast, the attendant got the warp back to Loryn and she tied it down. She then set the second warp while I offered to grab the lazy line. Luckily for me, the attendant said something that sounded beautiful in Italian and did it for me.

Within a few minutes we were secure and able to put out our passerelle. A very nice gentleman greeted us and told us to visit the yacht club office when we were ready. While Loryn and I cleaned up the boat, Simon and Sienna went off to do customs stuff. Within a few minutes they were back.

Sienna yelled out, "Mummy, mummy – we've received a present!"

She presented me with a huge tray of something wrapped up. We opened the package to find 10 freshly made authentic cannoli. Oh-my-gosh – was I happy or what? I couldn't believe it. So before stepping on

Sicilian land, I managed to enjoy one of the best cannoli I've ever had. But where did they come from?

My lovely husband had called ahead and asked if some cannoli could be delivered to the marina before our arrival. As soon as I started eating my cannoli I knew that I was going to love Sicily!

Every day I seemed to drift away for a bit and then come back and pinch myself. I just couldn't believe where we were and what we were doing.

Month one was over. We travelled from Gibraltar to Malta, via Algeria, and then on to Sicily. Since arriving in Sicily, we'd been to Marzamemi and Syracuse.

The new boat, the new and amazing sights and all the new smells forced me to be present much more than usual. I was definitely not sleepwalking on automatic pilot through my days anymore. I think, however, every once in a while I had to blank out just so that I didn't explode with new stimulus. Sounds funny, but everything was new and took a lot of attention.

There was no routine, no known comforts and very little that was familiar. By the end of the month, we all started to feel familiar with the boat, where most things are. We felt more settled.

We also started to develop a loose routine.

Around the breakfast table we would discuss our plan for the day. If were leaving port, we'd discuss the ETD (Estimated Time of Departure), what needed to be done and who's doing what. If we were staying put, we'd decide what we want to do and see. Usually there was a bit of time for Loryn and me to do some typing and for Simon to fiddle around on the boat. We'd have an hour or so with Sienna doing numbers and letters or helping her with an educational app on the iPad.

And I must say that I'm even becoming more comfortable with being around non-English speaking people. At first I was afraid to approach foreigners for fear of them not knowing what I was saying. Now I usually end up with the desired result. I was discovering that anything done with a smile tends to end up with a positive result.

Trying to sound Italian, I'd just add an "O" to the end of words. I'd point to an insane driver and yell out Crazy-O or Stupid-O. I know that I probably sounded like a complete nuttier but it was the only thing I could think of to do.

One thing is for certain, being around non-English speaking people forces you to FEEL rather than to HEAR.

No matter what, however, we have the ability to get to know our non-English speaking friends on Facebook. I can simply push "translate" below their comments on Facebook and lo and behold, they're changed to English. It's an amazing world we live in, isn't it!?

In my earlier life, I had more stability. Now, I had no idea where I'd be in five days, let alone where I'd be in a month. I didn't know what country I'd be in or what I'd be doing. And you know what? It didn't really matter – I knew that we're going to see new sights, meet new friends and grow closer as a family.

Yes, there were times when something would break and I'd think, "Oh no, how are we going to afford to keep doing this?" I'd worry occasionally about the fact that we were using our retirement funds to sail around the world, but overall, I pushed those thoughts aside and reminded myself that the universe was looking after me!

Everything is going to turn out great…and the journey to *get* great is going to *be* great. The time had come to let go and trust that life would play out just as it should.

There are no walls in the sailing community.

Imagine being in Sicily for the first time, moored up with a neighboring boat holding six Italians with only one speaking English. And then consider us – a yacht containing one Brit, two Americans and a Brit/American 3-year-old – all struggling to correctly say the town they're in, not to mention simple things like "hello, please and thank you" in Italian.

You wouldn't think that we'd exchange more than a cursory "bonjour" when we saw each other, but after a few days of smiling at our neighbors, something happened.

The smiles and random attempts at trying to convey some sort of meaning turned into something deeper.

Just after we arrived in Marzamemi, another boat came in – one with what appeared to have six Italians on board, three men and three women. The men just seemed to shout all sorts of foreign words. We helped them moor up and gave our best smiles.

Luckily for us, one of them, Stefano, spoke very good English. We met him later at the marina office and he introduced himself to Sienna, who was quickly becoming our 3-year-old ambassador.

With Sienna, everyone seems happy to talk to us...or should I say they're happy to talk to her!

From that quick introduction, Stefano became a new friend. The following day, Easter Sunday, we wanted to hire a car to drive to a nearby city – Noto. After approaching the marina attendant we realized that we couldn't convey our request. My husband's "vroom-vroom" noises accompanied with a wheel turning motion just didn't cut it. Our Italian was terrible and his English wasn't good enough. Thankfully, Stefano stepped in to help. He not only interpreted but he then went on to tell us where to go, how to get there, what to eat and what to stay away from.

He explained that in Italy, every 50 km the spaghetti sauce, meat dishes and wines are different, using different ingredients and different recipes – you can't get the same dish everywhere you go. Stefano also explained that spaghetti and meatballs are an American invention – if we see it offered in Italy, it's for tourists.

Upon our return from a day of sightseeing we were then greeted by our neighbors and given local oranges, cherry tomatoes and butter beans. Light conversations ensued with Stefano while the rest of us just smiled and kept waving hello to each other.

I wanted to talk to the others, but language was a barrier.

Whenever we'd see our new friends, we'd do our best to say something in Italian and they'd say something in English. Pleasantries were exchanged.

The day before we left Marzamemi, we went into the town and had one of the best meals ever! We had a pistachio/fish pasta to start and then for the main we had the most amazing stuffed squid and swordfish in the world.

Afterwards, we squeezed in an ice cream and Sienna not only covered her face in chocolate ice-cream, but she also covered her t-shirt, jean skirt, tights and the ground around her! Next stop – the showers...

When returning from the showers, I found a note left by Simon: "I've gone out sailing with the neighbors. Be back in an hour."

Well, I knew that it wasn't going to be an hour! I was happy that he was out sailing and Loryn and I hung out, put Sienna to bed and waited for his return.

When the boat returned, it was more shouting, shouting and yelling. I've never seen anything like it. The three men on the boat just barked all sorts of orders, responses and remarks. It was hysterical.

I didn't know what they were saying, but it certainly made me chuckle.

Soon after they tied the boat down, Loryn and I were invited aboard the boat to have a small glass of champagne. My husband explained that he didn't understand a word that anyone said but he had an absolute blast.

We all drank a few little glasses of sparkly and then Stefano said "I have the ingredients, but I need to cook dinner on your boat. My boat doesn't have a big enough pot or seating area!" Before long, we were all in our galley having a lesson on how to cut garlic, prepare a garlic oil sauce and properly cook spaghetti.

Stefano said to us in his lovely Italian accent, "There's three things in Italy. There's spaghetti, then there's pizza and then there's pasta." I questioned why spaghetti didn't fit under the term of "pasta" and he said "Spaghetti is spaghetti – it's in it's own category.'"

Not long after the lesson on cooking spaghetti started, there were nine of us seated around our table.

I didn't ever think that we'd have such a group so early in our trip. The wine was being drunk, the food was being enjoyed and we had a great time, especially considering the language barriers.

Stefano would translate a bit. Otherwise the others would talk and do a charades-type explanation. We would do our best to convey meaning and in the end, we all enjoyed being with each other even though we didn't share a common spoken language.

We had the language and love of food, sailing and now, friendship.

I told Stefano that I was going to add the evening to my top 10 of highlights of my life. I think I need to increase my top 10 to top 20 now as I'm experiencing so many incredible things.

Amazingly, everything that I wanted about this adventure was already coming to fruition.

There were many "AHA" moments on this journey. For example, when learning how to take the "bad" bit out of a garlic clove - yes, there is a bit you need to remove to avoid poor digestion and bad dreams, I told Stefano how happy I was to enjoy everyone's company. He replied so sincerely, "But this is what your life is now about. In the sailing community there are no walls – we're all sailors. We all speak the same language."

The day of our departure from Marzamemi, our new friends left a half hour before us. We caught up to them and while passing them we took photos of each other! Our boat yelled things in Italian and their boat yelled things in English. Originally, we thought that they might head for Syracuse, so that we'd stay together; however an hour later they caught up with us again.

The wind had died and they were heading for Cantania (our next port of call after Syracuse). To get to Cantania before nightfall they turned on their engine and while passing us, they handed over a bottle of sparkling wine and yelled out, "See you in Cantania!"

Later on we also found a bag of lemons and oranges sitting in our galley. We couldn't believe the kindness that was shown! What an incredible experience, one that I will hold close to my heart for the rest of my life.

[See Appendix A, 'V3. 'Sailing from Malta to Sicily' for a video link]

Chapter 9: Sailing to Catania in Sicily

Our next port of call: Catania. Originally our only reason to stop over in Catania was to get some repairs done, but we had made new friends who live there so I looked forward to a social visit as well.

For the first time, Loryn took the boat out of the marina. We were sailing from Syracuse to Catania in Sicily.

After getting into the open harbor, we raised our main sail and unfurled our genoa (front sail). The water was deep blue, the sun was shining and the smell in the air was fresh. Lucky for me, there were no swells so I didn't feel any seasickness.

Within a few minutes we were greeted by three dolphins that I named Moe, Larry and Curly. They stayed and played with us for a few hours. Every time I thought they left I'd see them poke their head out or swim across the bow. I spent some time with them by lying down on the bow and holding my hand out waving. I'm sure they had a conversation with each other saying something like, "Here's another really crazy human!" As with most animals, I love them and want to give them a hug!

And then the generator stopped working (a reoccurring problem!). We had worked on the generator for weeks. I thought it was fixed. Simon tried turning it on a few times and it would start but die out quickly. His prognosis was air in the lines. We needed the generator to cook lunch. Loryn was concocting a warm meal and I was eager to eat it! Fortunately, we could turn our engine on to power up the electric oven. Lunch was great but I was annoyed that our generator was broken again.

Then, just as we were getting into Catania waters, the wind started to blow and a little rain fell on us. There were some threatening clouds but what was amazingly more impressive was the mountain behind the clouds. To my utter delight we were sailing straight toward Europe's largest and one of the world's most active volcanoes, Mount Etna.

For as long as I can remember, I've always wanted to see (and climb) a volcano. I wasn't sure if I'd be able to climb Mount Etna, but just being next to it was amazing. I yelled over to Simon and Loryn, "Hey guys – not only are we sailing in Sicily but there's a freaking volcano right in front of us!"

Then disaster struck. As we prepared to enter the port, I released our main sail but it didn't come down (another reoccurring problem that was supposedly fixed in Malta)!

Thankfully, the winds weren't too bad – otherwise, we'd be in a potentially disastrous situation. You can't enter a marina with a full sail in windy conditions – there's no way to stop the boat. So…we got as close as we could to the shore, let out the anchor and prepared to send Simon up the mast. It didn't take too long to get the ropes sorted out.

Before sending Simon up the mast, we notified our new Italian friends we met in Marzamemi that we'd be late arriving in Catania. Our friend Stefano, who we eventually discovered was a retired Italian Navy Admiral, offered to help us moor up. Knowing that someone was coming to help us made me feel much more comfortable. We still had to hoist Simon to the top of the mast. Yes, I was scared, but on the other hand, I knew what I was doing and I knew that it had to be done.

Loryn and I winched Simon to the top of the mast. Luckily, we have electronic winches so all I really had to do was push a button and ensure the winch worked properly. Simon yelled down that the main halyard (rope) was, indeed, jammed again. We sent up another rope to release the tension on the current halyard allowing Simon to release the jammed rope from the main sail. Loryn and I then dropped the sail – yippppie! It was down.

While I started to slowly let Simon down, a rib of four men came out to greet us. It was Stefano, our other two friends Salvo and Mimo, and one other. I was so grateful to see them. Yes, we managed to solve our problem alone but it felt so nice to know that we had friends to back us up. Heck, it was nice to know that we were in the middle of Sicily and we had friends.

Stefano boarded the boat and helped us easily moor up in Catania. I'm so thankful he was with us – the commercial port seemed very quiet and I don't think we would have known where to go. Simon did a great job at lining us up along a concrete wall and it was nice to be able to turn the engine off and chill out. Looking around, all I could see were 18-wheeler trucks and trailers in addition to some large fishing boats. I also noticed a marina near us, but the boats were quite small.

While we were cleaning up, Simon yelled down, "There's a package here for you!" Simon handed me a package and said it was from Stefano. We took it down into our saloon and Loryn, Sienna and I opened it. To our delight, we discovered eight fresh cannoli.

After an incredible pizza dinner that evening, the night continued with a walking tour of Catania. We saw the city center, several amazing churches, a square with a central pillar displaying an elephant, a water fountain powered by water from an unknown source, a manhole cover where people opened and fished from (flows with fresh water and has fish in it), a castle with a noticeable lava line (when lava flowed around it), the second University in Italy (ever), a market selling local foods and several eateries and bars all very busy at 11pm on a Sunday night!

As usual, I walked around saying, "wow" or "holy smokes" over and over again. The whole day and evening felt surreal. I just couldn't believe how fortunate we were. Not only were we helped into Catania and greeted with goodies, but we were taken to see the real Catania with real Catanians. What a privilege.

I wondered how we could carry on around the world and experience life as amazing as this I then told myself, "Just go with the flow, Kim. Just go with the flow…all will be revealed." I suppose my thoughts at the time exposed a couple of things:

- I'm still a bit uncomfortable not knowing what's happening next. It's not easy for me to live life going from day to day. I am a recovering control freak planner – I used to have a to-do list and social calendar a mile long. And my business plans covered years. Not having an agenda, at all, is still unsettling for me!

- I have this belief popping up that life can't get any better than this, but I need to remind myself that it can and it will! Each new experience has the ability to be fresh and amazing. Surely nothing will replace our experiences in Italy, but that doesn't mean we can't have different and amazing experiences elsewhere.

Chapter 10: Sailing from Riposto, Sicily to Reggio, Calabria

After Catania we sailed north along the coast to a beautiful town called Riposto. We enjoyed a few days there and then our passage plan included viewing Sicily's beautiful northwest coastline, seeing the world's most amazing bronze statues on mainland Italy and then heading for Stromboli, a volcanic island located in the Aeolian Islands. Fortunately for us, we had two Italian crewmembers join us: Stefano and his girlfriend's daughter, Silvia.

Stefano managed to get us a free short-stay mooring on the mainland to quickly stop off to see the Riace bronze statues. As if on cue, a taxi drove up to our boat and offered to take us to the museum and back for a small fee. Considering that our 4-year-old daughter's (yes, Sienna had a birthday on this leg of the trip) little legs don't move too quickly, we opted to take the driver's offer. We could only stay at the mooring for a couple hours so we needed to be quick.

We were whisked off to the museum where the taxi driver made sure that we skipped the line and went straight in. I felt like royalty! Stefano stayed back on the boat to keep an eye on her. We literally moored up along a concrete standing where ships often moor. If we went to the marina we would have been charged and our travel to the museum time would have increased quite a bit. Silvia helped us to quickly find the exhibition and we watched a movie about the history of the statues. Then we entered an empty room that removed dust from us proving how valuable the bronze statues are.

Once the doors opened and the statues were in front of us, I was in absolute awe. Sienna yelled out, "You can see his willie!" and then giggled for a while. As a typical kid, she then started asking several questions like, where did they come from? How were they made? Why is a finger missing? What is the bite on his arm (location for a shield that wasn't recovered) and on and on. She's still too young to understand the significance of the statues, but she definitely demonstrated an appreciation for them. The Riace bronze statues are the most amazing artifacts that I've ever seen. The detail was incredible considering that they're super old. I felt a strong appreciation for the human body.

After spending 15 minutes with the statues, we left the museum and our taxi driver headed back to the boat. We asked him to stop off at a bakery for some fresh bread, so our driver made a diversion. He not only took us to the bakery, but he negotiated a discounted price for us. There was a lot of yelling back and forth and in the end we left with three loaves of fresh bread.

Before leaving the hands of our taxi driver, he gave us a bottle of red wine and a bottle of white. We all said "grazie" (thank you) and got back into the boat. Simon asked Stefano why the taxi driver gave us the wine and he replied that we paid a good amount for the trip and he was showing his appreciation. Again, I was feeling like royalty!

I put Sienna to bed and joined the rest of the crew up on deck. There was very little wind so we motored toward Stromboli. In the travel guides, I read that it's often possible to see flare-ups from the active volcano, so I was eager with anticipation. Would we see anything? Would it be too cloudy? What does a flare-up look like? Would we actually be able to see lava?

The sun went down and everyone peacefully sat in the cockpit. Loryn read her Kindle. Silvia grabbed a blanket and curled up on the seat to get cozy. Simon and Stefano chilled out as we progressed toward the Aeolian Islands. Around 9pm I went down below to read. It didn't take long for me to fall asleep, but I woke at 3am and re-joined the crew. Thankfully, there was enough wind to sail around the island rather than having to motor. The sea was flat calm and the only noise you could hear was the flapping of the headsail struggling to stay full.

All of us where trying to will the volcano to do something! There were clouds at the top, so we thought that perhaps we couldn't see through them. And then something happened. The cloud base at the top of the volcano turned orange and a rumbling sounded through the air. Loryn and I yelled out, "Oh my gosh – look, look, look!" Stefano joined us in the view but poor Simon was downstairs grabbing something.

Another 10 minutes went by and then suddenly a massive flare shot up, perhaps 100 meters into the sky and lava spewed out of the mouth of the volcano. I couldn't believe my eyes – I was watching a volcanic eruption from the absolutely serene surroundings of my boat. Furthermore, the backdrop was the Milky Way. The sky was blanketed with stars. I kept thinking, how lucky can I be?! We saw a bit more activity and noticed the sun was beginning to rise.

The volcano erupted and I was there to see it. My whole body felt energized with appreciation and awe. How many people get to see such a sight? I felt massively grateful. It didn't take long for tiredness to set in. Feeling exhausted from the day and night's events, I went back to bed. Upon waking up, I had no idea where we were. I noticed that we weren't moving, so assumed that Simon and Stefano must have anchored somewhere.

I got out of bed, climbed out into the cockpit to discover Loryn, Simon and Stefano all sleeping out in the fresh air. I looked up and noticed the massive volcano towering far above the boat. We were moored right at the base of Stromboli! Words cannot adequately convey how I felt. Every cell in my body had a perma-grin. I couldn't stop smiling and thinking, wow – this is the most amazing thing ever!

We pulled up the anchor and then circled the island in the daylight. We were able to see all the detail that we couldn't see in the darkness of night. Three sides of the volcano were covered in greenery and one side was full of a smooth blackness. It was very apparent as to which way the lava flowed out! And unbelievably, we saw houses and people who live on the volcano. I just couldn't believe that people would want to live there!

As if things couldn't get better, we then enjoyed sailing past the island of Panarea to Salina Island where we moored up in a marina. The whole crew disembarked with towels and toiletries. A shower was desperately needed for all! After enjoying a lovely, hot shower, Stefano directed us to a taxi and we were taken to the town of Malfa where we had an aperitif overlooking all the Aeolian Islands. The view was amazingly breathtaking. We were able to look out and view all the islands we had passed in the night.

Around 6pm, we left Salina Island and motored over to Lipari Island where Stefano treated us to a wonderful meal of pasta, fish and dessert. I don't think I can be any more grateful for my new friends, my family aboard, the amazing sights and the incredible food. I was totally in love with Italy and didn't want to leave.

We returned to Riposto to finally and hopefully get our generator fixed once and for all. We had engineers look at it in Gibraltar, Algeria, Malta and Catania – all without luck. Every time someone looked at the generator it would run for 10 hours or so (over a couple of days) and then it would just die out. Each time we'd think it was fixed, only to be disappointed. Fortunately for us, we were put in touch with a fantastic guy named George who was a massive help.

We really needed that generator. Our engine could power everything like the lights, oven, toilets, etc. however our system was not set up to work that way. Using the generator allowed us to create an alternative electricity source so the main engine could do what it does best.

We had guests! Actually, I think there have only been three nights in a whole month where we haven't had someone visit us. It's great. I've never had such a social life. Back in the UK, I felt like it was a chore to go out or have friends visit. It's not that I didn't like my friends, it's just that I was in a rut of working, eating dinner, watching TV and going to bed. And who wants to go out in the rain?!

Anyway, we went out with Salvo and Marisa, one of the couples we originally met in Marzamemi. Neither of them spoke English, nor do we speak Italian.

Language is not a wall or any barrier to friendship. None of us have to have walls if we don't want them. If the old stressed out control freak Kim was in Italy, never in a million years would I think I'd hang out with non-English speaking people. I'd be too afraid and think, "What could we possibly talk about?" And if I was forced to hang out, I'd probably make sure I either had a translator or some sort of communication.

That being noted, I do have an app but it's been too difficult to get WI-FI so we've had to make do. And that's a good thing!

Before I set out on my around the world sailing adventure one of my objectives was to connect more with people. I felt that I'd been locked away in the rat race for so long that I didn't know what human connection truly was. Little did I know that I was going to connect with people who speak a different language.

My cousin and I would try speaking Spanish, hoping that the words translated into Italian. My husband would try a bit of German, as Marisa lived in Germany. But mostly, we'd use our hands and do charades. Our attempts to explain things were hysterical.

Loryn and I would use any Italian words we could come up with and then act things out. By far, the funniest enactment was Loryn acting like an American Redneck. She was talking with a slow American southern drawl saying, "I'm going to go make me some grits." Of course, you'd have to be there to appreciate it but perhaps that example will give you an indication as to the fun we had.

Simon and Salvo hit it off from the beginning. I don't understand how, but they created some sort of sub-language where they whistled, made noises, spoke in their native languages and somehow knew what each other is saying.

Not once did any of us feel uncomfortable silences nor did we want the night to end.

We always came up with something to ask or talk about. And I suppose something far deeper than language was coming through. Perhaps love?

Even Sienna, when seeing Salvo or Marisa (or any of our new friends), yelled out their names and gave them great big hugs. And throughout the night she'd give them cuddles and, before bed, a goodnight kiss.

I hope Sienna learned something that took me almost 40 years to grasp. Connection with others isn't necessarily about speaking the same language. It's about being kind, wanting to spend time together and sharing love – no English required.

I'm so grateful. So, so, so grateful to have had this experience. Thank you, my Italian friends, for teaching me so much. You've changed my perception on life and people for the better.

[See Appendix A, 'V8. Riposto Marina' for video of us entering the marina]

Chapter 11: The Greek Ionian Islands

After our month-long sail around Sicily and the bottom side of the mainland Italy boot, we aimed *Britican* east to Greece. The plan was to start at the top of the Ionian Sea and work our way down before heading through the Corinthian Canal to Athens and the Aegean.

Our plan was to sail from Santa Maria de Lucia, Italy to Palaiokastrita, Corfu in Greece. The journey was estimated to take about 12 hours. We left our anchorage at 2am to give us ample time to find a mooring in Corfu in the daylight. Simon and Loryn got up while I stayed cozy in bed. Around 7am I took over and enjoyed a fantastic sail all by myself. It was bliss to be alone with the open sea all around me. It was also the first time I sailed our boat alone - yikes!

The weather was overcast, the seas were flat and the journey was quiet. Fortunately there was enough wind to have both sails out and achieve around 4 knots.

At one point I had two tankers lined up to eventually cross my bow. I couldn't figure out how to work the plotter. There's a way to look up ships and it will tell you if you're on a collision course or not. It also tells you when the ship will pass and by how many miles it will miss you.

Well, I just couldn't figure it out - perhaps because I was still waking up - so I diligently watched these two tankers that seemed miles away eventually pass in front of me about a half-mile away. If nothing else, it gave me something to do.

Suddenly, all the computer systems started beeping.

From what I could make out, we lost the GPS signal for a minute and then it came back. I just pushed buttons on the plotter and several of the other computers - things eventually stopped beeping. I then noticed that our estimated time of arrival (ETA) got longer or remained the same.

When I took over my helming stint the ETA said we had around 5 hours left and an hour later of sailing it still said we had 5 hours to go.

I felt as if my efforts to get us to Corfu were useless.

Looking at our speed, and relying on a plotter, we were doing 3.5 to 4 knots but our ETA wasn't reducing. I started to panic slightly and thought, "OMG, we must be going backwards – perhaps there's a tide or current pushing us?"

Being naïve, I pulled in the headsail (it's not hard – there's a button to push!) and started the motor to use our engine to reduce our ETA.

I didn't want to be floating around the Ionian Sea all day! A while later the ETA still remained around 5 hours. Simon woke from his rest, joined me in the cockpit, pushed something, asked, "'Did you lose signal?"' and then the ETA dropped to 2 hours!

Apparently, when we lost signal the tracking system stopped.

Simon then asked why are were motoring when there seemed to be enough wind. I had to tell him that I'm a goofball and didn't realize that our ETA was incorrect – I thought the tide, or something, was pushing us further away. Ironically, I noticed an island next to us come and go so that should have proven to me that we were certainly progressing in a forward manner.

I learned a big lesson: if the equipment doesn't seem to be giving you accurate information, check it out before using it to base your decisions!

Chapter 12: Our first stop in Greece – anchoring at Palaiokastrita, Corfu

I was super excited to see Corfu. Having been to some of the Greek Ionian Islands before, I knew what I was in store for, but Corfu was new to me.

It took us about 12 hours under sail to cross over to Greece. We left Italy early to ensure we had ample light to find a mooring in Corfu.

Simon decided to moor up in Palaiokastrita. We easily anchored in the bay – it was absolutely amazingly beautiful. The sea floor was sand so the water was turquoise blue, there were high rocks around us, and we were surrounded by a little fishing/tourism boat port, several tavernas and a few large hotels.

We anchored between a massive rock that came out of the water and some cliffs. The boat rocked from side to side quite a lot even though it looked very calm. During the day it didn't bother me but at night it was a bit much!

We took the tender out for a quick tour around the harbor and cliffs. It was the first time I rode in it and, wow, was it fast. Every wave hubby hit I yelled out a scream. In between laughing at me, Sienna just kept yelling, "Faster! Faster!"

Day two of being anchored in the bay, we got the tender out and motored ashore. We tied up where one of the small tourist sightseeing boats was missing. On shore, we got rid of our rubbish and found the first restaurant with WI-FI. Luckily, we didn't have far to go – it overlooked the little harbor and our beautiful boat on in the bay.

For the first time in months I connected to WI-FI that allowed me to upload and download larger files.

I was so excited – my online storage backup queue was massive by now. On the boat, I backup my computer to an external hard drive but once on land I attempt to back up to Dropbox, an online storage facility. I want to ensure all the photos and videos I'm taking are safe. In Italy, I struggled to upload a photo, let alone back up my computer.

While Loryn and I caught up with our emails and updated our families on Facebook, Simon took Sienna for a walk to find a grocery store. Not long after, they returned saying they had no luck. We were getting low on milk and had no bread left. It appeared that we landed ourselves in a very touristy town where the hotels and restaurants catered for everything.

That evening, we all boarded the tender and motored over to the strip of tavernas where we enjoyed our first Greek meal. The three of us adults ordered Kleftiko (stewed lamb) with a Greek salad and Sienna had fish and chips. Excellent!

In Italy, we ate home cooked food using readily available foods – pasta, seasonal vegetables, rice, potatoes and some meat. When we went out we invariably had either pizza or pasta. Most menus in Sicily had two pages of pizza, one page of pasta and then only one entre with pork, chicken and beef.

Before we left, we strategically put the bread served to us for dinner in my backpack. Thankfully we now had bread for our toast and eggs in the morning. Never had I even thought of doing that before, but then again never had I been somewhere that didn't have a grocery store!

The next morning we pulled up our anchor and motored to Gouvia Marina, Corfu Island's largest marina.

Wanting to check out the marina we went for a walk and found a cute little café bar. In fact, there were several to choose from right within the marina. My American background came out when I saw a cheeseburger on the menu. In fact, my husband and cousin joined me. Not expecting anything spectacular we were all surprised by the amazing taste of the burger. Oh-my-gosh – it was outstanding. Once again, it's probably because it's been so long since we had a cheeseburger that anything would have tasted great.

While out to dinner, Loryn and I started talking to the bar owners and Simon headed back to our boat with Sienna. We mentioned that we're collecting recipes on our travels, trying them out in *Britican's* galley and doing videos.

The bar owner's mother overheard us talking and went into the kitchen to handwrite a few recipes for us. Both Loryn and I were so excited to get an authentic moussaka recipe. Moussaka is like shepherd's pie – it can be layered with seasoned ground beef or lamb and has eggplant and potatoes.

Unbeknown to Loryn and me, Simon never made it back to the boat. He and Sienna were invited onto the boat next to us, full of Polish people. There was a little boy for Sienna to play with and Simon spent time tasting all sorts of Polish food and enjoying the company of those on the boat. No matter where you are, it always seems that there are new friends to be made.

The first full day we were in Gouvia Marina, we did some cleaning and general maintenance. In fact, the whole time we were at Gouvia Marina we took the opportunity to do various jobs. The weather wasn't great and the boat really needed a scrub down. Sienna helped a lot (we cleaned all the floors, cleared out some cupboards, opened the grey water tanks and cleaned them, etc.). For a break, we went for lunch and had the best salads ever! We also ordered a grilled squid that was AMAZING. It was my cousin's first taste of squid and she loved it.

At the supermarket I was shocked by the high prices. Not knowing what the cost of groceries would be, we made a novice mistake. We went to the supermarket at the marina and purchased very little – the total came to 116 euros. I fell onto the floor.

Later than day I found a huge grocery store on the main road – it was almost the same distance away. I was upset that I wasted so much money but also very happy – it was the best grocery store we'd seen since Morrison's in Gibraltar. It had two floors…everything we could ever want. Furthermore, there were loads of familiar brands so we knew what we were buying. Also, there was bacon and sauerkraut, something we'd been seeking for months.

While venturing outside the marina to the grocery store, I found a few local tavernas. I suggested to my family that we give one a go.

That evening, we went out to dinner and enjoyed another great meal. We all had local dishes – stafado, moussaka, grilled steak, and Sienna had slovaki. There were lots of laughs and we all really had fun.

For dessert, we ordered milk pie and it was amazing. If you ever see it on a menu, give it a go. My whole family thought it was excellent.

Sienna was in a particularly social mood. She spoke with the waiter, befriended another table of eaters and spoke to all the old boys sitting out near the outdoor grill. Sienna told one group of people that she was in Spanish school, that I speak Italian and that she has a sister and two brothers (Megan, Ethan and Mason – all friends of hers from back home). What an imagination! I guess her life isn't that interesting – she needs to make things up.

She had everyone eating out of her hands. The owner/waiter brought her ice cream, free of charge. And the guests all wanted to say hi to her. When we left I couldn't believe it when all the old boys yelled out, "Bye Kim," to me. She must have told them my name.

Of course, we always have an eye on her – she can't go out of our line of sight, but she can go and have conversations like a big girl. I get the feeling that she enjoys meeting people on her own – she feels like a real person rather than just a little kid.

Corfu Town is not just "nice."

Our original visit to the main city of Corfu Town on the Greek Ionian Island of Corfu was by taxi rather than by boat. While our yacht was safely moored at Gouvia Marina, about 10 miles north, we packed our backpacks and headed into the city.

Being new to the area, we didn't know if we could moor at Corfu Town so we took a nice little taxi ride to the city center. It might sound surprising, but going in a car was a novelty for us. We are almost always sailing or walking so having a car journey is fun.

Corfu Town is beautiful, magical, colorful, enchanting and downright special!

After the taxi driver dropped us off, my family and I started to wander through the narrow streets lined with restaurants, bakeries, butchers and tourist shops. Corfu Town is most definitely a tourist destination so the shops all hold the same made-in-China goods you find at any other tourist place; however, the shop fronts are at least in keeping with the style of the old city feeling.

I did discover quite a few one-off shops selling clothing, art, jewelry and a variety of knick-knacks. Those are the shops I enjoy!

Our first port of call was small little café for lunch. While walking along the main street we peered up a side street toward a square filled with restaurants, a church, official buildings and beautifully laid tables and chairs.

We stopped at the first café we found and pulled up a pew. The colors of the trees and shrubs drew me in – I immediately saw deep fuchsia, yellow and pinks among a beautifully laid out piazza. And there stood the most fantastic palm tree ever!

After a bit of discussion, we ordered a meat platter containing chicken and pork souvaki, turkey burgers and lamb, in addition to a Greek salad and some fries. While waiting for our food, a wedding finished at the church next door and we were able to admire a beautiful bride and groom. Even though I had no clue who the newlyweds were, my heart filled with loved and I silently wished them an incredible life together.

Our food came and went quickly. It was outstanding. How do we always get such amazing meals? Perhaps we're easily pleased or...we're so grateful for food that our gratitude creates more opportunities for more good food.

Our next stop was the seafront and the old fort. We looked out over a beautifully blue bay and cast our eyes on several sailboats moored at the foot of the old fort. The old fort in Corfu town was built by the Venetians and used by the British as a military hospital when Britain ruled Corfu.

After seeing the sailboats anchored, I asked Sim if we could anchor there. Of course he agreed.

We took some photos and made our way to the fort. We had a ball walking along the walls, enjoying the views and absorbing the history. The breeze was nice and the walk up to the top wasn't too difficult. Once we got to the end, we enjoyed a panoramic view over the Ionian Sea and Corfu Town.

The next day we were anchored next to the old fort. It was great to be anchored – I no longer enjoy the marinas. They're expensive, crowded, noisy and impersonal.

I can't explain how amazing it feels to wake up, open up our door at the top of our stairs and look up to a historical fort alongside the most blue waters I've seen. Every morning I had to pinch myself and express my gratitude for being able to sleep under the stars next to the incredible Corfu Town.

Needing a SIM card, printer, USB stick and a wireless keyboard, my husband dropped Loryn and me off for a trip to the town. We were like two little kids let out alone for the first time. We got our chores done – a quick visit to Vodafone to sort out our WI-FI and then a visit to Publix, a computer store and we were done.

We walked down the back streets enjoying the sights and smells of Corfu Town. And of course, we looked over the made-in-China stuff in addition to the handmade offerings.

Being without Sienna for the first time in months gave me the opportunity to dawdle, spend time looking at what I wanted to look at and stop off for a nice glass of wine! Loryn and I wandered around laughing and chatting – it was a nice little girly break.

Chapter 13: The magic of Fiscardo, Cephalonia

Fiscardo is a small town at the top of the Greek Island, Cephalonia; the largest of the Ionian Islands. Located to the west of mainland Greece, Cephalonia became quite popular after the book, "Captain Correlli's Mandolin" by Louis de Bernières, followed by the movie of the same name staring Penélope Cruz and Nicholas Cage.

Just over 12 years ago, I visited Fiscardo, a beautiful harbor village, when Simon and I did our very first flotilla vacation. A flotilla vacation involves hiring a yacht for a week or two. You get a yacht, are helped by a crew to leave and arrive in moorings, are told where to go and when to arrive at the next destination and for the course of holiday, you visit each destination with others doing the same thing.

There were around eight other boats in our group. We didn't sail around with them – we just met them at the final destination each evening. It was a great opportunity to have fun sailing during the day and then tell tales in the evening over drinks. Every boat always has a story – someone inevitably picked up the anchor of someone else's boat, another boat saw dolphins and someone learned something new.

A flotilla vacation is absolutely brilliant for newbie sailors!

I remember arriving in Fiscardo with Simon and another couple, Tim and Sonia. Previous to our trip, Simon and Tim took a weekend sailing course – a precursor to chartering a yacht. When we arrived in Greece I looked at the 33' yacht and thought, "Oh-my-gosh…are we really going to sail that for a week?" The yacht seemed huge and there were so many unknowns for me. I sailed a bit in the past, but I didn't really know how to sail. I was always a passenger – I sat up on top and looked pretty!

After collecting our yacht, named *Emerald*, we put away our clothes, poured a drink and I secretly said a prayer that we'd survive a week on the Ionian Sea. I was half excited and in love with the surrounding area and half scared about getting out and actually sailing. The next day, with no time to investigate the town and surrounding area, we left the beautifully idyllic Fiscardo.

We pushed off our mooring, motored out of the harbor and attempted to put up the sail. For some reason the guys couldn't get the sail up. They struggled to winch up the mainsail. I looked at the other boats and said, "Why are all the other boats going in the opposite direction?" The men quickly realized that they were going with the wind rather than going into the wind. Important note: to raise the main sail you must go into the wind!

We turned the boat into the wind, managed to get the mainsail up and thereafter we were hooked for life. Despite the fact that we had difficult start, that very first flotilla vacation gave us the bug.

Little did we know that we'd return to Fiscardo 12 years later with our own yacht!

This time around, however, I spent several days in Fiscardo and have found more of its magic!

When we first arrived to the area our initial intention was to moor on the island of Lefkas, an island above Cephalonia. The winds were too strong for the mooring so we diverted to Fiscardo. Around 7pm we entered the harbor, did a quick spin around and quickly realized that there was no room at the Inn! We left the port and sailed down the island finding an empty harbor where we moored for the night. We were surrounded by goats and that's it! The next day we woke and prepared to get into Fiscardo. Around 10:30 we entered the harbor and noticed a couple spaces free along the hard. I went to the anchor, Simon backed us up and Loryn, prepared to throw someone our warps (back ropes).

There were loads of people eating, walking around and enjoying the beauty of the boats. When we entered the harbor, people stopped to look. When we started to back up, and our bow thrusters sounded, people dropped what they were doing and stared. I felt as if we were the center of attention and I didn't like it! What if we mess up?! Fortunately, I managed the anchor well, Simon back up perfectly and Loryn threw the warps to someone who helped us out. For at least a half hour we had to work on getting our gangplank out, backing up a bit more and fiddly stuff. Meanwhile there were loads of people sipping their coffees and eating food a few feet next to us! We had a captive audience.

As we moored up, several people lined up to take our lines. Being private sailors, rather than chartering a boat, made me think we'd be all on our own. I was wrong. As we neared the jetty there were people on the jetty and along the boats next to us that all offered to take lines. Even the waiters at the restaurant were prepared to help in any way that they could. One guy got low on the stern of an adjacent boat to keep an eye on our rudder to make sure that it didn't hit the back ledge.

Within five minutes of turning off our engine we already made a handful of new friends.

The yacht next to us held two couples on a flotilla holiday in addition to a skipper who later introduced us to the seasonal flotilla staff. The waiters brought us nice cold beers and joined in on our discussions about our history in Fiscardo. And passers-by were quick to ask questions and find out who we were and how we came to sailing *Britican*.

Throughout our stay we were blessed to meet so many great people. One evening Sienna fell asleep at the dinner table. It was a very late evening and she was exhausted. One of the waiters pulled over a sofa chair and had us pick her up and lay her in the chair.. Next thing I noticed that Sienna had a coat over her body! The waiter covered her up to make sure she was warm.

That type of kind gesture didn't happen once – it happened day after day.

Sienna became friends with the son of the owner of the bakery. Soon she would come home with different cookies. She joined the local kids to catch a variety of marine life. Every hour or so we'd be graced with a small fish, a starfish and weird snake like fish with hundreds of legs.

Yes, most people are happy when on vacation and it's easy to strike up conversations. But I've been to many locations where the locals are not so happy to spend time with tourists. Fiscardo is one of those magical places where everyone – whether they're a tourist, seasonal staff or a born and bred Cephalonian – seems open to join in conversation and extend kindness.

The harbor is graced with around 30 eateries – each unique in character. Some offer traditional Greek food with a bright white and blue façade, where others provide elegant French food amid dainty tables, lace menus, white lanterns and freshly picked flowers. One of the flotilla staff members was a Thai foodie and invited us to join him for dinner.

Throughout our stay, we tested out various venues for breakfast, lunch and dinner and each time we moo'd like cows. Mmmmm. We ate everything from a fresh fish platter to moussaka to great salads. It would be unfair of me to recommend one place over another as they all offered excellent food and a unique ambiance. And there's certainly something for everyone. You can get a burger and fries, pizza or a kebob, or a gourmet four-course meal. There was often a child's menu, or I simply asked for a small portion of something and every restaurant was accommodating.

The one place worth mentioning, however, is the Captain's Cabin. We were fortunate to moor the stern of our boat right up to this restaurant. Not only was the food excellent, but the staff was amazing. If I needed help getting on or off the boat, they were there. They always greeted Sienna while patting her on the head. We'd even get served our beers on our boat!

The harbor of Fiscardo is lined with yachts on every side. Some yachts moor up to the hard, whereas others drop an anchor and then tie long ropes from their stern to a tree or hard standing. Looking out at the view, I can see sailboats, catamarans and a few powerboats. There are also several small Greek fishing boats. Behind the yachts on two sides of the port are beautiful restaurants, boutique shops, super markets and bars. Cars are not allowed, making the whole village a pedestrian's paradise.

Rising up above the town are a few small bed and breakfasts, homes and more restaurants. Of course, there's a lovely little church too. Unlike other popular towns there's no huge hotel or large establishment taking precedence over the views. In fact, aside from the town, the majority of the view consists of a variety of green trees, green mountainside and deep blue water. I love those long thin evergreen trees that rise up like long fingers – they're dotted all over the place.

Considering that we had several days in Fiscardo, Loryn and I decided to do one of the circular hikes promoted on signs throughout the town. After surveying the trail map, we decided to do a 4.7 km /2.5 hour hike leaving and returning to Fiscardo.

The trail had amazing markings – we never wondered which way to go. As we walked along, we enjoyed seeing stone walls on either side of the path, abandoned buildings and loads of greenery and flowers. We went up and we went down. We saw the sea from the top of the hills and we saw the sea from a couple amazing beaches. One of the beaches we discovered was accessible by foot only and the whole beach had white stones only. Loryn and I stood on the beach and had to use all our willpower not to run into the sea and swim!

After a couple hours, however, we realized that we inadvertently got ourselves onto a 10 km walk!

Instead of being close to the ending point we realized we were only half way. By the end of the walk neither of us could barely walk. I think it was about five hours when we made it back to the boat.

By the end of the walk we started getting delirious, but I wouldn't have taken back the experience for anything. We traversed Northern Cephalonia and saw goats, flowers, grasshoppers, snakes, trees, beaches and the sea. It was wonderful.

Before leaving Fiscardo, Simon's father, Keith, flew down from England to join us for a month.

We first sailed to the island of Zykinthos and stayed for an evening. We all participated in a Greek night enjoying traditional music and food. It was a fantastic way to welcome Keith to the beautiful country of Greece.

Our plan was to go east, leaving the Ionian Sea, headed for the mainland Peloponnese.

Chapter 14: Running the stadium track at Olympia, Greece

A few days before our arrival to the Peloponnese in Greece, I had no knowledge of what we'd find, nor did I expect anything of particular significance. As I've written, for the first time in my life I seem to live each day as it comes. I knew, however, that, at some point, we'd get to Athens and see the Acropolis.

On a Sunday evening, about one hour out of Parts, Greece's third largest city, we radioed the Patras Harbormaster looking for a berth. We were directed to a commercial quayside in front of a $30 million super yacht and a tugboat.

While heading toward Patras, Simon said, "Who wants to see where the Olympics started in Olympia, Greece?"'

It wasn't that long ago that Simon, Sienna and I stood in front of the butchers' in a British town center high street to watch the Olympic torch make its way through England. And the picture of my daughter holding the Olympic torch is also fresh in my mind. One of the parents associated to her pre-school had a connection and all the kids were able to hold one of the torches and get their photograph taken!

At the time of the Olympics in England we had no idea that we'd visit Olympia, Greece, nor did we have any inclination that we'd be living on a boat and traveling around the world.

Simon rented a car and Sienna, Loryn, Keith and I headed off to Olympia.

Not knowing what to expect, I was immediately blown away by what is called the "Sanctuary at Olympia." Dating back to the 10th century BC, the area flourished until 426 AD when the emperor Theodosius II closed all ancient sanctuaries.

My eyes walked down a very lush road and entered into the archeological site to see descriptive plaques, columns, building outlines, Greek works, Roman works and the site of one of the ancient wonders of the world! We saw the spot where the great statue of Zeus was located! Bonus – I wasn't expecting to see the spot of an ancient wonder of the world.

Except for Keith, my father-in-law, we all ran the distance of the track that naked Greek men ran all those thousands of years ago. Yes – the first Olympic games were performed by men only and they were naked! Women were not allowed to watch, let alone partake in the events.

The area filled with trees, flowers and lush green countryside littered with ruins – including mosaics. Most ruins had a plaque in English showing an image of what it looked like back in the day, so it wasn't difficult to imagine the spectacular beauty of the sanctuary.

At each plaque, Sienna would point out what the building looked like and we'd read out what it was for. One ruin was a gymnasium where athletes trained for running events and the pentathlon. Another building was called the Palestra where the sportsmen trained for wrestling, boxing and jumping. There was a place for the priests of Olympia, Baths, a Council Chamber and a Temple of Hera along with the Alter of Zeus and the Temple of Zeus. It was huge!

The museum at Olympia is different.

It's small yet the impact is profound. After walking into the main doors and passing the small-scale 3-D model of the grounds, you walk into a hall that has the actual pediments from the temple of Zeus. The pediments are the triangular tops of the front façade of a building.

The actual pediments were reconstructed in the large hall and it was amazing to see what it really looked like! Yes, some heads were missing and various bits were not present, but there was enough there to give you a first hand experience of what the building must have looked like in its heyday.

I had to pinch myself because I just couldn't believe something like this existed.

As I carried on through the museum, my eyes smiled at larger than life-size statues, metal objects, pottery and more. Sienna kept finding more and more goodies. She'd come up to me and say, "Mom, close your eyes!" She'd lead me to a statue or glass window and say, "Okay – open them now!"

Each time I opened my eyes I felt this amazing gratitude to be able to see such wonders.

The whole day was surreal. I suppose it's a good thing that I don't think ahead and don't know what I'm going to see and do. Perhaps if I did know what I'd find at Olympia it might have been anticlimactic? I'm not sure...

Seeing Olympia and running across the very first Olympic stadium, just as the Greeks did during the 10th Century BC was a definite top 100 highlight of my life. (Note that I started off at 10, then moved to 20 and now I've expanded to 100 highlights just so I can count all the amazing things happening on our journey!)

I know my family also enjoyed the experience immensely. If you're sailing around the Peloponnese, visiting Olympia is a must-do experience.

Chapter 15: Travelling through the Corinth Canal

The Corinthian Canal is a passage created back in 1882 and 1883 that connects the Ionian Sea to the Aegean. Rather than travelling south around the Peloponnese, you can pay a handsome fee to cut through Greece and pop out near Athens. Around 12,000 boats pass through the narrow canal each year, from small boats to tankers and large cruise ships.

Previous to the canal being in place, the ancients used to drag ships across the land on a paved road. I've been told that on the north side you can still see remnants of the road. Throughout history the Greeks and Romans drew up plans to create a canal but the task was too difficult.

For as long as I can remember, my husband always wanted to voyage through the Corinth Canal, so the lead up to the event filled us all with anticipation.

The night before our planned canal transit, and knowing that gale force winds were predicted, we anchored in the northeast area of the Corinth Bay, about one mile north of the canal entrance.

We anchored with our friends, Jim and Carole on sailboat *Nepenthe* while our friends on *Horizon* went toward Corinth to see if they could get a spot on the quayside. *Horizon* radioed us to let us know they got the last spot so we had to make do with our anchorage.

Around 9pm the winds started and they were forecast to increase to 7's and 8's (30 to 40 knots of wind or up to 50 mph) by 3am. When anchored in normal conditions, the boat swings around the anchor chain, usually swinging no more than 180 degrees with the bow facing the wind. If the wind changes, the boat may swing right around. When things are calm, it's a very slow paced swing and it's easy to ignore the movement. And at times, the boat barely swings at all!

When gales hit a boat on an anchor it's a totally different experience – it's somewhat scary!

Depending where the boat is on its swing and when the wind hits the boat you can experience different things. The worst is when the wind hits the side or beam of the boat and the boat gets slightly pushed over while it swings quite violently around the anchor chain. The background view spins around!

What kept me up all night was the possibility that our anchor might pull loose, causing us to drift toward land or out to sea. If other boats are close by, that increases my anxiety. There's a chance that their anchor may come lose and hit us!

Under normal conditions I sleep fine, but during gale force winds I find it difficult to get real sleep. I catnap, and whenever I hear the winds hit us, I pop up and look for spots on land that I've earmarked.

On the evening prior to our Corinth Canal transit we had gale force winds and a boat anchored too close to us for comfort. Simon and I slept in the cockpit so that we could keep a constant anchor watch. Around 4am I went to bed while Simon stayed up.

At 5:30am we started our discussions with sailboat *Nepenthe* and sailboat *Horizons* about the weather and the necessary requirements to enter the canal. No one on *Britican* or *Nepenthe* slept very well, and more winds were forecast. *Horizons* at least had the comfort of knowing they were tied down.

Carole on *Nepenthe* suggested that an anchorage on the other side of the canal would provide us with a safer harbor. We decided it was best for us anchored boats to make a move. The crew on *Horizons* chose to stay put and wait for the winds to die down.

We were exhausted, but the idea of going through the canal gave us all the energy we needed to get going.

When reading more about the canal I discovered that boats enter in one direction in convoy until they're all through and then the authorities open up the other end. So, boats go from west to east and then the east boats go through to the west. Apparently, the canal is open 24 hours a day every day accept Tuesday. On Tuesdays, necessary repairs are made to the canal.

After reading the Greece Pilot Book for sailors, we called the required VHS channel 11, using the call-sign Isthmia Pilot asking for permission to make the transit. Simon made the call on behalf of *Britican* and *Nepenthe*. The Corinthian Canal radio operator told us to leave the anchorage and call when we were one-half mile from the canal entrance.

By 7am we were pulling up our anchors and pointing our boats toward the entrance of the canal. For some reason I thought there would be locks or gates, but upon arrival we could see straight through the canal to the other side.

Simon entered between the red and green navigation lights and I noticed that a road was closed and a bridge reclined to prevent traffic from crossing the canal. Jim on *Nepenthe* radioed us to slow down a bit as the waters were rough. Upon entering the canal we were still experiencing gale force winds. Water was sloshing up onto the deck and I had to work fast to protect my cameras.

We slowed down as we entered calm waters in the canal. Not long after, the authorities radioed us to speed up. For the amount we had to pay to transit the canal I think we all wanted the trip to last for quite a while. While between the two high cliffs we felt absolutely no wind – it was blissful. The sun was coming up, the water was like glass, Sienna was enjoying breakfast and we all felt absolute awe as we motored down the beautiful Corinth Canal.

I took around 200 photos – several of *Nepenthe* and several of the journey. I was surprised by how narrow the canal was. And I didn't realize that the cliffs would be so high on either side.

On my SailingBritican Facebook page a friend advised me to take photos of the steps the workers used to get out. I wasn't sure what he was talking about, and after traveling for quite some distance I didn't see any steps.

Eventually I discovered what I was looking for. There on the side of the cavern were footholds going up and down.

Aside from high cliffs on both sides and calm waters in front of us, there wasn't much to obstruct our view. I took some photos of the rock, shrubs, *Britican's* shadow and all of the crew enjoying the passage.

When coming to the end of the Corinthian Canal we moored up on our starboard (right) side. I jumped off, got us tied down and then ran back to *Nepenthe* to take their bowline. Simon and Carole jumped off with the boat papers and went to the office to pay our dues. Our bill came to 347 euros to go 3.2 miles.

Feeling pressure to get off the wall within the exit of the canal, we slipped our lines and headed toward our new mooring in Kalamaki. Thankfully, the winds died down quite a bit and we felt more secure in the new bay. Although Kalamaki wasn't very picturesque, it was a more comfortable anchorage and we could watch all the boats entering and exiting the canal.

[See Appendix A, 'V4. Corinth Canal' for a link to a video showcasing our passage]

Chapter 16: Would we carry on after three months?

I don't want to live anywhere other than on my boat. I have lost all interest in owning an immovable home on land. Of course I have that "get out of jail" card saying that's how I feel today…perhaps tomorrow will be different.

We find a place to stay for a few days where we explore, do our grocery shopping, spend time swimming, work on the boat and enjoy time with friends. When it's time to move on, we do it all over again, but with a different backdrop, new things to explore and often more friends to meet.

Before we left on our adventure I felt that we'd make friends easily, but I didn't think it would be so easy and so much fun.

Every country we've been in, we've made friends who will most likely be life-long friends. In Italy, we spent time over the course of a month with three sailing couples. While in Greece we joined up with two other boats. I was sure the trend would continue.

And what I noticed from the other world cruisers is that the longer you're out sailing, the more friends you accumulate. Eventually you get to a point where you know someone in most ports of call.

I've also discovered that when a boat with a child finds another boat with a child, the two boats work together to organize play dates. For example, we met the sailboat *Horizons* owned by three-year full time world cruisers Vince and Barbie. On board *Horizons*, for a month, the owners entertained their niece Lalita and her nine-year old daughter, Sierra.

And on our seven-hour sail down from the Corinthian Canal to the island of Poros, Sierra joined us on our boat where the girls played doctor, PlayDoh, Barbies and watched a couple of movies. When we're anchored up they're out swimming or exploring our new location together.

Over 10 of us from three boats all organized a trip to Delphi together and it was great to see the girls climb to the top hand-in-hand.

Yes, the time will come when we move on or when Sierra has to go home, but it won't take long for another boat to come along with a child or children on board!

Since leaving England back in April, my daughter's social skills have gone through the roof.

She'll play with anyone speaking any language at any age! I've found her telling jokes to a table of old men and enjoying a nice swim with a 21-year-old girl. For the most part, however, she's running around with the local kids trying to catch fish, build sand castles or see who can run the fastest.

Before we left, Sienna would hide behind my leg when we met someone new. Now, she's so far in front of me that I'm behind her legs! She's happy to greet anyone and has definitely learned that it's okay to be confident and go up to kids and say, "Can we play?"

Thinking back...while in England, I took Sienna to an indoor play gym, crammed with children, and she was too afraid to befriend any of them. I had to crawl around the jungle gym with her for a few hours hoping I could convince her to make new friends. I was quite worried when we left for our adventure, thinking how am I going to help her gain confidence, but it really hasn't been an issue.

But what about Sienna's behavior?

Sienna's behavior went into a rapid tailspin two months into our journey. She started to freak out and we had a massive blow out one night where she lashed out, lost all control, smashed a plate and bit my arm drawing blood.

As you can imagine, I wondered if our trip was messing her up. I thought that I must be a terrible parent. And then I thought long and hard about how the transition was affecting us all. Heck – we sold everything we owned, up'd sticks and left on a boat destined to sail around the world!

Of course there were going to be some growing pains.

After the big blow out, I purchased some books on parenting from Amazon. Thank God for Kindle! The books all provided extremely helpful information and I was soon armed with several parenting techniques.

I'd love to say that Sienna's behavior changed instantly, but it didn't. I can, however, say that we never had a night as bad as the big blow out. Each day things got better and better. I started to listen more and she realized that I was always available to help. Our relationship grew stronger and we became closer.

I now feel that Sienna is a totally normal kid acting like several kids do…she would have had the same issues if we were on land.

Aside from all that, life on board was getting more "normal."

For these three months, it's been Simon, Loryn, Sienna and I who have lived aboard *Britican*. We now have routines and roles that we've organically fit into. Loryn does most of the cooking and we both clean together. I'm CMO (Chief Mom Officer), Simon looks after the boat and navigating. Loryn and I do all the ropes, sails, anchoring and mooring up.

We didn't even have to talk anymore; we just went about our tasks knowing what everyone is doing.

For example, when we first started, we had no clue about anchoring. We'd drop the anchor and hope it held! We certainly didn't communicate and no one knew who was doing what.

We couldn't really discuss our observations because we didn't know what we were looking for. Now, our confidence has increased and we feel comfortable doing what we're doing AND doing things with each other. And when I say all this, it goes for all our tasks – not just anchoring.

So –entering our fourth month of sailing around the world I'm happy to report that our expectations were surpassed. I wouldn't want to be any other place doing any other thing. For the first time in my life, if you asked me what I'd do if I won the lottery, my response would be, "absolutely nothing other than what I'm doing right at this very moment!"

Before moving forward, let me back up just a bit and mention Delphi. It's certainly a must-see destination.

Chapter 17: Visiting Delphi, Hydra and Delos

Delphi is an ancient Greek religious sanctuary sacred to the god Apollo. It's home to the famous oracles which gave cryptic prediction and guidance to politicians and individuals. Furthermore, it was home to the Pythian Games.

What's very interesting is that the site was first settled in 1500 to 1100 BC and considered the center of the world. In Greek mythology Zeus released two eagles – one to the east and one to the west – and they met in Delphi.

The site was abandoned during the 7th century AD and rediscovered around 1880 by French archaeologists. Lucky for us that they found it, as it's a remarkable place!

But how the heck did we come about visiting Delphi during our sailing travels?

After our stay in the commercial port of Patras, the third largest city in Greece, we made our way under the Rio-Antirrio bridge. The bridge links the Peloponnese with central Greece and is the largest suspended bridge in the world.

When we went under the bridge, heading for a town called Itea, we all went to the bow of the boat and enjoyed the view.

Interestingly Simon spent a couple weeks in Itea when he was seven years old. His aunt took him for a six-week tour of Greece and he remembers Itea vividly. Simon smiles and explains, "Itea is the place where I learned how to swim. My aunt popped my rubber ring and threw me in. It didn't take long for me to figure out how to float!"

When we moored up we found our friends on sailboat *Nepenthe*. And in Delphi, we met the crew from sailboat *Horizons* mentioned earlier.

On *Horizons*, three-year cruising experts Vince and Barbie were joined by their niece Marie, her daughter Seaira and Marie's best friend Cylinda. Cylinda was joining the crew for a couple weeks and Marie and her daughter for a month. We were all pleased to meet each other and it didn't take long for all three boats to decide to visit Delphi together.

So there were 12 of us heading for the bus station to Delphi. The ride took a short 20 minutes up the side of a mountain. We were all thankful at how close Delphi was.

I was very surprised at how lush the area was!

There were loads of trees and greenery despite us being on the side of a mountain. The village of Delphi was very quiet and rather old-fashioned. It didn't have a commercial or touristy feel to it. Of course, it was loaded with tourist shops, but it was simple.

After recently visiting Olympia, I thought that I'd be a bit tired of ruins, but I was wrong. Delphi was a magical experience.

While combining the history and the feel of the place, I couldn't help but feel like I was somewhere special. The path led us up higher and higher through a multitude of amazing ruins. There were temples, columns, an amphitheater and eventually we came across a beautifully well-preserved stadium.

Several of the building blocks were filled with ancient Greek words in addition to beautiful images. Around every turn there was a new an exciting view to take in. And Delphi is set on the side of a mountain so the views from the ancient city were absolutely breathtaking.

The Greek Island of Hydra

Imagine a cove with beautiful light and dark blue waters surrounded by etched hills and a beach with thatched umbrellas and sunbeds. And further visualize the beach full of day-trippers all leaving the yachties to absolute solitude by nightfall. No roads, no lights, no electricity and no mobile or Wi-Fi connection. No sign of any life in the bay.

Finding a beautiful, quiet peaceful bay isn't always easy.

So, when we anchored off the Greek island of Hydra we were very pleased. By 8pm we were joined with only a few other yachts. For the most part, we had the bay to ourselves. Not long after setting the hook, Loryn and I looked over to the mountainous island and decided that we needed to climb to the top! As the day was coming to an end we decided to wake early, swim ashore and hike as far as we could get. After a lovely night's sleep, we threw on our bathing suits, packed a bag with sneakers, socks, water and our cameras and headed to the aft of the boat.

Once there, we surveyed the distance between the boat and land. There was a small stretch of water we had to swim across to get to the island. Fortunately, we had a ship to shore line preventing our boat from swinging on the anchor.

The challenge, however, was to slide our bag across the line without it hitting the water!

After a bit of discussion, we fastened Loryn's backpack onto the landline. We then tied a sail tie onto the bag so that we could swim and pull the bag along. To increase the challenge we also decided to bring our coffees with us.

The swim to land was full of laughter.

Fortunately, the bag made it across dry and we were able to put on our socks and sneakers. We couldn't bring shorts and a t-shirt and it was hot anyway, so we scaled the hill in our bathing suits. No one was around to see us anyway. Rather than follow the main path to the beach, we instead went 'off-road' immediately and encountered some huge spiders. Perhaps keeping to a path might have been a better idea?

We eventually picked up a path and headed up the hillside. Our first stop was an abandoned house that may have doubled for a church. From there, we picked up a trail winding up the hillside toward an olive grove.

Then our climb went from easy going to hard work – we went off-road heading for the top.

At a certain height the hillside went from shrubs, thorns and grass and turned to rocks and boulders. Having to slightly scale the mountain, we kept going up and up and up. Finally, we hit the top of the mountain and WOW, the view was incredible. The hike was well worth the effort.

Upon our return, Simon welcomed us on board and said, "Let's release the land line, lift the anchor and head out!" Fortunately, we got all our work done (lifting the anchor, stowing the lines, securing the fenders and setting the sails) and then Loryn and I collapsed in the cockpit enjoying a nice, slow sail to the next island. I wondered what our next off-road adventure would be. Little did I know that we'd discover an uninhabited island, called Delos, that's full of ruins.

Visiting Delos

"Once you've seen one Greek ruin, you've seen them all," Or have you? What about visiting Delos, Greece?

Getting to Delos is not easy. You have to find a place for your boat in a marina or anchor off Mykonos and then take a water taxi over to Delos. Was it worth the effort to get there?

Let me tell you a bit about Delos before answering that question.

No one lives on the island of Delos and it's not a destination you'll come across by accident. Dating back to 2500 BC, Delos is one of the world's most important archaeological sites. It's the birthplace of the mythological sun god, Apollo, and his twin, Artemis, the goddess of the moon and the hunt. The island was the most sacred place of worship in ancient Greece.

In 426 BC, the Athenians decided to "cleanse" Delos, and its thousands of inhabitants were told to leave. No one was allowed to be born, die or be buried on the Holy island. Since then it's been uninhabited except for a handful of people who live on the island to maintain the archeological site.

When we entered the ancient site I thought, WOW – look at all the stuff.

Literally, there were columns, building footings, bricks, walls and roads all over the place. As far as the eye could see, there were ruins. A few modern houses and a museum were easily identifiable, but otherwise it looked like a junkyard of rock, marble and old stuff.

Some of the ruins had walls up to the ceiling, mosaic floors and columns within the buildings. It wasn't too difficult to imagine what they looked like back in the day. We also came across a few statues. The descriptive plaques dotted around the site offered an example of what the ruin looked like in its heyday.

What I find remarkable is that most buildings and statues were painted vibrant colors in ancient Greece. Even the Parthenon was very colorful. In my mind I always reflected on Greece as everything being white marble, but that was not the case.

Delos sprawled along the coast with a path leading up to the highest point on the island. Of course we had to go to the top! Sienna and I ran ahead of the rest of our crew to make it to the top first. To my surprise, we not only made it to the top but we also managed to stand without blowing over. The winds were seriously blowy.

After several hours of walking around, we made it back to our ferry to Mikonos. The crew and I were unanimous – Delos is a must see for anyone interested in Greek ruins.

Chapter 18: Is enlightenment in the cards, too?

Mornings on the boat are, and always have been, magical for me. Here's a typical day: I'll be sitting in the cockpit. The roosters are crowing and there are a few dogs barking. There's a low murmur of the crickets. I can hear waves hit the shore and the boat rattles slightly as the calm waters cause tiny movements. The halyards slightly caress the mast and a passing ferry can be heard in the far distance. Soft snores come from two of the bedrooms below.

The scents of local trees, the herb, sage, and last night's grill at the taverna lace the air. Although the temperature is mild, the smell and feel of the air indicate that it's going to be another hot day.

There's a castle high on the hill with an adjacent hill lined with very old windmills. Lower down the hill is a village with more windmills. Around 10 sail and motorboats are near us all lined up with an anchor in the sea and a landline tying them to the shore. There are boats anchored and islands further out dotting the sea.

We slowly swing on our anchor. I'm getting a 60-degree view without turning my head waiting for the sun's rays to hit a hillside or for the sun to make an appearance. Early mornings are so precious. They're so special and I'm not sure why I spent all those years sleeping through them.

As I ponder this new sleep and waking routine my thoughts open to all sorts of options.

Heck, I can do anything I want to do. If I want to wake at 5am, take five naps a day and sleep for three hours a night I could give it a go. And if and when that no longer suits me, I can change again. I suppose I've always had the freedom to choose my sleep habits, or anything for that matter, but the pressure of working, general life and exhaustion seemed to require a daily 12-hour respite.

Changing my sleeping hours is something I can alter allowing me to enjoy the peacefulness and serenity of the mornings...and what else? What else can I choose to change?

Selling up and sailing away not only took me out of the rat race but it also removed me from what is considered normal living distractions. I no longer have access to the news nor am I able to get caught up in my previous social-circle dramas. My mind isn't flooded with advertisements or over-stimulating television programs and movies. I no longer experience traffic jams, road-rage or people failing to cope with life. And for the most part, the weather can't give me cause to complain; the daily forecast is usually warm and sunny. From a work perspective, I'm far removed from office politics, and what a relief that is!

I have this newfound freedom that has cleared my mind and allowed me to choose different ways to think and live. It's as if I've cleared some space where I can be free of day-to-day stimulus and think about the more meaningful things in my life. Waking up to a magical dawn and sleeping routines is just one example.

On further reflection, my thoughts don't seem to spiral as much anymore. A thought comes in, I look at it and then it goes. Another thought comes in, I look at it and it goes.

Previously, I'd be off thinking of past failures and possible future disappointments or even world destruction.

Of course I think of my past. Often, I reflect on summer holidays with my family. I compare where I was to where I am now. Reminders of past events pop in all the time; however, instead of getting stuck into a thought they seem to pass through me. The same with thinking of my future. I'll consider what we're going to do for, let's say, Christmas, ponder a few options and then let the thought go. I don't spiral into a thought and get caught up in it. There's very little worry or fear present. I don't worry about where we're going or when we'll get there. My fears and worries about life are not completely gone, but they're not the way the used to be. Heck, I was afraid of everything.

I used to be so caught up with being successful, looking pretty and being a good mom/wife/friend/employer/etc. Now, none of those thoughts entertain my mind. None of those things apply to who I am anymore. Now, I look out at the blue water and feel gratitude, think about what I'll make for lunch or what activity Sienna, Simon and I can do when we moor up. We never know where we'll be in a couple days. Things change often and we all just go with the flow.

Wise people often suggest that silent meditation is used to quiet the mind and find enlightenment.

I've tried for years to both meditate and find enlightenment, and sitting alone with my thoughts caused me to think even more…and to get sucked more into whatever was bothering me.

I suppose, however, I've now found my form of meditation. It's not by sitting cross-legged, chanting OMMMM and watching my thoughts bubble to the surface. It's by sailing on the seas and living the lifestyle of a somewhat simple traveler – it's by living the life of my dreams. I feel so removed from the things I didn't like (gossip, news, politics, broken systems – banks, healthcare, education, bad food, depressing weather, etc.) and so close to the things I love (family, friends, local fresh non-processed foods, days spent sailing, nights spent star-gazing, new people, new sights and amazing memories).

Some people might say I'm escaping or hiding from life yet I feel like I'm, for the first time, really living life.

By removing myself from what most people call "normalcy" I can look back at it and realize how caught up I was by things that didn't make me happy.

Success no longer equates to making loads of money – rather, the word "success" means that I'm fulfilled.

And for me to be fulfilled, I don't need a car, loads of designer clothes, expensive haircuts or the largest TV screen. I don't even need a six-bedroom house. For me to be successful, I actually don't need much money at all.

What I do need is room to think my own thoughts, time to contemplate what I really enjoy and don't and then the balls to say that I'm going to go after what makes my heart sing. With this attitude it makes both my journey and destination remarkable.

I'm not advocating that everyone sell their house, buy a boat and sail around the world. I am however, suggesting that if you're not currently fulfilled with life, you don't have to keep living the life you're living. It's possible that the "normal" life doesn't necessarily suit you and it's time to find out what does. I've made massive changes in my life and, yes, it scared the crap out of me…but WOW, it was worth it.

One evening we found ourselves sitting with an Israeli family. We sat up late chatting about sailing, the troubles in Israel, and life in general. We explained how we had said screw it to our lives and traded it in for a new life on the seas. The family expressed their interest to do the same. They sail through the summer season (cruising and racing) and run a business in Israel making sailboat sails. In fact, they work for the largest international sail maker in the world.

We discussed how there are no walls, no boundaries, in the sailing community. Everyone is out to help every other sailor. Yes, we're from America or from Israel but there's something larger that we belong to. It's as if we belong to the world – just as everyone else does. Perhaps, however, when out on the sea, you realize it more.

Chapter 19: Homeschooling my daughter

If we were back in England, Sienna would be officially starting school at the age of 4. I think it's far too young for children to start school; nonetheless it plays on my mind that Sienna won't be following the same path as her friends.

I don't want her to be labeled as "one of *those* kids," and I am slightly worried that she'll either be too smart or not smart enough, if and when we eventually introduce her to the school system. However, on the flip side, I've grown so comfortable about the idea that I'm eager to get started. I love the whole idea of teaching her many subjects based on her current interests.

I'm happy to say that in the four short months we've been sailing around the Mediterranean, I've seen Sienna's skill-set explode.

Not only can she count to 10 easily but she can do it in three languages. She's no longer shy about meeting new kids or joining in with others regardless of language. Her vocabulary astounds me – just yesterday she asked me to explain "photosynthesis" and told me that we're on earth because "gravity" keeps us here. And her desire to learn and ask questions is amazing.

Thus far on our journey, I've been simply offering explanations to Sienna when she inquired about something.

We read loads of books and I've downloaded several educational iPad apps. She works on letters, numbers, reading, math and I have a few great sciences apps – they allow her to mix, freeze, spin, and burn things to create new elements or potions. Further, I found several apps about ocean conservation as I felt the topic was apt for what we're doing.

Aside from that, if I see a book on Greek gods or something kid friendly that would help her to learn more from the area we're in, I'll grab it. In Malta I found a couple of great coloring story books (about Malta) and in Greece we have a mythology sticker books and a fantastic ancient Greek encyclopedia that we flip through every week.

Today, however, I decided to make a concerted effort to test out the whole concept of theme-based education.

Rather than separate learning elements into subjects like math, science, English and so forth, the goal is to combine a variety of subjects using one theme. Let me explain what I did.

As Simon, Sienna and I were walking around the town of Kos, Sienna tried to pull a leaf off a tree. I quickly said to her "Trees have feelings! They can't talk, but if they did they'd say, "Hey – don't pull my leaves off!" I then asked Sienna how she would feel if I came up to her and pulled her finger off. After a long giggle Sienna started asking questions about trees.

Her first question was, "Why do we have trees?"

Like a game of tennis, Simon and I went back and forth explaining the benefit of trees. I explained that they help keep our air clean and Simon mentioned all the creatures that use trees as a home. And on we went.

Knowing that Sienna was interested in trees, I went online and found a great write-up on trees for young kids that came with a worksheet allowing us to fill in the blanks to describe the parts of a tree (roots, trunk, branches, twigs, leaves, crown).

I read the write-up as Sienna colored the tree on the worksheet. So far we already have had quite a few subjects coming in – reading, colors, nature, ecosystems, writing, science. I was actually surprised when Sienna was able to name all the parts of the tree without my help! While she told me what they were, I filled in the names. And when I said that the paper we were writing on was made from tree pulp, she said, "I already know that, Mom!"

After reading about the benefits of trees and their parts, I then copied her arm and fingers making a tree trunk and branches. We cut out the outline, pasted it onto a sheet of paper and then I found a template of small leaves that Sienna could cut out and paste onto the branches.

While she was cutting the leaves and using the glue stick to fasten them on the paper, I pulled out our jar of maple syrup and said, "Sienna – this is maple syrup. It's made from the sap or the juice of a tree!"

Excitedly, she wanted to try it. I then gave her a little spoonful and said, "Once you're done adding the leaves to your tree, let's make some pancakes and you can put the syrup on them and enjoy one of the most amazing delights of a tree!"

The pancakes tasted great and Sienna had a little lesson on cooking, too.

Then Simon and Sienna walked around the area finding as many different leaves as they could. The leaves had to be on the ground and each one had to be different; that was the challenge.

I'm sure I'll get better at theme-based education over time, however I feel that it was a great first attempt. Not only did I have fun doing it, but it seems like we all have a greater appreciation for trees now.

Chapter 20: Sailing around Crete

After learning about trees on the Greek island of Kos, in addition to enjoying the island thoroughly, our intention was to sail west to the picturesque island of Santorini. As fate would have it, the winds were not in our favor.

Blowing directly on our nose, there was no chance of getting our sails out. The thought of an eight-hour motor ride into wind and waves did not sound appealing. Furthermore, Simon and I were a bit concerned about finding a spot to tie onto or anchor. Apparently, there are very limited spaces for sailboats around Santorini.

The island is a volcano so it gets very deep very quickly, making it difficult to anchor.

It didn't take more than five minutes for us to agree to a 10-hour sail south to the island of Crete instead, where we could find a safe place to put the boat and take a ferry to Santorini for a day or two. Or, at least, that was the plan!

Our ground track to Crete was a straight line down. For the first half we did a steady 6 knots and the second half we were well over 8 knots, hitting 9 from time to time. It was our best sail to date!

Simon and I thought that we'd have to enter our destination marina in the dark, but we arrived several hours before our original estimate.

On the sail toward Crete we passed only one other vessel – a cargo ship that crossed our path within three quarters of a mile from us. Other than the ship, we saw a few barren islands and the rest was open sea.

I kept wondering where are all the other sailboats were. I later discovered that Crete is not a massive sailing destination. There are no charter companies and many of the anchorages and marinas are not adequate.

We were headed to a fishing village called Agios Nikolaos. Simon told me that he was there 36 years ago and all he remembered was a lake with restaurants around it and a little fishing harbor.

Unbeknownst to Simon, Agios Nikolaos was no longer a small fishing village.

Rather, it is now quite a loud and booming city. As we travelled closer to the marina, I could see houses, hotels, restaurants and buildings set against a mountainous backdrop, going east and west as far as the eye could see.

We easily entered the marina, were helped onto a berth and cleaned up a bit. I had earlier prepared eggplant parmesan, so we gobbled it down and then jumped off the boat to go for our first exploratory look. After hanging out in small bays and visiting quiet islands for months I felt as if my eyes couldn't handle all the hustle and bustle. There were so many people, cars, bikes and moving things – my head was spinning.

While moored up in a bay I didn't consider myself to be sensory deprived, but I think I was! It took a few hours for us to relax into the commotion. From the marina, we walked down the main strip to the fishing port, found a café overlooking the ferries and tour boats and enjoyed a glass of wine while Sienna, slurped down some strawberry ice cream. She then fell asleep at the table.

Simon and I chatted for a while and then took turns carrying Sienna back to the boat – back home. We all slept well and woke up early to adventure back into the city to find the legendary bottomless lake and look at all the shops.

Fortunately, the marina is very close to the city center – our walk to the famous lake and fishing port took 10 minutes at most.

Eventually we all got tired and hungry and stopped at a taverna on the lake. A lovely Scottish guy was welcoming people in and his charm did the trick on us. We pulled up a table, had a meal and opened our tourist book on what to see and do in Crete.

The ancient site of Knossos was high on the list and, of course, we'd have to visit one of the two huge water parks. We scanned the various options and realized that Crete is massive! We decided to hire a car for the following day and drive to Gournia, the best preserved Minoan town ruin, Mochlos, a little fishing village for lunch, and Vai, a beach on the east coast having its own palm tree forest. We also wanted to stop in Sitia, time permitting.

The next day, we collected the car and packed it with water, bathing suits, towels, maps and my camera. By 9am we were off on our first Crecian adventure.

Our first stop was Gournia.

Considering it's Crete's best preserved Minoan town ruin, you'd think there'd be more visitors.

During our hour-long stay there was only one other family walking around. Failing to have a parking lot or any concessions, the archeological site doesn't look like one that's visited by the tour busses. Seriously, there was nothing there other than the ruin that was actually a welcome surprise. No crowds, no "made-in-China" tourist trinkets and no distractions.

Simon and I were very impressed with the remnants of the Minoan town – we were walking on roads/paths where people walked 1800 BC and they were in impeccable condition. Further, the houses and buildings were rather high – some were above my head. In most of the Greek archeological sites we've visited only a few feet of building remnants remain. In Gournia you really got a feel for the size of the rooms, the layout of the houses and the way that the town was constructed.

The cost to enter Gournia was $3 each with children going free. I think it was well worth the fee. And knowing that they're still uncovering the ruin, I'm happy to contribute to its development. Who knows what's still there left to be unearthed!

Next stop: Mochlos, Crete.

A cove lined with traditional tavernas all uniquely styled in Crete tradition faced a once-connected island and miles of beautiful coast. I've always loved contrast – just looking at the sea can be boring. But when looking at the sea with islands, desolate beaches and through the windowless tavernas your eyes are spoiled with color, texture and contrasting patterns.

We walked the length of the row of tavernas and then settled on a tavern where the women were sitting outside preparing vegetables for their lunch and dinner guests.

Our lovely waiter gave us the history of the area and explained that the island across was a Minoan ruin. Depending on which way the wind blew, the ships would moor off one side or the other. Over time the land eroded, but during Minoan times there were two great harbors offering shelter from prevailing winds.

I ordered a traditional Cretian dish – I try my best to always experience as much localness as I can!

The dish was a brown rusk/roll, soaked in olive oil and then layered with stewed tomatoes topped with a dollop of lovely fresh soft cheese. The rusk was partially crunchy where the olive oil didn't penetrate, and partially soggy. The combination of flavors and textures was perfect!

Sienna enjoyed her drink and after an hour of observing the amazing views and soaking up the traditional Cretian feel, we decided to move on.

Off to Via Beach for some well deserved time in the sea.

As we twisted and turned along the motorway, we eventually made it to the east coast of Crete. We parked up, grabbed our seaside bags and went in search of a couple of sun beds.

While scanning the beach, we were elated to find two beach beds with an umbrella right at the front. Being on the beach front would allow Sienna to swim right in front of us without having to either be with her or constantly look through obstructions to make sure she was safe.

The beach is sandy and then it turns to flat slippery rock. Overall, it's a very clean beach with a nice ocean floor. Sienna wanted to play "Angry Shark," so she'd swim around chasing me while gnashing her jaws. I then would play "Kissing Shark," and I'm sure you can guess how that played out.

And then, out of nowhere, a massive milestone was achieved.

Sienna decided to take off her floatation device that she's been wearing faithfully all summer and have a go at swimming unassisted. After a few attempts, she made it a couple meters and then more and then more! I videoed her attempts and was so proud to see my little baby-cakes showing the first signs of swimming.

Being surrounded by water, our biggest fear is Sienna falling overboard. Teaching her to swim has been our number one priority all summer. We've tried and tried but as with most children, they'll do things when they are ready to do them. Thankfully, at Vai beach Sienna was ready to give it a concerted effort.

When we returned to *Britican* and looked at the weather forecast, we realized the winds would be too strong to leave the following morning.

We took a family vote and decided to keep the car for an extra day so that we could explore some more on the amazing island of Crete.

Checking out Crete – Knosos.

After a very sound sleep, my family and I woke ready for day two of our Crete explorations by car. Our first stop was the ancient Minoan Palace of Knosos.

From what I was told, the archeological site is very busy and very hot so it's best to arrive as early as possible to avoid crowds and the heat. We entered the town around 10am and by then it was already heaving and hot. Oh well. At least, I knew what to expect.

We grabbed some cold waters, entered the site and walked along the palace grounds avoiding the herds of people as much as possible.

Overall, I was seriously impressed with Knosos. Out of all the ruins I've seen over the past few months (Olympia, Delos, Delphi), this one was very different from the traditional Greek archeological sites. Knosos has whole structures, vibrant colors, and meatier buildings. In other words, the site doesn't look like a pile of rubble with a few columns sticking up.

You can see three floors in one of the buildings. There are staircases, alters, columns with rooftops. The mind didn't have to stretch too much to envision what the palace looked like during its heyday. And the restoration, although it's controversial as the architects used modern materials, helps you to really envision the colors. I loved the fact that some of the columns have been painted – it gives me a feel for what the place really looked like.

A few interesting tidbits about Knosos…

Very little was known about the Minoan civilization before excavations on Knosos and another palace called Phaestos. Everything known previous to finding the palaces was passed down through Greek tradition and mythology. When the English archaeologist, Arthur Evans, discovered Knosos around 1900 he opened the floodgates of the Minoan past. They found loads of artifacts, texts (which they still haven't deciphered), and clues as to who the Minoans were and how they lived.

Based on what archeologist have discovered, Crete appears to have been first inhabited around the 6th millennium BC – that's considered the Neolithic period. The Minoans lived from 2600 – 1100 BC and this is when the palaces were built.

After sweating from every pore of our bodies, Simon, Sienna and I then put our focus on cooling down at a water park. Within an hour, we were in our bathing suits and all fighting for the next water slide to test out.

There are two water parks in Greece, both within few miles from each other. We decided on Aqua Park simply because we spoke to a local woman with children, and her 4–year-old preferred Aqua Park.

The slides were brilliant. Simon did every slide and I did almost all of them. There's one that drops vertically and then goes up the other side and you slowly make your way down to the exit – it's a big long 'U' shaped slide. I took one look at it, listened to the screams and decided against it.

As for Sienna…well, she didn't have a confident day.

Some days she's open to try anything and other days she's quiet and a bit closed down. On this particular day, she did make an effort, but she was put off by water splashing in her face.

I'll give her credit as she did go down an adult slide once with Simon holding her and once with me holding her. Both times she loved the ride, but at the end when she went splashing into the water, she became distressed.

By 5pm we were ready to peel off our bathing suits, hop back into the car and head home.

Just before Agios Nikolaos I noticed a sign for Elounda and quickly asked Simon to turn into town.

We walked around the town looking at menus and I yelled out, "There's snails on the menu!"

Our tourist book on Crete mentioned that there's a local dish of snails but it's hard to find them at the tourist restaurants. The book instructed us to find a more traditional taverna. Based on my observations, every restaurant in Crete is for tourists, but some are less blatant. Not once have we found a place that doesn't have five sets of menus (English, German, French, Italian, Russian).

We sat down at a lovely taverna looking out at bay containing the island of Spinalonga. Victoria Hislop wrote a fiction-based-on-fact book about this island. Apparently it was a leper colony up until the 1900s!

I've had escargot several times and I quite enjoy it. Heck, if you put enough garlic on anything it tastes good. The snails I got in Elounda, however were different. First of all, when I've ordered escargot in the past, I usually got 6 to 12 snails. Second, as mentioned before, they are usually loaded with garlic. The snails from Elounda were cooked in a rosemary infused olive oil and covered with a 2mm layer of sea salt. The snails looked like they came out of someone's back garden rather than those I've had in the past. They were chewy and when I pulled them out of the shell, there was a bit of a slime spring-back as the snail became unattached to the shell. Overall, they tasted really good but I felt there were too many. There must have been 75 snails on my plate! As an appetizer that would have been far too much. Luckily the snails were the only thing I ordered. After 20 of them the flavor and consistency just got to be a bit too much. I could have eaten more, but I needed something else.

Would I order them again? Yes – as long as I could share them with someone.

My husband was daring and had one. Sienna, said to me, "Are you crazy – that's disgusting!"

After two full days of land-based exploration, we were ready to take to the seas again. Hopefully the winds will be in our favor and we'll be able to leave Agios Nikolaos.

Chapter 21: A lesson on comradeship among sailors

After living aboard our boat for over five months, I witnessed over and over again a bond that exists with sailors and makes my heart smile. No matter where we turn up, other sailors are always around ready to chat or eager to lend a helping hand.

From Agios Nikolaos, we sailed to Bali and then on to Rethymno, Crete. It was quite rough but we were able to sail rather than motor into the wind. After several hours, we entered the commercial port of Rethymno to pass through into the "marina". I put the word marina in quotes as it's not quite a marina – you'll see why as you read through the story.

I was thankful to be in the calm waters of the port yet nervous as we couldn't figure out who to call on the VHF to request a berth. The pilot book had no information nor did any of the websites detailing Rethymno marina. Usually someone on a tender will come out to greet you or someone will be around waving their hands to show you where to go.

Simon circled in the commercial harbor while I rang the only number I could find – the Rethymno port authority. Fortunately, a lovely woman told us to radio 67 on the VHF. Incidentally, we noticed the VHF call sign being displayed at the exit to the marina rather than the entrance! How frustrating.

Anyway, Simon called up, requested a berth and was told that no one could help us moor up until 7pm at night – five hours later. Apparently, the attendants were busy with a commercial vessel. Looking around, there was one tanker and one ferry in the port and no people for as far as the eye could see.

Needless to say, we prepared the boat and I got ready to do all the warps (ropes) myself.

The marina told us where to go, so we slowly started to back our stern into a spot. The wind was blowing very strong and it was hard to determine if mooring lines were available. Mooring lines are used to tie onto the bow of the boat and act as an anchor. Getting these in place is what keeps the boat from swaying or moving backwards onto the jetty.

Thankfully, there was a sailboat next to our mooring spot. Simon yelled over asking for help, and a woman and man jumped off – Lily and Richard. Sim had to back in several times as the wind was pushing the boat. Further, we had to back into a specific spot to get the only remaining mooring line. I managed to get a line to shore and secure the front mooring line but I couldn't get the massive rope around our winch to tighten it.

The mooring line started off as a tiny little rope, that was tied to a larger rope and that large rope was then tied to a very large rope. I couldn't get the very large rope onto the boat and around the winch...and I couldn't winch the smaller rope as the knot wouldn't go around it. It's as if I pulled up a knotted mess and wasn't strong enough to get into a position to help attach the rope to our boat.

Our boat was moving from side to side and Simon had to continuously push forward to prevent us from crashing on the jetty.

Richard offered to help, and I was so appreciative. The couple, who were flying a Belgium flag, not only wanted to help us, but they also spoke English.

Richard jumped on and struggled for at least 10 minutes with the mooring line to pull it tight.

I thought if Richard struggled I'd have no chance at getting it tight. Lily worked hard along the stern to fend the boat off from hitting the jetty and hold the lines. I helped Richard and then helped Lily and could feel my stress rising. It must have taken us around 45 minutes to get our boat secure.

Never had we experienced such difficulties, but these were just the start!

Later, Richard and Lily explained that it's a very difficult mooring. The wind blows you into and along the jetty – and it doesn't help that most of the mooring lines are broken or missing. After taking time to get settled, Simon took Richard and Lily a beer and enjoyed chatting with them and discussing sailing stories. We were fortunate to have them over for an evening to hear about their background. They live on their boat in Egypt during the winter and sail around the Mediterranean during the summer. Richard, who is French, is a kite surfing instructor by day and a musician by night - we were honored to be serenaded by him with his electric guitar! And Lily, from Belgium, is a lovely woman who has had quite a difficult few years, having recently lost her husband of 25 years.

After a nice evening of drinks, a good sleep and a walk around the town the following morning, we returned to the boat as the wind started to blow.

The wind changed completely and was blowing off the shore in gusts.

Everyone's boat was moving from side to side and we all had to put fenders along the stern of the boat. I tied three fenders onto the ladder railing and then tied the bottoms together with a bucket that I sunk with water to keep them from floating up.

My main concern was the integrity of our mooring line!

If it broke, our boat would go smashing to the right, hit another boat and possible smash into the jetty. With wind blowing a 35 ton boat, nothing's going to stop it!

Considering that there were so few mooring lines, and the fact that the marina was not maintained, I feared the worst.

Our first idea was to take our anchor out and drop it. The issue with that was the ocean floor was full of old mooring lines, concrete blocks and who knows what. The risk of losing our anchor was high. And the depth was too far for us to swim down to check things out.

To my amazement, Richard yelled over to us, "I'll go down and see if I can find another mooring line for you guys." At first Simon thought he was going to swim down but then realized he had tanks. Within a half hour, Richard had his tanks on and was scouring the ocean floor to find a line for us.

After 15 minutes of looking, he came up and explained that it was an absolute mess.

All the lines are knotted up and all over the place. He then suggested that we run one of our warps from the boat to the master cement block at the bottom of the sea bed and back. Fortunately, we have a very long yellow ship-to-land line that made it from our boat to the master chain block and back again!

Once we secured the second line to the boat, *Britican* stopped flying about so much and we could all breathe again.

We were then able to return the favor and help our new friends affix another bow line onto their boat.

I say this all the time – you don't know what you don't know. Every day is such a learning experience for us. For five months we'd had absolutely no problems mooring up stern-to. We'd never had an issue with winching the mooring line up. We'd never had a situation where the wind blew strongly from one direction one day and the totally opposite the next day. We'd never entered a marina and had no one there to help.

However, the one thing that has been consistent has been the assistance we've received from other sailors!

Talking about assistance. While we were in Rethymno, I emailed our new friend, Admiral Stefano, explaining that we were making our way from Greece back to Sicily. I inquired if he wanted to fly out and join us for the trip. Within a couple days, Stefano rejoined us on *Britican*.

Chapter 22: Discovering Monemvasia

My friend, Carol, had emailed me about a tiny island off the Peloponnese called Monemvasia. She said that her family enjoyed a few holidays in the area and it was not to be missed.

While Simon and Stefano were discussing a route from Santorini Island (yes, we made it to Santorini after all!) back toward the Ionian Sea, I piped up and asked, "Can we stop at Monemvasia?" Errrrr, in actuality, I said, "There's a place on the east side of the Peloponnese that starts with an 'M' and I've been told it's worth checking out."

The guys looked on the map, I put my finger in the region of where I thought we needed to go and we pulled up anchor from Milos Island to set sail for Monemvasia.

None of us had any idea on what to expect in Monemvasia.

For the first half of the journey, we sailed a steady 6 knots. A storm was growing to the north of us and we all watched a tornado start to form in the clouds. A long line of clouds spun and started to descend toward the sea. We kept an eye on it while nervously increasing our speed.

At first, the sight of a tornado was exciting but then I wondered, "what if"?

What if the tornado touches down and becomes a water spout? What if it starts to come toward us? Stefano asked Simon to start tying things down – just in case. After 20 minutes, the funnel cloud disappeared and we all let out a sigh of relief.

Once we passed the storm front the wind died and the engine was turned on.

Eventually, we could see the coast of the Peloponnese and a tiny island jetted out before our eyes. And then I heard Simon yell out from behind the binoculars, "It looks like a walled city." We all took turns looking and becoming more excited about our destination.

Just as I went to get my camera, I saw a huge splash out of the corner of my eye.

I excitedly said to Stefano, "Did you see that – look over there..." And then suddenly a tuna at least four feet long jumped out of the water two more times. The sun hit the silver grey tuna with such a special light. The jumping tuna against the deep blue Aegean sea background made a spectacular sight.

By the time we stopped looking out for the tuna to jump again, we were upon the island of Monemvasia. I went to the bow of the boat with Sienna and we took several pictures of the island and surrounding area.

Our first attempt to moor up was in a tiny harbor to the left of the island.

The pilot book outlined the depths and if we could get inside the outer wall, our keel and rudder would clear the ocean floor. Unfortunately, the wall was full. There were several smaller sailboats moored stern-to along an inner jetty, but the pilot book and our iPad navigational app noted depths of under 1 meter. Our keel is 2.6 meters.

Not wanting to run aground we aborted our initial berthing plans.

After consulting our pilot book, we looked at anchoring in the area but then noticed a couple sailboats tied up on a jetty along the other side of the island. We headed around the island and went side-to. The pilot book mentioned that a ferry and hydrofoil used the jetty, but no one seemed to stop us from taking a spot.

What we've discovered is that you often have to start mooring up and someone will either yell at you to go away or help you out. In this particular circumstance, a policeman eventually showed up, told us we were welcome to stay, but asked all three boats to move from side-to to stern-to, thus taking up less space.

A couple of hours after initially trying to moor up, we were finally tied down!

That's one thing about sailing – things that you'd think would take minutes often take hours!

Once the engine was turned off, I took the time to appreciate my surroundings. To our stern was a beautiful rock mountain – like a mini Rock of Gibraltar – with infinite sea as a backdrop. To our left and right I saw grass-bottomed rock-topped mountains. Off our bow was a small town at the water's edge.

The kind policeman told us the best restaurant to go to – I'm sure it was his brother's or uncle's restaurant! He said if we stay on the island, we'd pay more than if we walked across the bridge to the mainland.

In medieval times, the island was connected to land by a drawbridge, but today it's a nicely paved road. We walked over to the mainland, turned left toward the marina and picked the restaurant in the middle of two others. We were all exhausted by the time we finished but the Admiral promised Sienna an ice cream.

Walking through the town I noticed a couple of fruit markets, a grocery store, some boutique shops, a creperie, some coffee shops and several tavernas. It was a cute little town. There was also one of those old fashion butchers. When we walked by the butcher, he was carving up some sort of carcass – the whole thing was laid out on the counter and passers-by could see the cuts he was making with a meat hook and knife. Personally, I like to buy my meat all wrapped up and ready to cook…

We stopped at a café, ordered three coffees and Sienna enjoyed a chocolate ice cream. As she ate it, she kept saying, "I'm not tired," and then proceeded to do the nodding dog. Her eyes would close and her head would fall to one side or the other.

That night, Stefano carried Sienna back to the boat while she slept on his shoulder.

In the morning, we all woke and did our chores. After lunch, we put on our hiking shoes and headed for the walled city.

I wasn't expecting anything so when I walked through the walled gates I was simply awestruck.

Monemvasia was like many other islands in the Mediterranean – everyone owned her at one time or another. In the 1400s the island was even sold to the Pope. It seems that the largest influence on the town that can still be seen was when the island was under Venetian rule, when they had the island in the 1500s. Then the Turks took it in the 1600s…and then it went back to the Venetians and then back to the Turks. The town was liberated from Ottoman rule in 1821 during the Greek War of Independence.

It was one of those days where all you could hear me say was, "Wow – look at that view," or "Holy smokes, can you believe how beautiful that is?"

The town was devoid of cars so it was easy to calmly walk the cobblestone pathways exploring various ruins, new buildings (in traditional style), churches (of course!) and enjoy the surrounding blue sea.

Aside from a few satellite dishes here and there, the town seemed like a movie set.

There was nothing out of place – the buildings are all made of the same stone and materials – old and new. Patches of colorful flowers weaved through the winding corridors – beautiful pinks, oranges, greens and yellows against the stone walls oozed life into hard rocks.

Smells of slouvaki, grilled fish and Greek salad wafted through the air. And when the breeze blew you'd get that strong Mediterranean smell of dust, trees and organic herbs.

And the sounds? There were no sounds. We were fortunate to hit the island on a quiet day. I've been told that ferries and cruise ships stop by, but we were the only boat on the quayside. There were more workers on the island than there were visitors. What a brilliant present – no crowds!

The four of us walked around, admiring the beauty of the island all feeling grateful that we stopped on this gem.

After our explorations and an obligatory ice cream, we made our way back to the boat. Stefano offered to look after Sienna so that Simon and I could experience one of the romantic restaurants on the island by night. It would be our fourth time out for a private meal in six months – as you can imagine, I was overjoyed at the idea.

Simon and I strolled back into the walled city, enjoyed a meal overlooking the sea and a full moon. We sat there saying, "Can you believe that we're sitting here right now? Can you believe how much or lives have changed in just one year?"

We were in the very initial stages of letting the idea fill our imaginations. Never in a million years did I come close to speculating everything that's happened in the past year. The great friends we've made, the amazing ruins we've visited, the incredible foods we've tried and the endless views of sea and coastline.

Chapter 23: Our first fishing story - from the Ionian Sea to our dinner table.

"What is that noise?"

Everyone started to look around. We were quietly sailing along Lefkas Island in the Ionian Sea doing around 6 knots. The sun was hot, the air was salty and the humidity heavy.

Stefano was helming. Simon was lying in the cockpit. Sienna was down below playing on the iPad and I was up on deck reading a book.

We kept hearing an odd sound every 10 minutes or so. It sounded like a little kid screaming, but we were too far away from land to hear people making noises.

"There it goes again....what is that?!?!?" I yelled out.

After scanning the environment I noticed that our fishing pole had a line out and something was on the end of the line! Earlier that day, Stefano put a lure on hoping that we might catch dinner. It was the third time we had a line in the water. None of us knew what it sounded like with our fishing reel letting out our line!

Suddenly, we rushed to the back of the boat and the two guys took turns reeling in the line.

Was it a tuna, or perhaps just a plastic bag?

After a good 10 minutes or so, the prize was landed. It was a Dorado, or Mahi Mahi.

Stefano got the fish on board, quickly killed, gutted and cleaned it. I secretly thought, "Thank God I didn't have to do that!" When I was younger I had no issue killing and cleaning a fish, but now I have troubles killing a fly. The only thing that doesn't bother me is terminating the life of a mosquito.

Stefano caught, killed, cleaned, cooked and served fish to us aboard *Britican*! Can my life get any more magical?

Chapter 24: Six months living on the sea

As we entered our sixth month of living on the sea, I looked back in astonishment when I realized that it was three years since I quit the rat race and one year since we formally decided to sell-up and sail away.

My whole life was consumed by stress, making money, spending money and living in the fast lane. I worked hard and I partied hard. How could I go from working 80 hours a week, constantly pushing for results and fighting to become bigger and better, to someone with no company, no known future and no identity. How could I go from being someone to being no one with no idea or vision for what was to come?

Looking back to this time last year, frustration was exchanged with nervous excitement.

I had spent enough time away from my company to rise from the ashes.

After I left the rat race, I spent a couple of years soul searching, doing consultancy…writing a book ("**How Life Really Works**"), I was part of a lovely business group full of Managing Directors (better to hear their issues than have them as my own!) and I started a small company with a friend to give me something to fill the void.

I suppose I needed space – those two years – to come off my corporate lifestyle high. I needed to deprogram myself from the budgets, forecasts, HR issues, legal matters – the early starts and late finishes, and on and on. I needed to lose my ego.

In contrast to my old life, it was so difficult to wake up every morning not knowing what the plan was.

For almost two years I felt as if I was a feather blowing in the wind. During the transition it's as if I was just spinning my wheels, but now I can see that I had to allow myself to break down so that I could build up a new me.

I'm not sure if I can put into words how things happened. Let me try…I knew that I had to change my life so I set out, in shotgun fashion, to start over again. While going through the process I felt alone, lost and afraid that I threw out everything that meant anything.

Essentially, I set out to trade one life in for a totally different one.

I did some serious soul searching. For the first time in my life I started to take time out for me. I started to listen to my body and watch my thoughts. I started to really contemplate what I liked, what I didn't like and on and on.

For me, the issue of being successful wasn't on the agenda anymore. I proved that I could make money – financial success. After contemplation, I realized that the way I chose to make money wasn't in line with the type of person I am.

Heck – I owned a multi-million-pound currency exchange company! Ask me if I knew the names of currencies in other countries or the exchange rates. I usually didn't even know what the USD to GBP rate is. I was successful because I studied how to start and grow a company – the type of company didn't really matter. I was successful because I never gave up.

I kept pressing forward and that "pressing" eventually wore me out!

That being said, taking time to contemplate my past allowed me to realize where I went right and where I went wrong. Over the course of two years I really started to understand what made me feel fulfilled and what didn't.

I started to pay more attention to my love of sailing…and everything that came with the lifestyle attached to sailing. Having the ability to move my home when I wanted created a spark in my heart. Being able to sail at night under the moonlight and feel the freedom of great open expanses brought a smile to my face. Knowing that I was truly one with nature and surrounded by nature felt amazing. And living in gym shorts, no bra and a holey sweatshirt also felt right.

I have no regrets. I freaking love my life. I love the new "me" and I love the direction I'm going – whatever it is!

I have no idea about how my life will unfold, but that's okay.

Instead of controlling everything, I'm truly living my life one day at a time. I have no plans, no forecasts, no budgets…Just me, my family and the open sea.

And what do others think of this new "me"?

Many readers of my blog, like Grainne below, asked me if it feels like I'm on permanent holiday or if it has become normal:

"Hi Kim,

Just thinking about you as I start my new job tomorrow (primary school teaching) after a long summer off, and it made me think what it must be like to be on what seems to be an endless holiday. I wonder if you think of your trip as an endless holiday too, or does routine become as much a part of your life as it does for everyone?

Grainne"

I wrote back to Grainne explaining that her question was a good one! When we're walking around a new location I do often think I'm on holiday. When we're sailing, I actually feel as if it's like I was taking my daily walk – that's normal now.

Some days I feel as if I'm flowing with life and everything is perfect. Other days, I'm tired or cranky and I struggle to last the day. Overall, however, I feel so free and open to accept new things into my life.

When I was in the corporate world, my future was just like my past – very little changed. Nothing changed because I was so tightly wound into a pre-scripted life. Now that I'm on the open seas I believe that anything can happen. Tomorrow I might meet a new best friend or have a meal that is out of this world. I might have an incredibly memorable time with my daughter or perhaps write an article that strikes a chord with someone who then feels compelled to get in touch.

In some cases I do feel like I'm on an endless holiday; yet in other ways I feel like I'm just living life with a different mentality/ attitude. I suppose I could have had this approach to my corporate life but I was so stuck that I needed something very different to pry me out of my stuck-ness…if that makes sense.

Another reader wrote:

"Kim,…I now realize it is difficult for me to fully understand that *Britican* is your HOME now and not a means of transportation…I bet many of your readers have the same problem – we fail to really comprehend your family's new Modus Vivendi, so far different than the established model.

Michalis"

Michalis is a beautiful soul. He follows us along on our Locator and when we get to a new destination he tells me the best places to go and what to look out for. Being in Greece, I feel as if I have the Gods on my side. Everywhere I go, there's someone to direct my family and me – especially Michalis.

In response to Michalis, yes I think it is hard for others to comprehend our new life – heck, I have a difficult time writing about it. We have good and bad days, but overall I feel as if we're doing the right thing. We're living a lifestyle that feels right and we're truly making the most of our time on this wonderful Earth. And that is the key point. For many of us, we have the ability to go out and do what our heart craves...but things get in the way – usually fear, money or security (or all three).

We've been able to push the worries to one side and say, "screw it, we're going to go out and find a fulfilling life! We're going to do what makes our hearts sing."

I suppose only time will tell if we've made a wrong decision. But look at all the people who work all their lives, fail to find fulfillment and still end up old, miserable and starving.

Chapter 25: Sailing around the world isn't fun when you're not sailing!

Here's my recollection of our time in Preveza, Greece when we unexpectedly got laid up.

We're on an adventure of a lifetime – we're sailing around the world; however, we're NOT SAILING RIGHT NOW! We're laid up across from the town of Preveza, Greece with engine troubles.

Our generator, engine and even our outboard on the dinghy are out of commission.

I can see Preveza but can't get to it – the town is across the water from us. We're actually stuck in a marina with two restaurants and a shop that sells 10 items.

There's no place to walk to and there's nothing to do.

While on the boat, we have to listen to a massive crane haul boats out all day long. The crane drives up within two feet of the boat, blows exhaust and dirt all over us and makes a loud noise. Once a boat is hauled out, the attendants spray wash the hull and all you can smell is yucky fish smell.

Alternatively, we can go hang out at the marina restaurant but the waitress there is the most miserable person I've seen in months. Perhaps she is a reflection of how I feel or even what I look like.

We've been stuck for about 10 days and have perhaps five more days before we can leave. So far, Sienna has been great. Fortunately, I got over to Preveza one day and we found a playground (with other kids) and toy store. And for a couple days she had a friend to play with at the marina.

But to say that it's been easy to come up with ideas on how to entertain my daughter, I'd be lying. We've done every paper craft for kids that you can find on Pinterest. We created a TV set and I recorded Sienna doing "Hello Kitty News" – 15 times! We've played on the toddler playground (a tiny plastic play area behind the marina) as long as I can stand it. And now whenever I hear Sienna say "mom, can you play with me?" I shudder.

The whole entertainment task starts at 8am and ends around 10pm. By the time the day is over there's no time left for me to just be by myself. And I must say that Sienna does play by herself – sometimes for hours! And when forced, my husband will take her out for a while. But I think it's the fact that I'm constantly on call that I'm struggling with.

To have a whole day to myself would feel like absolute bliss.

As far as Simon is concerned, I often find him playing a game on the iPad and feel enraged. The boat is a mess, there are loads of things to do and learn. And when someone isn't directing him on what to do, he plays on the iPad. My daughter never calls hubby to play. He talks to people walking by the boat, grabs a coffee with the guys or gets to focus his attention on learning about all the repairs we're having done.

We have one guest and my husband on board and if I don't make anything for lunch, no one else does it. And when it comes to dinner, if I don't make anything (or source the food and recipe for hubby to cook) we go out to eat.

Man...can I get any more bitchy?

Of course, there's the cleaning aspect but in all honesty, I actually like to clean right now. It's the only thing I can do where I'm alone. If Sienna wants to play, I have a valid reason for saying no.

I suppose I could lock myself in my bedroom and say I'm cleaning and read a book instead, but overall I feel like there's so much to do that I can't really relax. And when I do sit down and open a book, I hear a request for a task that seems irrelevant. I just want to yell, "Do it yourself," but I don't.

And then there's my writing and updating my blog, doing my emails, looking at Facebook and Twitter. When people see me on the computer, they quietly say, "She works too much." It drives me nuts because getting to do my website is my version of playing an iPad game. I like to work and yet I get criticized about it.

Then there is the guilt.

Right now we are getting the most amazing service, making new friends and sorting out our fundamental boat systems once and for all. I should be grateful and feel full of happiness.

I am grateful. VERY GRATEFUL. But I was not always happy living through it. Originally, our engine work was going to be carried out when we made it back to Sicily. I have arranged for Sienna to be around other kids, we'd have a car and places to go. We just happened to bump into some amazing people who are helping us in innumerable and invaluable ways.

Looking back, I didn't do enough.

I didn't pay enough attention during my Diesel Marine Engine Course and I didn't research the most important things to know before taking over a used boat.

Yes, we had a 35' Moody sailboat for a couple years but the systems contained within were simple. In fact, everything was relatively easy. We did the standard maintenance ourselves and then paid someone to give the engine a look over every year.

We never "wintered" the boat, as we used it year round. We simply took good care of her and she took good care of us. We'd bring her out of the water, do the antifouling, change the anodes and so forth. Furthermore, when we received our boat, she was old but in good shape.

Our small thirty-year-old 35' sailboat was a walk in the park compared to our 11-year-old 56' Oyster.

We should have found our own marine engineer, skilled in the electrical and mechanical aspects of diesel engines, and flown him or her out to the boat to inspect it before purchasing, in addition to getting the $2000 marine survey we paid for... but then again, we needed our money to buy the boat.

And then, we should have connected with some full time live-aboard cruisers and, if money was no object, paid someone to fly out to the boat and look over the whole thing – to go up the mast and look at the rigging, to check out the steering and propulsion systems, to go through the inventory and make sure that all the rigging was on the boat, to look at the expensive things to ensure they were in good working order.

Unfortunately, for us, money was an object and we had a limited supply of it.

We would have still purchased the boat, as we are totally in love with her, but at least we would have known what needed to be done to maintain the integrity of the systems.

Instead, we've been sailing and motoring around all summer with seriously congested engines, dangerous rigging and something so terrible that I'm embarrassed to admit it...

We've been sailing around the Mediterranean all summer with our stern gland packing box locked closed (I'll explain what this is in a moment).

I can just hear all the captains of the world snickering thinking, "What a bunch of idiots. They know nothing. They're going to sink that boat."

I'm okay with having the sailing world laugh at me. If I don't write down our mistakes, what's the sense of me writing anything?

Yes, most of our experiences are amazing and those are great to share, but it's the massive errors that need to be shared. If we all share our good AND bad times, perhaps we can help others to avoid feeling like I feel right now: the biggest idiot in the world.

Let me tell you about the stern gland on a boat. If you have an inboard motor that turns a shaft attached to an external propeller, that shaft will pass through a stuffing box, or stern gland. It is used to cool and lubricate the shaft while preventing water from coming into the boat.

On our boat, the stuffing box doesn't look anything like a box, but rather a set of round shaped clamps around the shaft. Inside the "box" is a thing called packing that really looks like wide waxy rope. In our stuffing box, we have three lengths of wide rope set in a circle to be packed along the shaft.

The way it works is that you compress the stuffing box and packing so that enough water from the outside comes in to lubricate and cool the shaft, but not so much to sink the boat.

Depending on where you get your information, I've read that the drip rate should be one drop every minute to one drop every hour while the shaft is in operation, and it shouldn't drip when the engine is off.

Yes, the water does drip into the boat and it's designed to do so.

Aside from the stuffing box there's also a grease aspect. On our boat, we manually turn a handle to force grease into the stern gland. You're supposed to do it every day if running the engine heavily or once a week with moderate use. You turn the handle until you feel pressure.

Faithfully, we've been doing this job but in our ignorance we didn't witness the water drips. In our Oyster manual, it says that we need to see it drip once an hour. Can you imagine putting your head in the hull as you're motoring along waiting for that one drip?

Needless to say, our stern gland was not dripping but we didn't realize the implications.

Previous to getting our boat, someone must have closed the packing box tight to eliminate the possibility of water entering the boat. If you're going to leave your boat for a long time or when you winter your boat, you'll want to tighten the box.

HOWEVER, YOU NEED TO WRITE YOURSELF A NOTE TO REMIND YOURSELF TO UNTIGHTEN IT AND MAKE SURE IT'S WORKING.

When we picked up the boat in Palma, Mallorca with our professional skipper, our broker asked if we had questions. We spent a few hours figuring out the mammoth electronic breaker board, finding the grey and black water tanks and outlets, pulling out all the safety equipment and so forth. Our heads were a mess.

Both Simon and I were excited and terrified at the same moment. Just looking under the floorboards in the saloon, we found nine truck sized batteries running all sorts of things. We had a generator, engine, inverters, battery chargers, heating system, fridge and freezer systems and I haven't even mentioned the whole "how to sail the boat" aspect.

I've come to realize that sailing the boat is the easy part!

Anyway, no one thought to check the stuffing box.

Yes, we turned the greaser like it said for us to do and we did this faithfully. I'd often look for a drip or water in the bilge and I think I did see it…but I didn't understand what I was greasing or why water needed to drip.

So…all summer we've been overheating our propeller shaft.

It's a miracle we didn't burn the boat up or completely destroy the shaft. When we pulled out our packing, it came out black –burnt to a crisp.

If you have issues with your stuffing box, the results could be catastrophic. We're talking about a broken shaft or even massive amounts of water entering the boat.

As a side note, I discovered that I'm not the only person in the world who didn't understand the existence or importance of a stern gland. Apparently, it has a very bad reputation for be an inferior piece of kit but that's because the majority of boat owners don't know how to properly service it.

Many boat owners keep pumping the stern gland with grease and completely fail to realize the importance of tightening the unit (supposedly three times/year) and repacking the stuffing (or rope).

Apparently, old packing material is the number one cause of problem leaking, and shaft wear and damage, as noted by Bears Marine Development (boating hardware specialists).

If you don't spend the $20 on new packing, the result could be thousands of dollars on a new propeller shaft.

It's recommended to change the packing in the stuffing box every two years or sooner if there's excessive leaking. Don't just tighten the packing box!

In the end, our propeller shaft was found to be fine and our experience and wisdom has increased.

Chapter 26: The presence of angels

My mind feels all jumbled. There's so much I want to say but I'm not sure if I can detangle it. The events of my life over the first few months as a new boat owner seemed to be guided. If I didn't know any better, I'd think that there's an angel looking out for my family. Something somehow prevented us from serious engine failure. More on that to come...

Every day we woke up not knowing what the day would bring us. A coincidence here and there is one thing; coincidences every day is another.

Generally speaking, however, our plans never played out the way we thought they would. That's the sailor's way.

In my first six months of being a new boat owner live-aboard sailor I quickly learned the skill of flexibility and flow. To be a happy sailor, you must drop your need for achievement. And in this context, I mean getting to a destination or having a plan come to fruition.

Try as you might to get to destination A, if the winds, weather or engine gremlins get in your way, you'll surely end up in destination B – if you get to any destination at all!

We would often think we'd stay in once place for two days and it extended to nine days. Once we stayed two weeks longer in a particular area because we ran into good friends and couldn't pull ourselves away from them.

On another occasion, Simon and I tried several times to sail to Santorini, the one "must do" island on my Aegean bucket list, but the winds wouldn't allow us to go. However, we did eventually get the island when the weather was perfect AND we had a crewmember on board to man the ship while we toured the island. Everything worked out perfectly and had I become upset that we missed Santorini it would have been wasted energy.

I no longer even speculate about where we might be in two days – thinking about it is futile.

So instead of sailing up the coast of Italy, we were moored up along a hard in mainland Preveza, Greece, watching all sorts of engine and generator pieces and parts leave our sailboat.

Totally unexpected, we had a complete overhaul of our engines in addition to serious fixes made to our rigging.

To put things bluntly, our generator and engine had not been property serviced since the boat was built 11 years ago. The injectors had never been taken out and looked at. The heat exchangers had never been cleaned. Some of the anodes had never been changed. The diesel pump had never been opened. And that's just naming a few of the issues.

When taking the heat exchanger off the generator, our engineers found almost a kilo of salt in the tubes and two impeller blades.

The whole unit was completely clogged up and the anode crumbled like a cookie.

Furthermore, all the safety components to shut the engines down were decommissioned.

For example, instead of our generator turning off if it overheats, the sensor was disabled so it would continue running.

Previous to buying the boat, we were given the receipts for the services and a log of previous maintenance.

Either the receipts were fake or the previous owner paid a lot of money for nothing.

The receipts we have are from a marine servicing shop in Palma de Mallorca and one of the listed items is: "Drain cooling water, dismantle heat exchanger, pressure test in workshop, clean, assemble and fit to generator." That was clearly not done last year. Our engineer questions if it was ever done during the life of the boat!

We did the right things – or at least we thought we did. We had a marine surveyor spend around 12 hours inspecting our boat with a fine tooth-comb. He told us there were issues but nothing out of the ordinary.

Is it only me who thinks it's strange that a marine surveyor didn't realize the engines were in such a bad state?

When taking various bolts off the engine/generator (holding the injectors, water cooling system, etc.) the paint chipped off indicating that the bolts had never been loosened!

In the course of six months, we had over ten "engineers" look at our engines due to leaks, failures or malfunctions. A few of them suggested we simply needed new engines…that "they are worn out". If any of the engineers took the time to look deeper into the engines they would have realized why there were issues.

The whole reason we purchased an Oyster was due to the quality, craftsmanship and reputation of the boat.

Having a child with us, safety is number one on our priority list, and Oyster is known to be one of the safest (and heaviest) boats there is. And a Perkins engine is one of the best engines there is. If maintained correctly, it will go forever.

I find it so hard to believe that someone (the previous owner) would have paid so much for a boat and then failed to take care of it. Then again, we'd been sailing around for six months assuming everything was up-to-date, but it was far from it. Ultimately, we are like the previous owner – ignorant about the state of our equipment.

To say that I felt stupid, vulnerable and inexperienced is an understatement.

How could this happen? How could we get so far without knowing/realizing that our home was cracking underneath us? How could such an expensive sailboat be mishandled so badly and for so long? How could so many engineers look at our engines and fail to express the dangerous state it was in?

Perhaps the majority of the marine world is full of sharks?

Engineers can create a quick fix; send you one your way and they know that the next time it breaks you'll be far, far away. I'd really hate to believe that the bulk of the industry is that disingenuous.

But our current engineer took ten minutes looking at our engines and riffled off all the problems immediately.

He explained that the reason the others didn't mention various things could have been because the jobs are very time-consuming, dirty and there is very little space to work. He said it's easier to tell you to get a new engine – they make more money and don't have to do any of the messy stuff.

In fact, I've discovered that it's common practice for marine engineers to tell you that you need a new engine, pull it out, fix and sell it on and then sell you a new engine. The engineer makes profit on both the old engine and the new.

We naively thought that we'd get a boat, learn how to sail it and maintain it – we'd make sure everything was working well and then once we were confident, we'd leave our backyard (the Mediterranean) and head out around the world.

Through all our various minor problems, the confidence in our engines reduced by the day.

We've always been willing to stop for a while, sort out the problems properly and then get going again, but until now every engineer failed to come up with a solution or take the time to actually look at the engines properly.

In Palma, Mallorca, we had engineers look at the engine to make sure we'd be good to go for our trip to Gibraltar. From Gibraltar we paid engineers to look at our engines before our trip to Malta (850 miles). How is it that neither of these supposed professionals looked at the fuel and water-cooling systems? HOW?!?! I've learned that it's not even hard to look. Yes, it's hard to repair/fix but to look is relatively easy.

When taking our Diesel Marine Engine course our teacher told us that we needed to watch the engineers work. He showed us how long it takes to clean a water cooler/heat exchanger unit and stressed that we needed to make sure they do it properly. He mentioned that most engineers run pipe cleaners down the tubes (if that!) pushing the gunk to the end rather than taking the unit off, soaking in acid and removing the gunk from the circuit.

Now I realize that our teacher wasn't kidding.

When our generator water cooler was taken off today, it was filled with a solid mass of gunk. Our injectors are all covered in carbon. The list goes on.

To keep myself from crying, I mentioned to our current engineer that we must have one hell of an engine and generator for them both to still be going! He agreed with me and confirmed that we do, indeed, have angels looking after us.

What was the sequence of events that brought us to this new engineer in Preveza, Greece?

Several months back our hot water heater developed a small leak and then turned into Niagara Falls. A reader of my blog, and a 56' Oyster owner also, gave me the name of a contact in England that helps Oyster owners source parts – a great guy named Andy Willett from a company called Stella Maris Yacht Services.

After emailing Andy in a panic, not only did he help us find a replacement but he talked us through rerouting our fresh water supplies so we could use our taps.

Furthermore, Andy helped us to find someone in Greece that could help us install the new boiler.

After a couple of months, we arrived in Kos Marina, Greece, where Andy's contact, Pierre, was waiting for us with our new boiler. Pierre not only helped to install our new boiler, but he changed a broken areal, installed new waterproof speakers, taught us how to grout the teak, changed a water tap, put a new water pump in, demonstrated how to clean the chrome and what supplies to use. The list goes on.

Throughout our time with Pierre he was so helpful and genuine. In his French accent he would say, "That is shit" if he thought so. I painted the windows as there was a rust issue and hubby got the wrong paint – gloss. Pierre let me know that he didn't think it was good and told me what to do instead. I liked his attitude about things – he told us how he saw things. Furthermore never did we feel like we were paying too much. His prices were reasonable – they were normal.

Keep in mind I'm still talking about a sequence of events here.

So fast-forward to September when we pick up our friend Stefano, a retired Italian Naval Admiral (and have I yet mentioned that he was also a helicopter pilot?), in Crete. Remember, we met Stefano while sailing in

Sicily in April where he became our Italian angel. If he wasn't helping us with translations, he was teaching us to sail or cook spaghetti.

We've adopted Stefano as part of our family, so having him on board was a real honor.

So Stefano, Simon, Sienna and I sailed to Santorini, along the Peloponnese and eventually to the Ionian Islands. While sailing to Leftkas Island our main halyard broke and Simon spotted oil in the bilge.

What the heck?

Simon called Pierre in Kos, hundreds of miles away, who perhaps would know someone in the area. Pierre had a great contact near us. Simon made the phone call and within a couple of hours a new engineer, Andrea, was on board while we were moored up in the middle of Spinola bay.

Interestingly, the new engineer was Italian and an ex-helicopter pilot (coincidence or what?), among many other talents.

Simon explained our issues to Andrea, who inspected the engine and made a phone call about our rigging. All the while, I was down below making videos with Sienna.

Next thing I knew, there were three new Italian people on our boat. Two were going up the mast; one was looking at the engine.

Andrea had called a rigging specialist – no, he's not a rigging specialist...he's a world famous sailor, who happened to be sailing by teaching a group of eight people about advanced skippering. It was Vittorio Malingri, one of the most respected sailors in the world. One of his accolades is sailing solo around the world in the Vendèe Globe race. He also crossed the Atlantic Ocean in something similar to a Hobie Cat.

Vittorio is friends with Andrea and even though he was teaching a course, he took a detour as we needed serious help. After a few hours of going up and down the mast, a temporary solution was created; however the work we had done on the mast in Malta and later in Catania was inadequate.

It seems like we had "experts" repair something that works for aluminum masts rather than carbon fiber masts…apparently, there's a big difference. Carbon fiber is a rather new material in the sailing world, so let this be a lesson if you have it – you need to find someone that knows about carbon fiber.

After Vittorio looked at the problem, he could see an easy solution and it wasn't expensive. He explained that the small thing could cause massive issues and even damage the rigging beyond repair. Apparently, we were very lucky to catch the issue now.

As you can imagine, I was now thinking "what the heck" in a different manor.

I was thinking, how the heck did we end up in this particular bay at this particular time to get access to the people we need that will help us most?!

Each day, Andrea taught us how to take things off, what to do to service various items.

He explained that engines are very easy to look after. The main things to maintain are the fuel and water systems. If you keep on top of maintenance, engines will run forever.

He explained that he'd cleaned the generator – the outside. And then he would clean the engine and repaint them both. Andrea, a 6'4" big guy, then stated, "I will only clean your engines once. If you come back to me and they're dirty, I will not help you!" I swore up and down that Simon and I wouldn't let him down.

What have I learned from all this and what advice can I pass on to you?

If you haven't purchased a boat yet, find a marine engineer, above and beyond a surveyor, and pay them to tell you what condition the engine is. Get one through recommendations and let them know that they won't be the engineer fixing the engine. Perhaps by saying so, they'll have no ulterior motive. (Look how cynical I am!) Better yet, if you can find a marine engineer who lives on a boat (like Andrea), get them to look at your engine or engines!

If you have a boat now and you're not sure about the state of your engine, I urge you to pay for a recommended engineer to spend a week taking things off the engine (or engines) and looking at them. Learn how to check the water-cooling system. Know where the anodes are and how often to check/replace them. Learn how to take the injectors out and determine if they're okay or not. All of these things are very simple now that I've been shown how to do it.

If you pay for servicing, I recommend that you watch everything the engineers do. If the water-cooling/heat exchanger system does not come off the engine, there is a problem – it cannot be serviced while still attached! When I'm more knowledgeable about all the things that should be covered I'll compile a more comprehensive list. As it stands now, I'm only part way through my experience-based training.

Above and beyond all the stuff about the engine, I think the largest lesson I've learned is to trust in the flow of life. I know that probably sounds corny, but by not having set plans, everything seems to sort itself out. My husband and I knew that we needed to sort our engines out but we didn't know how. Amazingly, life had a way of bringing us to the best place at the best time!

Every day we wake up and have no idea what will unfold...and by doing so the most amazing experiences take place.

I'm 100 percent confident that we're getting the best job for our engines for the most amazing price possible. The universe seemed to deliver us here and we didn't put obstacles in its way.

When we leave our mooring, Simon and I will know the exact state of our engines. We'll have a calendar of all the maintenance checks and we'll have confidence that our engines will see us around the world.

Chapter 27: Sailing from Greece to Sicily

After all our repairs were made it was time to head toward Sicily. By October most live-aboard cruisers hole up in a marina for the winter.

We had sailed 3,283 nautical miles in seven months. It's been one heck of a first sailing season for us with our new boat.

We've made some incredible new friends, seen some absolutely amazing sights, enjoyed countless sunrises and sunsets, enjoyed fresh, local incredibly tasty food, gotten to know our boat and have essentially broken ourselves into our new lifestyle on the sea.

The time has now come, however, to find a cozy corner of the Mediterranean to "winter" ourselves and *Britican*.

Originally, we would have been preparing to cross the Atlantic Ocean with the Atlantic Rally for Cruisers (ARC) crossing; however, early in the season we realized that the boat wasn't ready for such a long trip (three to four weeks). And, it was less expensive and easier to get our boat in shape in Sicily rather than in the Caribbean or remote areas of the Pacific. (Our boat is European so once we left Europe it would be harder to find parts and people who knew how to fix it, and our plan is to eventually head into the Pacific.)

So, we lived aboard our boat in Sicily waiting for summer when we enjoyed another season in the Mediterranean.

Our recent journey from Greece to Sicily was very tranquil.

The week before our departure, we endured massive thunderstorms, high winds and flash flooding so I was initially concerned about getting a window in the weather to make the crossing.

Prior to our lifestyle change, cooking was not part of my skill set. I'm proud to say that that has changed. In preparation for our trip, I spent a day preparing meals for the journey. I made shepherd's pie (a ground beef mixture on the bottom with carrots, celery, peppers, onions and Britican Galley Beef Blend covered with garlic mashed potatoes and cheese on the top), a hearty chicken soup (with the Britican Galley Chicken Blend – of course!) and chili with very little chili powder. Unfortunately, I purchased paprika at the local Greek supermarket rather than chili powder – heck, it's all in Greek…how was I to know?

In Greece the days were still quite hot but the evenings drop quickly in temperature. I thought some nice warm comfort food would make the transit even more enjoyable. Also, I still got seasick so having the knowledge that a good meal was coming up made me feel better. Essentially, I daydream about food all day long while we're sailing.

Looking back, I could have cooked on our voyage across. We had very little wind and it would have been nice to have something to do, but it's better to prepare for the worst. By having meals ready, all we had to do is heat them up. In a storm or turbulent seas, it's almost impossible to cook, as my cousin Loryn discovered. She tried to cook fried eggs in a Force 8 and I wasn't surprised when she got egg on her face.

There was enough wind in the Ionian Sea to raise the main and genoa, so we put our sails up as soon as we could. I sat in the cockpit, looking out at the deep blue sea, and quietly said, "Boy, have I missed you!"

Simon set the navigational instruments and like the dashboard on a car, we could see the estimated time of arrival (ETA) and distance to weigh point in Syracuse, Sicily. Our ETA read 48 hours and our distance was 281 nautical miles. It was better than the 800+ nautical miles we had to do from Gibraltar to Malta!

We all said our good byes to Greece. We'd definitely miss the exceptional food, great new friends and overall feel of Greece. What an incredible country for sailors…It's probably my number one destination for sailing in terms of variety, value for the money, facilities and great people.

Although Greece doesn't have the funds to maintain many of their marinas, at least they have many harbors, mooring buoys and anchorages dotted all over the place. Further – it often costs nothing to tie off on a town quay. That definitely can't be said about Italy or the Balearics.

After dinner, Simon went to the aft cabin to get a bit of rest and chill out with Sienna. The two of them watched a film. Stefano and I kept watch in the cockpit. We saw a massive moon come over the Greek mountains – it was definitely a sight to behold.

We chatted about the stars, constellations, the position of the moon and sun, navigating by the stars in addition to me practicing my Italian. Stefano must be so tired of me saying "come sei dichie _____" or "how do you say _____"?

After midnight I went to my bedroom and cuddled up with Sienna. We allow her sleep in our bed during night sails so she looks forward to them rather than not. She sees it as a treat to sleep with her mom and it gets her focus away from nighttime rolling, noises and disturbances.

The following day, the wind started to die so we got our gennaker out. It's a very thin sail that can be used with winds blowing between 10 and 15 knots. Using our heavy genoa, the sail would flap and fail to fill up with wind whereas our gennaker fills up perfectly and lets us gracefully sail in light winds.

We have around five additional sails on board and that's on top of our main and genoa (front sail). The gennaker is kept in our forward berth (bedroom). To get the gennaker out, we simply pull it up through the forward hatch and then attach it to the various points, unfurl (unroll) it and trim as appropriate.

Our gennaker is blue and white and adds a bit of color to our journey. With the gennaker and the light winds I felt as if we were in a fairytale. As far as the eye could see there was no one and nothing – no another boat and no land.

Unbelievably, however, 120 nautical miles out from Greece, with no land in sight, a rather large bird started to swoon us.

First of all, I was surprised to see a bird at all. Second, I darn near died when Simon yelled out, "'It's an owl!"

What the heck is an owl doing during the middle of the day circling us – a boat in the middle of nowhere? In my usual moron fashion, I started to yell out "whoop, whoooo," to let the owl know that he or she was welcome to rest on our boat. We often get birds stopping on *Britican* for a while to regain their strength to carry on.

Needless to say, the owl didn't stop, however we did have two finches rest on our safety lines and one robin stopped by a few times to say hello.

We put out breadcrumbs and a little dish of water. Either the birds were migrating or perhaps they were on a tanker or cruise ship and found themselves stuck out at sea. We're always happy to accommodate new guests – as long as it's not a giant squid – the one that my mother warned me about after watching a National Geographic special!

Aside from our flying friends, we also watched three pods of dolphins go by.

They all seemed to be feeding so they didn't sail along the bow like usual. One pod did come over to say hi but quickly carried on. I tried my best to get a picture but they all seemed to be swimming very fast!

We also spotted a couple of massive turtles just floating along. Every time I see them I feel as if they're just going with the flow. It doesn't look like they have the ability to navigate very well – they just flow by looking unconcerned about anything.

Half way through our trip the wind died completely.

The Ionian Sea was a millpond. Stefano said that in the 40 years of being on this sea he's never seen it so calm. The forecast called for very little wind, but there was nothing. Not even a breath of air coming from any direction.

Sadly, the decision was made to turn the engine on after 23 hours of sailing. We all discussed that it would be a good thing to give the engine a good running-in and ensure that all the fixes were, indeed, fixed.

The engine went on and we motored along across the flat calm Ionian Sea.

Around 4pm the following day and after two failed attempts to reel in a big fish, we made it safely to Syracuse, Sicily.

Just as we anchored, the wind started to blow and would you believe that it was too windy to leave the boat? We had over 24 hours of no wind and then the time when you want it to be calm, the wind decided to blow!

The plan then was to head to Marina diRagusa along the southeast cost of Sicily where we'd stay put for the winter among several other live-aboards. I was told that it was quite a nice community, and I looked forward to discovering yet another new chapter of our amazing around the world adventure.

Chapter 28: Living on a boat in the Mediterranean

Previous to our decision to sail around the world, I had no idea that there are thousands of people winter their boat and themselves in the Mediterranean. I assumed that people either sailed around the Med all winter or left their boats there and flew home.

I soon realized that there are those who live on land during the winter and only use their boat in the Mediterranean for holidays or during the summer. I've met quite a few consultants who work during the winter and save up so they can sail during the summer months.

And there are loads of retired couples who spend the full summer island hopping and then head back to land over the cooler months. These seasonal sailors almost always have their boat pulled out of the water and stored on the hard over the winter season.

And then there are the "live aboards".

These people live on their boat full time. Most of the live aboards that I've met do not have homes in their native land. They've taken to the sea full time and live a somewhat nomadic life moving slowly or quickly from one destination to another. Some travel far, perhaps around the world, and some have spent years just sailing in the same area.

In the Mediterranean, most live aboards find a marina to live in over the winter months. The weather becomes treacherous with high winds, torrential rainfall, cold temperatures and turbulent seas. Additionally, all the areas that cater to sailors shut down for the winter, so even if you wanted to sail around there'd be a lack of facilities and services.

Taking the boat out for a sail here and there is fine, but overall most live aboards in the Med dock up for the duration of the winter.

Many marinas offer a special deal from October to April. Thus far Greece and Turkey seem to be the least expensive at around $3,000, Sicily comes in at $5,000, Spain is around the $7,000 and we were quoted over $10,000 for Malta. These prices for a 56′ boat include the full six months but do not include water and electricity. Smaller boats pay less as the price is based on the length of the boat.

I have also met quite a few Americans who winter in Algeria or Tunisia because the EU won't let them enjoy Europe for more than three to six months at a time.

And during my recent stay in Rethymno Marina, Crete I discovered that our neighbors winter their boat and themselves in Egypt!

Every time I talk with live aboard the world seems to open up more and more. My first question is always, "Is it safe to winter in Northern Africa? Is it safe to winter in Egypt?" The answers are always the same – "Yes, it's very safe."

Apparently, in a marina you're not really part of the country you're in. You're surrounded by other Brits, Americans, Kiwi's, etc., and the host country wants you there as you're spending money to keep the local livelihoods going. It's a win-win for everyone.

So we decided to settle in Sicily. Welcoming children into local schools from the marina is a normal occurrence.

I took Sienna to see if I could get her into a pre-school, although I couldn't speak the language. I sputtered out "Barca" (boat) and did my six fingers for months and added with "Auito" (help). I was received with a welcome smile, a bit of English and an iPhone translation app where the teacher and I discussed options.

As a side note, and to describe the amazing people we're surrounded by, after Simon and I dropped off Sienna on her first day we stopped by the marina office. Everyone around the marina speaks perfect English so we asked a staff member to call the pre-school to ensure our daughter was okay and we understood everything correctly.

Not only did the staff member give us a great report but the marina office offered to become a point of contact if there were any issues.

Later that day the marina office rang me to request my email address. A few minutes later, I received photos that the pre-school sent to the marina and then the marina forwarded to me! They were of Sienna, having fun, smiling and laughing. Let me get back to the world of live aboards.

Generally, live aboards keep their boat in the water for the majority of the winter only to have it hauled out for necessary out-of-water work. On a yearly basis the haul needs new antifouling painted on, anodes need to be changed and a good check of the shaft, rudder and prop areas needs to be actioned. During the out-of-water work a boater might fly off to see relatives, find a hotel or remain on the boat using a ladder to get aboard.

Within the first couple weeks of arriving in their designated marina, live aboards prepare their boat for the winter.

Instead of winterizing, or shutting down the boat, they shut down bits of it and do a variety of tasks to ensure the winter is as comfortable as possible. For example, most boats remove their sails, halyards and sheets (all the ropes). By removing the sails, you reduce the amount of resistance to wind that you get so the boat won't blow around as much. You also protect the sails from damaging SUV rays.

The ropes all need a very good wash with fresh water and to be stowed away for next season. Small ropes, called mousing lines, are used to replace the ropes that go up the mast and through all the fittings. When the next season starts, you simple tie the halyard or sheet (ropes) onto the mousing lines and pull them back into place.

We wintered our water maker as there was no use for it for the six months we'd be at the marina. With a nice supply of water off the jetty we'd fill up our tanks with a hose as needed.

We also tackled our biggest issues - repairing leaks, changing faulty pumps/switches and addressed the long list of to-do's.

After all the preparation tasks were taken care of, we created a weekly/bi-weekly/monthly routine to ensure that the boat stayed in good condition. For example, every pump needs to run on a weekly basis. That means that it's important to run your air conditioning and freezer even if you're not using it. Pumps seize up if they're not used regularly.

Furthermore, it's absolutely imperative to run the engine not only in neutral but also have it tick over in forward to make sure the shaft moves. This moves the salt water through the engine and gets the oil to splash around a bit. It also moves the grease along the shaft and propulsion unit. The generator also needs to be turned on and loaded up (turn lots of things on) for a few minutes.

So...we paid around $800/month to live in paradise.

Additionally, in the marina we chose, every morning at 9am there were announcements about excursions, goods for sale or wanted items, any medical issues, lost and found and upcoming social events. Every Tuesday and Friday the boaties would meet at one of two bar/restaurants for a drink and nibbles.

There was loads to do, we met many great new people, I honestly can't imagine ever going back to the way I use to live my life. I'm truly a nomad and loving it.

Month seven. Can you believe it?!

As we approached our seventh month of living full-time aboard a sailboat, I found myself living with yet another set of circumstances, in new surroundings, with yet another routine to figure out.

The cruising life is certainly different than the live aboard marina life.

The marina staff and its residence (60 percent live on board over the winter) were amazingly kind, generous, knowledgeable and helpful.

The surrounding area is gorgeous. We had beaches, a lovely boardwalk leading the town center and all the important shops close by. The grocery store, hardware store, bakery, butcher and all the restaurants were in walking distance. We were able to get Sienna into the local Italian pre-school. Sim and I thought the experience would be an excellent opportunity for her to learn a new language, integrate with local children and give us a bit of space to work on the boat. It was a good decision.

[See Appendix A, 'V6. A child living on a boat' for a video I made about Sienna's experiences]

Chapter 29: Home for the holidays!

For a couple of weeks leading up to Christmas that first year, Simon, Sienna and I flew to England to spend the holidays with friends and family. For live aboards traveling home for the holidays, here are some tips that helped me.

1. Be prepared to experience a lifestyle conflict. After living on a boat for quite a bit of time it might be hard to adjust to life on land.

2. If possible, arrange a gathering in a central location where you can invite everyone to come to you rather than trying to make the rounds to all of your family and friends.

3. If you're going to buy presents, buy them online before you arrive and have them shipped to a friend/family member so you don't have to fall prey to the pre-Christmas shopping rush.

4. Schedule in time for yourself – every few days make sure you have a rest day or a few hours to just read a book or veg out. If you don't schedule it in, the time will be taken up. Hubby and I booked a spa day/night at a hotel to make sure we took time out for ourselves.

5. Don't feel bad if friends and family can't relate to you and your lifestyle – that's normal.

6. Realize that each visit might be more about simply spending time with friends/family rather than gaining a close connection. It's a time of stress, deadlines and endless preparations. Many people who you meet with will be more anxious and stressed than usual.

7. Be easy on yourself. Don't get upset if you can't see everyone and/or make everyonc happy. Do the best you can and

give yourself credit for making the massive effort to get home in the first place.

Let me tell you our story about leaving our live aboard boat community to go home to England for the holidays.

During the lead up to December, Simon and I couldn't decide if we wanted to fly to England for Christmas. Initially, we wanted to fly my father-in-law down to Marina di Ragusa so that he could join us on the boat or at a nearby holiday apartment for the festive period.

Unfortunately, his health restricted him from flying, and I was invited to attend a party with some of my best business friends. Of course, several of our friends wanted to see us and I was missing them.

We didn't want to leave the sunny, moderate weather. Nor did we want to leave our friends or the amazing planned festivities at the marina. We felt so comfortable, and the thought of flying felt as if we were leaving a vacation rather than leaving our live-aboard life.

In the end, we decided to fly to England for three weeks over the Christmas period. Simon and I couldn't bear to think of my father-in-law being home alone.

Travelling isn't for everyone, but those of us who venture away from home have a massive opportunity to not only see new things and experience new experiences, but we also discover just how amazing our home was to begin with. As I always say, you don't know what you don't know. If you never get out of where you are, you'll never realize how good you have it.

These are some of the things I missed about living in England:

- Toilets have seats on them (In Italy it's rare to find a café, bar or restaurant with a toilet seat!)
- You can flush your toilet paper down the toilet (on the boat and most places in the Med, you need to put your toilet paper in a wastepaper basket)
- You can shower without turning the water on and off to conserve water.
- There is a massive variety of FOOD! Curry, Chinese, Thai, Sushi, roast dinners, parsnips, and big coffees.
- It's great to go into a shop and have the ability to read packages in English – it doesn't take all day to figure out what I'm buying!
- Being able to use my phone and not worrying how expensive the call is going to be is so relaxing.
- Unlimited Internet that is actually unlimited and works is a breath of fresh air.
- Being able to find things that you want easily allows me to walk around chilled out rather than always having my radar on. In the Med I always have a list of things I need in my head and I'm always looking out for a shop that might have them!
- Not having to figure out what language you need to speak for pleasantries (please, thank you, hello, good bye) makes going out that much more relaxing.
- Seeing the British countryside – there's nothing as beautiful as England when the sun comes out!

On the flip side, however, after the bombardment to the senses is over, there is for some of us a realization of why we left in the first place. And interestingly, all the things I listed above become normal very quickly. At first it feels amazing to flush toilet paper down the toilet, but by day three it's as if you've never had it any other way.

If you've ever moved from one location to another you'll know what I'm talking about. It's as if your circle of awareness expands and the thought of going back to where you were before sends a chill up your spine. The same can happen while thinking back on a previous job or perhaps a previous partner. You've moved on.

My circle of awareness started in Rochester, New York. It then expanded to San Francisco, California. Thereafter, it expanded to Aylesbury, England and now it's grown to not only include several countries around the Mediterranean but it also encompasses an alternative lifestyle of living on a sailboat.

I left England to live my dream because I was fed up with a lack of meaningful connection with others, unhealthy food, negative media, and broken systems (health service, banking, education, etc.). To me, the world seemed broken and I wanted to find a new world – one that is less filled with fear, negativity and systems that didn't make any sense.

Within the sailing community, I've certainly found a different world. I've discovered people who are similar to me and perhaps running away from the modern world of commercialism, fear, stress, broken systems. Let me rephrase that and say that perhaps we're all running toward something more authentic and fulfilling.

For the most part, sailors aren't living in a world based on fear and broken systems; they're instead living in flow. They naturally generate a community of kindness, friendship, support and authenticity.

Most sailors I've met don't watch the news and aren't influenced by the barrage of negativity emitting from the TV, radio or Internet media outlets. Conversations among sailors tend to reflect on the weather, sailing stories, interesting things to do in the area, tips on future locations, food, our past lives (on land) and anything troubling us.

When you're living on a boat, there's always an issue – how do you get stains off the hull? What's the best way to clean the curtains? Where can you get gas for the oven tank? And so on. The issues are not emotional or heavy – often they're the next thing to do and learn so they're treated in a positive manner.

While in the UK, I caught the flu and watched a bit of TV to try and take my mind off feeling like crap. In the course of four hours, I cried six times – every charity commercial made my heart break and the news made me feel unwell. After nine months of not watching TV, I felt as if I wasn't prepared for the overwhelmingly strong messages used to get viewers' attention.

The sad thing is that if I lived on land and saw the charity commercials often I probably wouldn't bat an eye at them – I would just turn off my ability to feel, as it's the only way to protect oneself from all the negative messaging out there.

Having a break from TV made me realize just how hard the modern world has to work at getting our attention.

Going nowhere fast – are we?

Most cruising sailors don't try to get anywhere fast and it's reflected on land just as much as on sea. We all know that our best-laid plans often won't pan out – either the weather or the wind will hamper our efforts. Furthermore, getting anywhere by sailboat takes quite a long time. Over the nine months, I've slowed way down. I move slower. I walk slower.

And I even talk slower. I'm truly going with the flow rather than trying to force anything.

Contrast my slow pace with my workaholic city girl past and you'd see a massive change in me! I use to speed walk everywhere I went. In London, I'd race up and down the escalators in The Tube. I was always rushing and it wasn't because I was late. It was simply because I always felt as if there wasn't enough time in the day. Even when I forced myself to slow down I could feel my blood race through my veins yelling, "Hurry up"!

You can choose to rush or you can choose to go a speed that says, "I have all the time in the world." In the end you get the same results but the slower journey is much more relaxing and far more beneficial to one's health.

During our stay in London, hubby and I enjoyed the sights of London with our daughter. Watching all the people speed by made my head spin. Everyone was on super drive, whereas we were all dawdling around absorbing the views. As our time in London progressed I felt myself start to speed up.

When you're in an environment where everyone is racing around it seems impossible not to join the race too. I don't want to race. By the time we left London I couldn't wait to get back to the boat. I felt my whole mind and body start to speed up, and I didn't want that anymore!

Being in England caused me to also miss the sense of community in the boating world.

On a boat, whether you're at a marina, in a bay or passing another boat you almost always exchange pleasantries, start up a chat and more often than not make a new friend.

In England, my sense of community consists of my friends spread throughout the country. I feel very close to my friends and it's lovely to see them, but in between, when I'm walking along the High Street or doing some shopping I feel a lack of connection.

When we landed in England we spent the first weekend visiting Sienna's friends. Upon seeing her various groups of friends she immediately went up and hugged them. There was no shyness or an uncomfortable first few minutes. All the children acted just as they did before we left as if no time passed.

As a whole, Sienna seemed to just go with the flow and she was happy when she was with her friends, happy when it was just she and Granddad watching TV and even happy helping my dear friend, Ene, rake the leaves in the back garden. She didn't seem any happier than when she was with her friends in the sailing community. I was pleased to see how stable she seemed.

The one remarkable difference I noticed, however, was her ambivalence to Christmas – especially in regard to presents. When I asked her what she wanted from Santa she couldn't really give me an answer. After a couple days she told me that she wanted a toy truck.

Contrast that to last year where she gave me a list of every toy she wanted, and the list was not short!

Due to the fact that she hadn't seen a commercial in over nine months she didn't know what she wanted. I really don't think she cared too much about the presents she received, yet she seemed grateful.

And hopefully my constant repetition about family and friends being "all I want for Christmas" will reinforce the values I want her to hold.

Two days before we returned to the marina from our three-week holiday, Granddad asked Sienna if she'd rather live in England or on the boat. Sienna responded with, "I want to live on the boat."

The second we left the boat, Simon admitted that he didn't want to leave. He said he had a knot in his stomach. Throughout our time in England he said he was okay. I could see that he enjoyed his time with friends and family, but overall the trip was very stressful.

I asked him if he could ever live in England again now that we've left and changed our lifestyle. His answer was yes, but definitely not in the near future.

Chapter 30: Ten months of living on *Britican*

Sienna was flourishing. She's growing up around people who are inspiring and eager to take the time to send positive words her way. She's growing up in a beautiful environment.

In the marina, she had a range of friends aged 2 to 80 who come from Italy, Poland, New Zealand, Britain, America, Canada, Holland, France, Spain, South Africa, Germany and on and on. She doesn't see color, language or nationality as a separator but a connector! One evening we'd visit a boat of Brits and the next evening we'd have a French couple over.

Her grasp of the Italian language was coming on in leaps in bounds. Interestingly, however, she kept trying to teach me new Italian words, only for me to find out they don't exist! Yes, Sienna was also developing a great sense of humor.

Social skills are definitely low on my worry list now. And as far as education goes, that's quite a low worry too. Every day Sienna learned in her pre-school, and then we used an online homeschooling website called ABC Mouse to ensure she was doing letters, numbers, math, music, reading and more. We spent time every day writing letters, creating pictures or doing a craft session. Often, other kids from the marina or the town came over to the boat and we painted pictures, played with stickers or created props for a play.

From what I can make out, Sienna seemed to be on par with other children her age. If and when I discovered she should be doing something, I make more of an effort. For example, I noticed that another four-year-old was really good at writing his name, so Simon and I spent a couple days with Sienna helping her to get better at writing her name.

Recently she wanted to know how are clouds are formed, how do you make chocolate, where do beans grow, where do you go after you die and when you have a baby, do you poop it out?

If I know the answer to her question I give an explanation and then I'll follow it up with more information that I can find on the Internet. We also have some amazing apps on the iPad that help with everything from the human body, outer space and some great science games, math, reading, art and music.

And as for Simon and me, we've made some amazing friends who will be friends for life. We've learned to slow down a bit more. We've started to find the funnier side of life rather than taking things so seriously. When something breaks on the boat we laugh instead of doing what we used to do – cry!

For the first time in my life, I finally got it.

I've inched my way around life slowly and at many times going in the wrong direction. Heck – I think I've fallen off the tree and have had to climb back up it over and over and over again. I might be premature in saying this but I feel as if I've finally found my wings. I've finally become a butterfly.

Chapter 31: Going back to the States

Considering that the boat needed to have several weeks worth of work completed, I thought it would be a great opportunity to fly with Sienna to the States to visit with family – especially my grandparents, mom and brother.

For the past 16 years, I've been flying from London to New York to visit my friends and family, experiencing a variety of feelings. Returning home often presents a bombardment to the senses, an awareness of nostalgia, and memories of why I left mixed with the love for those I left. It usually takes me a few days to balance out as I go a bit crazy eating foods I've missed and mixing with loved ones in familiar places. By travelling back to America, my home, I was pleasantly surprised to see and feel like a different person. I had fundamentally changed but didn't realize how massive the change was.

For over a month, Sienna and I spent time with my family in North Carolina. My mom, stepfather, brother and his family all live in the Raleigh–Durham area, so while Simon managed a refit on the boat, we girls spent time on land enjoying long hot showers, eating cheeseburgers and hot dogs, and spending as much quality time with our family as possible.

Sienna was offered a space at her cousin's pre-school, so for a month she enjoyed her first taste of the American school system. The transition from her one-room 10-pupil class in Italy (Italian speaking only) to the massive school (hundreds of children) with state-of-art outdoor playground must have been an interesting one.

I was amazed to hear my daughter's accent change from British to American so quickly! Within days, instead of saying "water" she was saying "waaader" and rather than "lift" it quickly became an "elevator." And instead of everything being "lovely," life simply became "awesome."

As if Sienna had lived in America her whole life, she joined in with the neighbor kids running around the neighborhood, made new friends at school and acted like any other child.

The biggest issue I faced was Sienna's dislike for her baby cousin, Emma. For some reason, Sienna avoided my 18 month-old niece like the plague. Sienna announced, "I don't like babies," and feeling embarrassed I didn't know how to deal with such negativity. She ignored her cousin and at times I saw her push the baby aside. I couldn't understand why she felt so strongly about babies – aren't little girls supposed to love babies?

Eventually I realized that Sienna was jealous. Instead of me being available all the time, there was someone else who took precedence over my little princess Sienna. Although I felt uncomfortable with her negativity, I could see that we were learning a massive lesson.

Through the course of our stay with my brother and family, Sienna had to learn how to not only share toys with her cousins but to also share me. There were times when she asked if I loved her more than her cousins and at one point she threw a fit because I couldn't leave the baby unattended to play with her.

At first I thought that all our time together on the boat had created a self-important, attention-seeking monster, but then I realized that she's just a child and it's my job to help her learn a life lesson.

By the time our stay came to an end, Sienna was a best friend to baby Emma. She learned how to share my time and enjoy baby playtime. The two girls took baths together, had tea parties and loved to chase each other around the house. Sienna also learned how to take responsibility for a younger child – to look out for the baby.

Our time at my brother Bryan's house forced a great lesson upon us. Sienna learned that my love is always present even if I'm not. For me, the situation reinforced that children are quick learners. Watching Sienna learn to share, reduce her expectations for me to physically be present all the time, and take responsibility for a younger family member was great to see unfold.

Yes, I was horrified to see my daughter act so negatively toward her baby cousin, but on the flip side I'm now very proud to see the transition that transpired.

Being in the States allowed me to compare who I used to be with who I am now.

My new life is far better than I could have ever speculated. It is so amazingly fulfilling that I often have to pinch myself because I feel like I've transferred over into a heaven on Earth and the old me was living in hell.

No…I'm not going to sit here and preach that everyone should sell everything and go sailing.

What I am saying, however, is that once you stop doing what you SHOULD do and start listening to who you are/what you want/what you like and start doing what makes you feel alive, your reality drastically changes for the better.

And my life is not easy. I don't have fun all the time. Things are not perfect.

I have struggles, bad days, bad weeks and bad times. Overall however, all the bad things (if I must label them as bad) are so worth the life I'm now living.

How things have changed for me:

1. Going with the flow

Since leaving my old life, I've had to learn to seriously go with the flow, especially when you're sailing. Your intention might be to get to destination B but more often than not you end at destination C or D or E or get nowhere at all. The wind could be wrong, there's a storm coming or the engine dies!

What I've learned is that by going to the flow, wherever I end up is a great place with the option for amazing experiences.

I've lost my attachment for things to go the way I want them to go. Now, I accept whatever happens, knowing that wherever I end up will be fine. Sailing and the boat taught me this lesson, and it's expanded through to my normal life.

For example, when I arrived in North Carolina to spend time with my family, I had a mental list of all the things I wanted to do and see. The morning after I arrived I woke up to a snowstorm that shut the whole state down. Mom and I had to cancel our shopping, spa, lunch day and stay home instead. I just went with the flow and mom and I had a ball. In fact, usually I run around and get tired but this visit we hung out at home and actually created a whole new product line for my Sailing Britican store. The old me would have been annoyed at the snow, complained to anyone who would have listened and sulked around.

The new me went with the flow and enjoyed every moment.

Another example – Bryan and I flew up to Rochester and he caught a bug on the way up. He was down for the first two days so I had to visit family without him. I was sad that he couldn't join me, but I spent quite a lot of time with him sitting on the sofa. We sat around joking, laughing and having a rather enjoyable time. The last two days we were in

Rochester, *I* got sick! It was no big deal. I let the illness take its course and just chilled with Bry.

All in all, we didn't do much, yet the time we spent together was priceless.

The old me would have wallowed in self-pity thinking, what a waste. Instead, I spent loads of time with my grandparents, and that was priceless, too!

And finally, the day came for us to leave the States and a huge storm hit the whole East coast. Our flight was cancelled and rebooked for a couple days later. The old me would have been livid. I would have been attached to getting back to the boat – to my hubby, friends and boat. But the new me just went with the flow. Due to a change in the flight route I was able to see my dear cousin – he met us in Boston and we enjoyed a couple hours together – something that wouldn't have happened if the storm hadn't hit.

2. There's no hole to fill

Back when I lived in my big house with my fancy car, I always felt I had a hole to fill. Simon and I would spend our free time shopping to buy things that would ultimately be left in a cupboard and usually forgotten. I spent years feeling the need to buy more shoes, more clothes, more house stuff and then, once I gave birth to Sienna, I had to buy more and more so that she could have the best of everything.

More, more, more, more. Holes, holes, holes…there was always a hole to fill!

During my various excursions on this trip to the States, when the snow disappeared, Mom or Bryan would ask if they could take me anywhere to get anything. Usually my response was, "nope – I don't need anything." It's so funny… I live on a boat so there's no room for anything. My clothes are sun bleached, full of rust stains (from drying them on the metal safety rail around the boat) and falling apart. When something eventually passes the point of no return, I make a mental note to replace it.

I don't watch TV anymore. No more TV means no more media and that helps me to avoid society telling me what I should have. Since I stopped watching TV I've stopped feeling so inadequate. Furthermore, my craving for fast food has totally stopped!

I think that I was actually living a lie – I wasn't being the best me I could be and therefore I always felt I had a hole to fill. Once I said, "screw it – I'm going to live life the way I want to live it," that hole has totally disappeared.

3. Time to be present

I really can't stand it when people say that want to live in the "now." It sounds so corny. But…that's where this line of writing is going. For some reason my past no longer haunts me and my future is more about going with the flow. I choose to believe that everything works out; therefore, there's no need to spend time worrying or speculating.

I ruminate and get caught up with things every once in while…but in contrast to the old me, the transformation is nothing short of a miracle.

The old me was either feeling emotional pain because I was wronged as kid OR I would be experiencing increased stress levels because something didn't go the way I wanted it to go. Neither of those things had any real meaning in my life! Thinking of the past or speculating about what might happen in the future was and is a total waste of time. I was so distracted by emails, drama, the news, being right, being perfect that I never just lived life as it came to me.

Now, I have all the time in the world to engage with people. I can take 20 minutes to explain something to a child or engage in an interesting adult discussion. Furthermore, I have time to really look a sales clerk in the eye and respond genuinely to casual conversations. The smiles I get when I truly engage with people are deep and full of energy.

I don't know how I became so distracted by non-life, but now I can see the difference. Boy, can I see the difference.

4. Acceptance of my past

Up until this past visit, every time I visited my hometown I went through a constant good/bad judgment game in my head. I'd justify my decision to leave home by picking out all the bad things about Rochester and, more significantly, I'd remember all the bad experiences. My thoughts would sound like this, "This city is a shithole. How do people live here? How do people live with so much snow? My time in school was the worst time of my life. I hate this street. I hated my life here…."

During this trip I didn't make any judgments. I felt myself wanting to do so, but instead of thinking something was good or bad, I just kept saying to myself "there is no good or bad – there's just my interpretation of it."

I didn't look down on people who live there. I didn't think I was better for getting out. I didn't feel anything accept for a genuine happiness to be able to spend time with my family.

My mind didn't spiral. I just went with the flow and, by doing that, my past record of judging everything as either good or bad, black or white didn't exist anymore.

It was weird. It was empowering. It was beautiful.

So…it had been eleven remarkable months since I left land. Yes – it's cool that I was sailing around in a boat, but what's more impressive is that I was now flowing with life. Rather than paddle insanely up a raging river, I let life take me where it wants to take me.

I haven't written this to say, "look at me – look how great my life is...." I've written this book because I'm a born-again human. I've realized that life can be amazing and I want anyone out there who doesn't feel alive to realize we all have the opportunity to make changes...to improve our quality of life.

Sure, I speculated that I'd make several new friends as we sail around the world. What I didn't realize is that the friends I'd make would be so close. I didn't understand that new relationships could provide such depth, warmth and love. And furthermore, I didn't comprehend how hard it would be to leave my new friends.

Chapter 32: Back to Sicily

We returned to Marina di Ragusa after visiting the states, and prepared to leave for our next destination. I felt a variety of emotions. Even within the space of an hour I felt sadness, anger and even a tinge of excitement. And a whole bunch of other things, too.

These sentiments reflect the range of feelings and emotions I went through prior to, during and after leaving our winter home:

- **Sadness.** Due to leaving so many great people and a place that I learned to feel at home.

- **Heartbreak.** Leaving a few amazingly good friends pulled at my heartstrings. I know it might sound unlikely in such a short time, but I made a few friends at the marina who I know will be friends for life. We laughed together, cried together…shared our problems. In those short months I felt closer to them than I did with friends I've had all my life.

- **Connection**. During the lead up to leaving, I experienced more hugs over a couple of days than I've had all year, and they were all great hugs! In many cases I initiated the hugs, as I'm a hugger and not a kisser. Many people make fun of Americans for a whole range of valid reasons, but I must say that we are a nation of great huggers (and hug initiators). I'll take a hug any day over the European two-cheek air kiss!

- **Guilt**. I couldn't help feel like I should have made more of an effort to have spent more time with my marina friends. When I was hugging several people either I or the other person would say, "we should have gotten together more!"

- **Anger**. Part of me felt angry about our lifestyle decision. At one point I became irritated that I chose a sailboat cruising life…I didn't know how painful it would be to say goodbye. I didn't realize how much my heart would hurt. At times I thought, I don't want to make more friends if I'll have to say goodbye!

- **Emotional**. Watching my daughter's Italian pre-school teachers visit us on the boat to say goodbye was tough. One of the teachers had so many tears that you couldn't find dry spot on her face. It was so emotional!

- **Anxious.** It's our first sailing trip of the season – 40+ hours non-stop from Sicily to Greece. I thought...Will we actually be able to leave? Will the boat be okay? Will we get out of the marina? Will the weather be okay? Am I saying goodbye to all these people thinking we're going to leave, but in actuality, we won't be able to leave for another week or two (due to weather)?

- **Worried**. Worried about how my daughter will adjust from going to having loads of very close friends around to none. At school she had friends, but she also made friends with a few English speaking children with whom she became very close to.

- **Apprehensive**. What about my seasickness? Will it come back in full force or will I pick up where I was last year?

- **Overwhelmed**. A massive workload of getting the boat prepared – clean up, stow away everything that's been out for six months, prepare home-cooked dinners, buy provisions for the trip, and get meals/snacks ready for my daughter. Hubby had to get the running rigging on, put the new sails up, service the winches and make sure everything was ready to go.

- **Excited.** We were moving on. We were heading to the next open door. Our Marina di Ragusa door was closing and it was sad, but when one door closes...

While the boat was leaving the marina...I felt:

- **Relief.** The heartache of knowing I was leaving started to lift as I didn't have to think about it anymore. I was still sad but there was a sense of closure. I had spent a couple of weeks knowing we might leave, and it was hard to live in that space. Our departure provided me with the opportunity to know that I didn't have to say goodbye anymore.

- **Nervous.** I couldn't help but wonder how my seasickness would play out (yes, I know I shouldn't think that way, but it's hard not to worry about it when you have a serious track record).

- **Free.** Whenever I'm on the sea I feel a sense of freedom. There's no Internet connection, no phones, no noise – other than waves hitting the hull, sails flapping in the wind and the bow breaking on the water. When we finally got our new sails up and the engine went off, I felt totally free.

Between leaving Sicily and arriving in Greece I felt:

- **Sick. Sick. Sick.** I couldn't lift my head up off the bed despite taking an anti-seasickness pill. Fortunately, I didn't puke, but I didn't feel good either. The whole trip sucked. I definitely believe that stress makes seasickness come on faster and stronger.

- **Pleasure.** Enjoyment found in eating the food I cooked and snacks. Out of the whole 40+ hours, I only felt a glimmer of happiness when I ate. I'm now wondering how I'll ever make it across the Atlantic. I have noticed that as the season advances I get better at handling my seasickness. I still have hope.

- **Numbness.** You'd think you'd have time to think when you're seasick – right? You're just lying in bed, often trying to drift off to sleep, thinking of things that might make you feel better. For me, I'd think of food. Otherwise, I'd think about what a sissy I am. I'm on an around-the-world sailing adventure and I turn green so freaking easily. How am I going to cope? Otherwise, I just felt numb.

While arriving in Greece, I felt:

- **Excited.** I was very happy to see the sight of land AND friends waiting for us on the jetty! The sights made my heart and body smile.
- **Comforted.** The view of a place I knew well made me feel comfortable. We've returned to Preveza, Greece. Our friends were on the jetty to meet us and my heart expanded with even more smiles.
- **Joy and relief.** Our friend had his daughter with him! Mila, from Italy, has just turned five and looks just like Sienna (about to turn five). Mila was on our boat within seconds of tying up. The girls played on our boat, went to the park and played on Mila's boat. Last time we were in this area I had to take our dinghy over to the town of Preveza and find friends for Sienna at the playground. It didn't go so well…the children were sparse and the homeless person napping on the park bench didn't want to play! My worries of Sienna being stranded in a marina without a friend were totally unfounded!
- **Forward-looking.** I'm not at Marina di Ragusa anymore so I'm not being reminded of the people who are no longer with me. Yes, I miss everyone, but on the flip side there are other things for me to focus on.

Cruising life is full of hellos and goodbyes. And at times, the goodbyes can be heart wrenching, HOWEVER, the pain of leaving only lasts a few days.

The transition from living in the rat race to living full time on a sailboat has taught me some amazing lessons. One of the largest lessons I've noted, thus far, is my ability to consciously choose life's course rather than live life on automatic pilot. In the past I thought I was making choices, but after reflection I was simply being distracted by life rather than living it.

Let me explain how I came to this realization. But first I have to back up a bit to show you where my line of thought started…

I've been debating as to whether I have more options with my current lifestyle than I had in my previous rat race life. And taking that a bit further, I've asked myself if there are too many choices more apt to complicate life rather than simplify it.

Since selling up and sailing away, endless possibilities have opened up. And with those endless possibilities I've had to seriously increase my decision-making skills. My romantic notion of sailing into the sunset and doing nothing couldn't be further from the truth.

Sailing around the world certainly isn't simple – our new lifestyle of doing nothing is anything but "doing nothing!"

Not only do I have a multitude of destinations I can go to at almost any moment, there's my choice on when I leave for the next destinations and what kind of weather I want to travel in (high wind, low wind, etc.). And what time should I leave – during the morning or late at night? At this very moment, I have the option to move our home to Greece, Malta, Turkey, Croatia, Spain, France, Portugal or Africa.

Then there are limitless choices on how to spend my days, too – do I visit with friends, make new friends (that's more spontaneous but you must be out and about to allow for that to happen!), explore my surrounding area, go for a bike ride, take a swim, try a new cuisine, go grocery shopping, read a book, work on my blog/shop, write an article, create a new product to sell, do a cooking video for my Britican Galley YouTube channel (see Appendix A for a link to the channel), work on my latest book, clean the boat, fix something on the boat (that list is endless), have alone time, have family time and the list goes on and on.

In my old life, I had a limited amount of choices on where I traveled for work (home or the office) and I had to work no matter what the weather …and sadly, I worked almost every hour of the day. I seriously didn't know how to do anything other than work.

And the way I spent my workday was dictated by whatever project was requiring the most attention. Yes, I had choice about what I did, but it was almost always dictated by employees, clients or suppliers. In most cases, I don't think I had to think much, but rather, I just reacted.

But was I reacting to life in my past rather than consciously choosing life's path?

Yes…I think so.

And what about the weekends in my old life? Yes, I had the choice on what activities to do with family and friends – exploring, socializing, and spending time together. But making time to make a new friend? That almost never happened. My choice of friends was mostly a done deal – I had no reason to increase my circle. Furthermore, where would I find the time to deepen another friendship?

Home management forced many of my choices down the path of laundry, shopping, cleaning and gardening. My week was mainly broken up into my career with a tiny bit of extra activities in the evenings, and then the weekends where I recovered from work, got the house in order and socialized a bit.

Sure, I had choices, but my choices seemed much more limited. My life seem unconscious...it just happened. Life was very routine. I didn't stop to think.

Now, I wake in the morning and think about how I feel. I scan my body to simply feel the sensations of having a body. I then take a look at my mood – am I happy to be alive? The answer, thankfully, is almost always a yes.

The old Kim would wake up, jump out of bed after oversleeping, rush around the house like a manic and if I had time to pay attention to my mind, my thought would be, "life sucks!"

I never in a million years knew that I had the capability to check in with myself! Feelings? What were those?

Life was go, go, go...do, do, do.

So, what do I feeeeeel like doing now?

Back on the boat...after checking in with my body and mind, a routine I never had time for before, I ask myself what I want to do right now and the rest of the day.

On a typical morning, I'd wake at around 5:30 and decide to either go back to sleep, watch the sun come up, do some writing or yoga, start breakfast or read. That's before I even started to consider what the plan for the day might be.

I now ask myself what feels like the best choice for me in the moment.

At first sight this might seem like living the dream. Who wouldn't want to be able to "choose life's course" (the motto of SailingBritican.com)?

Yes, it is a blessing but it can also be somewhat of a curse. With choice comes opportunity cost, and opportunity cost can quite a demon.

Opportunity cost = the loss of other alternatives when one alternative is chosen.

We have so many choices and consequently so many alternatives that we're missing.

But this is where the importance of flowing with life comes in (that I talk about incessantly).

With this way of living, we need to teach ourselves how to consciously "choose life's course." We might have loads of choices, but perhaps there's a limit to what we feeeeeel like doing.

As long as we check in with ourselves, get to grips with where we are emotionally, physically and mentally, survey the choices available and then choose what feels best at the time, I think we're on the right path.

Looking back, I don't know how I lived the way I use to live. Instead of analyzing my life, figuring out if I was in the right job or spending my time in a way that fulfilled me, I just kept busy – I just made sure that I was distracted by life rather than living life. It's as if I didn't want to ask the question, "Am I happy?" because I knew if I did the answer would be "no" and then I'd have to take responsibility for my unhappiness.

I might have a billion options now but my overall distractions have been greatly reduced. There's no TV, no news, no advertisements, no "keeping up with the Jones," no world problems…And more importantly, I'm not working for the sake of working. I now LOVE what I do to earn an income.

Speaking of an income, it's important to note that I'm not retired. I don't want to be put in the "lucky for some," category. I'm still working...I still have to create an income so that we can carry on with this lifestyle.

The difference now is that I'm consciously choosing when I feel like working and what that means. I'm checking in with myself and determining if this moment is the right moment to write an article OR go for a swim. And because I'm doing the kind of work that I love (writing, blogging, growing my nautical themed shop, Sailing Britican Store) I actually WANT to work...I enjoy working. I also enjoy all my other options, too.

So... that's how sailing full time has taught me how to take my life off automatic pilot and consciously choose life's course.

[See Appendix A, 'V5. Preveza Refit' for a video detailing our refit.]

Chapter 33: Taormina Bay in Sicily – An anchorage that has it all!

After Greece we headed down to Malta to finalize some necessary tax paperwork and then eventually returned to Sicily for a short stay in Taormina.

Just below the ancient city of Taormina, which is below the ancient town of Castelmola, there's a lovely bay that offers great holding, and during the summer season you'll find first class mooring buoys.

The water is crystal clear, the amazing views include Mount Etna, a cliff top Norman castle, a spectacular coast line filled with cliffs, caves and mountainside, a train that weaves its way along the coast, Toarmina main street up above and the town of Giardina Naxos down along the beach front.

This bay is definitely a hot spot during the summer but it's worth a visit.

Once anchored in the bay or tied onto a mooring buoy you'll have loads of options on how to spend your time.

Aside from swimming and sunning, you can take your dinghy along the coast and explore caves, massive rocks and land formations. The coastline truly is breathtaking due to the contrast between the blue sea, the dark cliff walls, the black caves and then the grass, trees and countryside above.

When facing land, if you take your dinghy to the left, just past a concrete wall you'll find an area where you can beach your boat in Giardini Naxos. There are large boulders to navigate between, but they're clearly visible. Once your dinghy is secured on the beach, it's worth visiting the bakeries, cafés, restaurants and grocery stores.

If you walk toward the beautiful train station (get off your dinghy and head right) you'll follow a very tiny sidewalk up under a bridge, over a bridge and then you'll get to an amazing butcher. The butcher owns a farm nearby and all the meats are local, fresh and outstanding in quality and taste. If you see meatballs on sale, BUY THEM! They are the best meatballs I've ever had in my life.

Just after the butcher's, there's a rotisserie chicken shop – Oh-my-gosh…the smell of rotisserie chicken gets me every time.

And speaking of indulgence, there's also a low cost alcohol shop directly across from the beach where you'll need to leave your dinghy. I discovered a bottle of Sicilian white wine in the shop for $4 so I purchased a couple to serve during a boat party we had one evening. We all enjoyed the wine.

Not all cheap Sicilian wines are good, but I'd have to say that most of them are!

The day after eating too much rotisserie chicken and drinking far too much wine, you might want to take a nice 45-minute walk down to the main area of Giardina Naxos. You'll find even more amenities with large busy beautiful beaches there.

No matter what, however, get yourself on a bus up to Taormina to see the incredible Greek and Roman amphitheater and ruins. I've seen loads of amphitheaters – this one has the best backdrop EVER. You look out through Greek/Roman ruins to see the sea in the background. It's one of those views you wish that could bottle.

Unfortunately, the fee to see the amphitheater is high. I think it was around $40 each. AND…they use the venue for proper concerts so the seating area is covered with plastic seats. During the summer this place is packed! And I mean jam packed.

The town is beautiful but it's one of those places that is 100% touristic. Every shop has tourist items, there are beggars, and you'll find people at every corner selling the latest "made in China" strange toy. Your best bet is to visit the area off-season, but failing that, I think the ruins and the views from the main street are truly amazing.

After a tour of Taormina, you can also go up a little further on the hill and visit Castelmola. We enjoyed a few Sicilian delights at the restaurant while taking in more amazing views. The cobbled streets are lovely and the tourist goods seemed more authentic than Taormina.

Aside from visiting Giardina Naxos, Toarmina and Castelmola, you can also take a train to a variety of destinations. The train weaves along the cost and it's a great way to see the coastline from land rather than from the sea.

For $12 I took the train to and from Catania with some girlfriends to visit the market.

Fortunately for me, there were several boats in Taormina Bay that I knew. After wintering in Marina di Ragusa we had made many friends. So…during our last stay in Taormina bay, I joined a Canadian, Brit, Turkish and Dutch woman on a girls' day out to Sicily's second largest city, Catania.

We had the best day enjoying the massive Catania market. I found loads of designer clothes for only a couple of dollars! All us girls tried things on, threw items to others that we thought would look good and were full of giggles.

Chapter 34: Sailing through the night

After meeting up with friends we made while wintering at Marina di Ragusa, Simon and I headed across the Ionian to Greece once again.

With it being just the two of us (and Sienna, of course), I had to do some night watches.

At midnight, Simon came into our cabin and softly shook me awake. He quietly groaned with a tired voice, "Kim, it's midnight – time for your watch." I spent five minutes lying in bed allowing all my systems to activate.

While at the Catania market with my friend, Aylin, she told me her thoughts about night sailing. She explained that she didn't like the darkness – it really scared her. She arranged with her partner to sail up until midnight, as she felt okay until then, but afterwards didn't feel comfortable. Her partner would then take over and when the sun started to come up, she would be awakened to do another watch.

During her discussion it got me thinking about night sails.

It seems that there are no rules. You do what works best. Another girlfriend explained that she just can't sail at night alone. Not being able to see scares her, so the arrangement she has for long sails is for her partner to sail at night and she sails during the day.

And it seems like professional crews do three hours on, six hours off depending on how many people are on board.

Considering my serious bout with seasickness, I didn't do any night sails alone during the first year. We always had crew with us so I wasn't necessarily needed. Instead of sailing in the moonlight I laid in bed trying to sleep through the passage.

Now that we were three months into our second sailing year on *Britican,* and Simon and I were the only competent sailors, I had to up my game.

Simon doesn't sleep that many hours anyway so he was happy to start off at night and finish the early morning shift. So, we ate dinner, I went to bed, Sienna went to bed and then Simon woke me at midnight.

I then did my watch and woke Simon at 3am. He carried on until I woke around 6 or 7am to once again take over. After a discussion and coffee, Simon would go back to bed for a nap and perhaps throughout the day I'd take a little catnap in the cockpit.

Life not only slows down when you're doing long passages, but your routines change completely. When we're anchored near land there's always something to do – something that has my attention. Either there's a ruin to see, groceries to get, friends to visit or articles to write. While sailing, there's very little to do – mainly because I simply can't do it!

My day-to-day activities change; sleep patterns, eating routine, so much more. Life seems more present – you observe how you feel and then go with the flow. When you're tired, you sleep – when you're hungry, you eat and when you're in awe with the beauty surrounding you, you simply take it all in.

One night's watch was an especially magical moment for me. For my first time, I did my midnight to 3am watch in the pitch black. There was no moon, and making out the horizon was almost impossible. Simon debriefed me with, "I haven't seen a ship or any lights all night. It's very dark out. A couple dolphins jumped up along the side of the boat and scared the crap out of me. I heard the splashes and eventually made out their silhouette. Other than that, we have light winds across the beam (side of the boat) and all is quiet."

He then added, "Oh yeah, look up!"

Although my eyes were still adjusting to the pure darkness I looked up and my heart almost burst with awe.

The stars were so bright and beautiful…and there were so many of them! I looked around and almost felt frightened due to the difference in my expectation. I looked around and shouted out, "Oh-my-gosh – did you see the Milky Way?"

Instead of seeing a light thick strip cloud-like image, I could see more depth in the Milky Way – it looked massive, expansive, and glowing with beauty.

I never had I felt so overtaken by the view I experienced.

And it didn't stop there.

Before Simon dropped down below to find his soft space on the saloon sofa (I'm brave, but not brave enough not to have him close by!) I again yelled out, "Look at our wake! Did you notice the things glowing?"

While looking over the side, stars would form and leave just as quickly as they came. They were small dots of phosphorus. I'm not sure what they are actually, but they glow in the dark. Perhaps it's a type of plankton.

So I had stars in the sky and stars alongside the boat!

After what felt like an hour of being totally present and absorbing the night sky I looked at my watch and discovered only ten minutes had past. I thought, "Crap, I have two hours and 50 minutes to go! What am I going to do now?"

So, I consciously listened to all the sounds – the sea foam rising up and ebbing away through each wave we passed through, the dark waves hitting the hull, the light warm wind blowing past my ears, the boom creaking with the inconsistent flow of air and the sails occasionally deflating and reflating again.

On the port (left) side of the boat, when I put my head around the spray hood I could smell diesel, the whiff of a salty sea dog and humid ocean smell. On the starboard (right) side of the boat I could smell a sprinkle of olive trees, remnants of our earlier dinner, and fresh water dew.

I seriously couldn't see much at all so my nose went into hyper drive. As my watch went on and my stomach started to wake up I even started to smell the food I was thinking about. I smelled fresh tuna with wasabi, ginger and soy sauce (earlier that day we had a school of tuna with us for over an hour!) And at one point I smelled a filet mignon.

How did I feel to do a night sail with no moon?

When I first started doing night sails I thought I'd be scared. I also thought I'd feel like a speck of dust in a massive desert, but to my surprise I didn't feel fear and instead of feeling insignificant I felt connected with life.

At times I just felt love...I felt love for life, love for the Earth and love for having the opportunity to experience the freedom to cross a sea using wind as my fuel.

So...is sailing through the night scary, exhilarating or boring?

My answer is all of the above. Sometimes it's scary when you can't see a thing and hear a splash. Other times it's amazing when you breathe in the massive amount of stars, and when the watch gets toward the end it can sometimes be a bit boring.

No matter what, I am grateful for the experience - overall, it was flat out freaking amazing.

Chapter 35: Back in Greece!

Our plan, after doing necessary tax paperwork in Malta, was to visit Sicily and then head west, knowing our Atlantic crossing was imminent.

That being noted, we went east instead and spent yet another wonderful month enjoying the Greek Ionian Sea. Friends that we met in the Aegean, sailboat *Why Knot*, sailed their boat to the Ionian, so we had to sail back to Greece to spend time with them!

The Greek Ionian has such a pull to it that it's not surprising to hear about people who set sail for a world circumnavigation and 10 years later still haven't left.

A great anchorage and harbor that missed our radar on previous trips was Port Kastos. In years gone by we mainly focused on the larger islands – Corfu, Cephalonia, Zakinthos, Meganisi, Ithaca and Paxos.

Port Kastos ticks many boxes:

- It's quieter than most other ports
- As long as a flotilla isn't in, there are usually several spaces to moor up in the harbor
- The anchorage (outside the harbor) is lovely, so even if you don't venture into the small town, the surrounding views are beautiful
- There's a selection of tavernas and cafés
- The food we enjoyed was not only authentic Greek food but also it tasted divine. Our friend Stefano and I enjoyed stuffed tomatoes and fresh fish. The tomatoes melted in your mouth and the fish had a lovely flavor.
- Although many people were unable to speak English (strange for Greece!) all the menus were in Greek and English. It was kind of nice to be able to practice speaking the few Greek words I knew.

Usually, I try to speak Greek and the other person, says, "no – please speak English so I can get better at it."

- There's a café/bar on the beach within the harbor that offers a lovely view out into the harbor and surrounding area. As the sun sets, you can enjoy a drink (wine is always my choice!) and appreciate a golden pink color cast a glaze on the land and sea.

- A small grocery store offers all the basics. On a second visit we took two of Sienna's friends with us and the grocery man helped the children pick out ice creams. As we were leaving, he threw in three free candy bars too!

- There's a playground for children to play on – it's a bit dated but very roomy. In the evening the local and boat kids seem to mix easily and enjoy playing.

- The church and cemetery have quite a bit of character – my daughter and I enjoyed a wander around. Many of the graves have pictures of the deceased on them. Sienna would comment, "that man (or woman) looked like they were kind."

On our first visit to the area, we anchored just outside the harbor. Within the small port you can moor stern to a wall or put an anchor out and run a stern line to the beach. Either way, our boat was a tad too large – the chances of our anchor going over or under someone else's was high.

Anchoring is our preferred mooring – especially if there's light winds.

I'd rather have space to swing naturally, privacy to go about my routine unnoticed and cleaner water to swim in. Mooring up to a wall is great if you want to get on and off the boat easily and quickly, but other than that, there are more negatives than positives.

As a side…I tend to write about the places I'm impressed with rather than those that I'm not. I think it's important to realize that not every harbor is nice – some of them smell, are very noisy or are in a bad state. Many tavernas are not very nice – many of them get a constant flow of tourists, no matter what, so they don't pride themselves on good food. And so forth.

Based on my visit to Kastos Harbor I was very impressed with the simplicity, peacefulness and light-natured buzz about the area.

But there were some negatives. As with any harbor, when the flotillas come in it can be a bit nerve wracking if you're worried about an anchor going over your anchor or a boat getting too close. Not a week goes by where I don't hear a story of a chartered boat hitting a live-aboard cruiser's boat… That being noted, if you worry about flotillas, simply anchor outside the harbor.

Finally, there are tourist boats that enter the harbor to let their guests have a wander around. They boats are relatively small, but it's possible to be enjoying a very quite lunch and then suddenly find yourself surrounded by a few more people!

After spending a month with our friends on *Why Knot* we said our goodbyes and headed back to Taormina, Sicily, preparing to head west into the unknown.

[See Appendix A, 'V7. Port Kato's' for videos showcasing the area]

Chapter 36: After 15 months of living on our boat...

After slightly more than 5000 nautical miles of sailing, visits to six different countries, a six-month stay in Sicily, trips back to the States and to England, and meeting some really amazing new friends, how does it feel to be living full time on a boat?

Here are my thoughts:

I'm much more relaxed.

When we first started out I was a recovering control freak. Now, I've realized that I don't have to control anything. Life is going to play out the way it's destined to play out. Plans are what they are – and they are going to change. I just don't feel the need to control anything anymore...it's not who I am.

Every day I wake up and just let the day unfold. There's no need to force anything. Sometimes I pop into the old Kim and get uptight about something, but my issues are usually short-lived. This lifestyle seems to force you back into going with the flow.

I'm less concerned about money (in general).

My whole life was built on the premise that I must make money to be happy. I worked, pushed, forced, cajoled and kicked my way through life trying to become more and more successful. Ultimately I made a bit of money but I didn't enjoy the journey as much as I could have. That being said, it's been very hard for me to shed my obsession with making money.

When we first started out I worried for months about how we'd be able to keep sailing. I'd get stressed, try and come up with various ideas and then I'd become a nightmare to be around.

Now…I seem to have a sense of knowing that things will work out. I don't know what we'll do when our savings run out but I'm not worried about it. Living on a sailboat is so inexpensive that our savings isn't reducing as much as I thought it would. I've been slowly building up my Sailing Britican Store, magazines approach me for commissioned articles and I've written a couple of books. These things build up and over time I'm sure we'll have enough cash flow to keep going.

I'm just not so worried about it. Furthermore, I don't have this mindset to be "successful." I don't want millions…all I need is a bit of monthly cash flow. I don't need money for the things I used to value (like watches, cars, gadgets, clothes, shoes…) None of those things are important on a boat!

Simon and I are massively more comfortable about how our boat works (mechanically, electrically, etc.).

This is a big one. When we first took possession of the boat in Palma, Mallorca and sailed it to Gibraltar we had NO CLUE. One of our circuit boards (electricity panel) has 44 switches. The other panel has 12 with a variety of twisty knobs. There's a battery bank of nine batteries! We had to figure out the water maker, black/gray/fresh water systems, davits, windless, hydraulic system and on and on and on… And then there are the navigation systems – the autopilot, plotter, radar, GPS, Nav 6, AIS… We have three computer screens (two inside and one outside) and around 12 different Raymarine devices.

Notice that I haven't even mentioned the "how to sail the boat" bit yet!

We were totally and utterly overwhelmed when we took over our boat. Yes, we had a Moody sailboat before, but the Oyster is a whole different ballgame. The sailing bit we understood but all the mechanisms were new. And having to learn about our engine and generator was a massive learning curve.

That being noted, our voyage last year provided us with an outstanding learning ground. We made many mistakes but we also met many teachers. I'm so proud to say that Simon and I know so much more than we did before. Of course, there's loads that we don't know…but not only have we learned about our systems, we've increased our confidence to the point of being able to problem-solve.

Last year, something would happen and we'd simply yell, "Help!" Now we know enough about troubleshooting that nine times out of 10 we're fixing things ourselves rather than paying someone to do it for us.

I'm totally fine with anchoring – in fact prefer it now. When we started out, we stayed in marinas. I was too scared to anchor – what if the anchor didn't hold? What if we were swept out into sea or, worse, what if we were dragged onto the rocks?

After my good friend Elaine from sailboat *Why Knot* taught me how to use our anchor alarm, I started to feel much better about anchoring. You just set the alarm on your GPS system when you drop the anchor. If you move, the alarm goes off and it will wake you up to survey the situation. So…if we do drag, we know about it instantly.

After months of anchoring, I now love it. I enjoy the peaceful setting, privacy, ability to swim and ease of anchoring. We don't have to put fenders out, tie ropes on, panic as to whether someone will be on the jetty to help. We simply find a patch of sand below the boat, drop anchor, make sure it's dug in and the job's done.

I'm chilled out about food, preparation and eating.

This was another biggie for me. Not knowing how to cook before we left on our adventure, I was always in a state of turmoil about what to buy at the store and how to cook it. I never learned how to throw things together… Fortunately for me, I had my wonderful cousin with us for the first five months and she loved to cook! She gave me confidence with food and helped me understand what goes well together.

Now, I have my main recipes that I cook often, and I also go on the Internet and get new ideas. I've become an expert at making bruschetta, tatziki, and hummus!

And thankfully, I have my mom's spice blends that I sell in my Britican Galley shop so when I have to make a quick dip or spice a chicken, seafood or beef dish, I just use a tablespoon of the blend.

So for me, cooking has now become a very enjoyable part of my life. Before, I thought it was a necessary evil, but I actually enjoy preparing food. I seriously never saw that coming.

Cleaning the boat is easier – I know what products to use, how to use them and when.

I was totally overwhelmed with the amount of cleaning that is necessary to keep a boat presentable. I thought by trading in our six-bedroom house for a 56′ boat would reduce my cleaning time massively. Oh how wrong I was.

I have to vacuum the boat every day – yes, every day (not that I do it)! The amount of dust that appears from nowhere is insane. The bathrooms need a good clean every couple days and the kitchen (and doing dishes) never ends.

My two biggest tips I have for cleaning the boat (and I'm only talking about the inside right now) is to buy a handheld Dyson. Also, get those bathroom/kitchen wipes. I know that those wipes are causing landfill issues and that is a big problem…HOWEVER, using those wipes keeps chemicals out of the sea, they're quick and easy to use and if you use one every couple days the bathrooms (heads) don't get out of hand. I vacuum the bathroom and then use a wipe – it's the quickest, easiest and most environmentally safe (for the sea).

The topside of the boat is a whole different beast. If the rains come from the Sahara Desert, you'll have a boat full of red sand. After a day of sailing, there will be salt, dirt and dust all over the place. My big tip for the top of the boat is to use Permanon.

Perhaps my biggest take-away about cleaning on a boat is to not underestimate how quickly boats get dirty.

I'm even more convinced that new friends await us at every new port.

I had posted on Facebook that I was feeling very low due to saying good-bye to sailboat *Why Knot*. Many people wrote very kind words of support. And a friend whom Simon and I met while sailing the Ionian last year, Mick Burrow, responded with some really comforting words:

"For you, Simon and Sienna.

The one thing you must remember is you are leaving friends in the Mediterranean you didn't have before and they and we will always remain friends.

You are also moving on to new adventures and new friends and cultures.

Embrace it and enjoy the experiences."

Sometimes I fail to feel grateful for all the amazing friends who I wouldn't have had in the first place! Shame on me. I suppose I still crave non-change... I find a new friend and I just want to keep them. I want the world to stop spinning and life to just be simple. Sure – over time that wouldn't be very nice, but the combination of having to keep moving forward and say goodbye creates loads of change. It's not always easy.

The community feeling is getting stronger – almost everywhere we go, we know someone.

It's great to be down below doing something while anchored in a bay and hear, "*Britican*, is anyone home?" When I pop up, it's a friend we've met in a previous mooring or while staying in Sicily.

Every few bays we go to, we'll see someone we know. And often when we're sailing around we'll see a friend pop up on our AIS. Once you join the sailing community you truly realize just how small the world really is.

Furthermore, I keep in touch with many of my sailing friends so I know where they are. Often they'll be a few hundred miles away, if that. Knowing where people are offers me the feeling that we're never alone!

I'm more comfortable with entertaining a young child full time.

Life with Sienna has become easier and more enjoyable.

Possibly the hardest transition I had to make was going from a workaholic production machine to a stay-at-home mom on a 56' boat!

I traded in my laptop for a dolls' house, my overly logical mind for Legos, and my full time adult conversation style for kid talk.

In a nutshell, I've had to learn how to play again. It hasn't been easy – there's always something else that needs to be done rather than playing or doing school work, but I've slowly relaxed into it. Doing schoolwork is a breeze – it's just part of the day now and we enjoy working on numbers and letters. Sometimes Sienna doesn't want to do it but we usually find a way to make it fun.

Sienna has learned how to play more by herself and that's great – she's not reliant on Simon or me 100 percent of the time like she was previously. When it's just the three of us, Sienna's behavior is, for the most part, really good.

When we have friends over or are moving around with another kid boat we often have issues, but I think it's because Sienna is staying up later than usual, learning social skills and trying to make sense of her world. Emotionally, I'm not sure if she's maturing as quickly as her counterparts, but she'd be the same if we were on land.

Overall I'm absolutely convinced that she's getting the best possible upbringing we could give her. I have no doubts and absolutely no regrets.

My relationship with Simon is good.

We're further settling into our roles and are closer to knowing who does what. I handle most of the cooking, cleaning and figuring out how to make some money. He handles the boat servicing, maintenance, passage planning and sailing. We both share responsibility over Sienna. As for romance?! We'll it's just too darn hot for that! (Kidding!)

Over the past year we've been doing our own thing. I've never been one for teamwork but I feel that I'm starting to warm up to the idea. Rather than do things on our own, Simon and I are helping each other and it's added another element to our relationship.

Some days he chews too loudly and leaves his wet towel on the floor for the 1000th time which drives me nuts, but those moments are few and far between. Thus far this experience has definitely helped us to grow closer – in fact, as a family we are much closer than we ever were before.

I'm feeling scared about moving to pastures that we're unfamiliar with but I keep reminding myself to stop thinking too far forward. Live for today – eh? So here's to more travels, more hellos, more goodbyes and loads more of living life!

Chapter 37: There's no "I" in team, but there is a "Me"

Growing up I had a chip on my shoulder and believed that if I wanted something done well, I needed to do it myself. I also felt very alone and as if the responsibility for the world was on my shoulders.

Therefore, when a problem occurred, I'd respond in one of two ways:

1. Hubby – that's your department, you sort it out.
2. Hubby – back off, I'll do this.

For example, while our engines were being ripped apart for three weeks, Simon laid in the bilges assisting and constantly learning from the engineers.

Even though I love engines and tinkering with them I felt as if it was his duty to understand the engines and I was relegated to looking after Sienna.

Simon was the man so he could have fun and I'll be the parent. It was black and white in my mind – Simon will do the engines, I'll cover Sienna. I didn't see any other alternative. That's my "you sort it out," reaction.

Regarding my "back off" reaction, let me tell you about our anchoring blow out.

Simon went to the front of the boat and started messing with the anchor while I was down below. We entered a bay, it was dead calm and he wanted to anchor to let me carry on with what I was doing.

Big mistake – messing with my anchor!

Yes – it's MY anchor.

Again, it's black and white – doing the anchor is my job. I've done it hundreds of times. I know how I want it done. I can ensure it's dug in…I

236

will ensure the correct scope is used (you let out 3x to 5x the depth in length so if you're in 10 meters, you'd let out 30 to 50 meters – closer to 50 if it's blowing).

Now that I've had an epiphany, I've realized that I didn't understand the concept of teamwork!

The belief that I had to do everything myself created an environment that hadn't been very nice. I had to deal with MY problems, MY daughter, MY life…Thankfully I have qualities that must make up for this massive short falling because my husband smiles at me and says "I love you," even when I'm ranting about things being MY responsibility.

Since we're forced out of our comfort zones (having to solve various problems) it's easier to analyze our lives and to reflect on what's good and what's not so good (my lack of understanding on teamwork).

Here I was, thinking that I was perfect only to discover I have a teamwork impairment.

Up until now, everything in my life was MINE. And don't get me wrong – I'm not selfish at all. I'm just a bit of a loner. I do things my way or you can hit the highway…YOU CAN'T HAVE THAT KIND OF ATTITUDE ON A BOAT!

So in an effort to ensure OUR daughter learns about teamwork AND to allow me to share responsibility, work together with my husband and survive this around the world sailing adventure, I'm going to have to change my belief!

My point is this – going on this around the world adventure is causing me to grow and learn in ways I could have never predicted. I speculated about how we'd learn about sailing, new cultures, history and meet new friends, but I didn't consider the person I'd have to change into so to make this trip a success.

Chapter 38: Sailing the southwest coast of Italy

After 4000+ nautical miles and 16 months sailing around the eastern Mediterranean, it was time to start heading west for our imminent Atlantic crossing set for November.

The ultimate plan was, and still is, to circumnavigate the world. Although we could spend a lifetime in the Mediterranean, we had to push on.

To appease the part of me that doesn't like change, I kept thinking that we'd end up back in the Mediterranean eventually and when we do, we could hit all the wonderful spots that we missed the first time.

The Med has everything and it feels very comfortable. If it wasn't for the fact that we've paid to cross the Atlantic with the ARC (Atlantic Rally for Cruisers) I think we'd extend our stay.

Anyway, the day came when we had to leave known waters, long-term cruiser and local friends and push past our stupid, but always present, nagging comfort zone.

We left our safe space in Taormina, Sicily, our last comfort spot. Our sites were on Salerno to see Pompeii before carrying on west. We slipped into the Messina Straight (waterway between Sicily and mainland Italy) and eased over to the Tyrrhenian Sea.

As fate would have it, and the amazing "go with the flow" lifestyle of sailing, we actually arrived at our first destination welcomed by friends.

I kid you not – there's something very weird about being a full-time cruiser. If you don't make friends within a couple hours of being moored up, you're most likely going to bump into someone you know anyway.

Our first stop was Reggio, Calabria. We received word that Simon's friend, Mick Flynn (Britian's most decorated front-line soldier and author of *Bullet Magnet*) was there. A couple of years back, Simon met Mick aboard a sailboat on the British Solent to complete the practical Ocean Masters qualification.

Mick sails a lovely 30-year-old Ketch. Within an hour of mooring up in the marina, we were aboard Mick's boat meeting his beautiful wife, two very handsome sons and their gorgeous girlfriends. And of course, a drink turned into a few drinks and then we all went for dinner. The night ended around 1am or 2am. We had a brilliant time and, although we were out of our stomping ground, life felt comfortable.

After we left Reggio, Calabria, Simon, Sienna and I were on our own.

It felt strange sailing to an unknown port but what felt even stranger was the fact that it was just the three of us. During the first year we rarely sailed alone – we always had at least one friend with us – sometimes many. And if we didn't have friends on board, we were near other bowtie friends.

From Reggio, we made our way out of the Messina Straight and up the Italian coast to Vibo – we stayed in Marina del Sud. The lower western Italian coast doesn't have any marked anchorages and there are very few marinas.

Furthermore, the marinas are not cheap.

In Vibo we had to pay $350 and boy did that hurt. I couldn't help but think of the inexpensive cost of Greece where a town quay is $10 (if anyone ever comes to collect the money) or the $0 cost of anchoring.

However, for the first time in our sailing adventures, upon entrance to the marina, one of the three attendants on an adjacent boat and said, "Do I have your permission to get on your boat and help you?"

I was bowled over! Usually I'm throwing the back lines, picking up the slime line, running to the front of the boat and securing the boat while Simon keeps *Britican* steady in the waters.

Through all the commotion I usually trip on something invariably embarrassing myself, stub one toe, forget to breathe and end the process hyperventilating.

A mixture of stress, bad footing and low fitness cause my many issues!

Arriving in Marina del Sud in Vibo, Italy was different. I barely had to do a thing. A lovely Italian boy secured the front of the boat while I merely threw the back lines and secured them back on the boat. I didn't have to move more than four feet the whole time.

Here I am worrying that it's just Simon and me handling the boat and that we're in a new destination, but in the end there was nothing to worry about (as usual). Mooring up was a breeze.

While Simon parked the boat, we heard drums in the distance. The attendants explained that we arrived during a festival with entertainment, music and fireworks.

It was one of those pinch me moments – how amazing can life be?

We had no clue where we were or what to expect. To our surprise, we arrived to a wonderful weekend festival. The attendants at the marina were excellent. The town was alive with activities and we took in the sights and smells of southern Italy.

As we enjoyed our first ice cream/beer/wine, Sienna, Simon and I were privileged to see a procession pass with these most amazing 12′ tall figures. They were papier-mâché bodies that people put on top of their shoulders. The two figures paraded around the town for the full weekend asking for loose change.

And the night before we left, one of the marina attendants came to our boat with three candles to be placed in the water when the Virgin Mary was brought around the harbor by boat. Unfortunately it was a bit too windy so many of the hundreds of candles blew out, but just the same it was an impressive show!

Before leaving Vibo, I secured a few sausages and ground beef in addition to vitals such as milk, bread and water. We were fortunate that the shops opened for a half-day during the festival – usually everything shuts down for the entire duration and it's hard to get provisions.

The town of Vibo itself is well-kept, clean and offers a range of cute little shops.

There's one small grocery store, a few butchers, bakers and fruit shops. One shop offers meat and cheese and the selection is impressive.

After a couple nights in Vibo we headed north to the town of Cetraro, Italy.

Following 12 hours of bad wind we eventually made it to Cetraro. Again, the cost of the marina was eye watering, but we didn't have many options – it was Pompeii or bust!

We moored up with the boat tied down along the side. There were four attendants this time and I didn't have to do anything other than throw the ropes. So – one massive benefit of sailing the southwest coast of Italy is the assistance you receive. It's the best we had experienced to date.

The boat in front of us was trying to pull a very ripped front sail out of the mast (furling unit). The whole genoa was ripped to shreds. Over the past couple of days the winds were gusting and the storms were terrible. By luck, we had managed to avoid the bad weather.

We wanted to stay in Cetraro as there's an old town, museum and a Lidl (Lidl is a discount grocery store that all full time cruisers look for). But…the clock was ticking and our mission had to stay set on Pompeii.

Ever since I was child and heard about the magically preserved Roman city I felt the need to see the archaeological site of Pompeii. I watched all the History Channel documentaries on Pompeii, read about it in books and studied it in University. Simon felt the same about it – we just had to see it considering it was so close.

Furthermore, I'm always up for seeing another volcano! Mount Vesuvius is located next to Pompeii so we could kill two birds with one stone.

We sailed for another 12 hours. Each day we were pushing on to the next suitable mooring. For the most part, the three of us read books, watched movies, prepared and ate food and absorbed the lovely views of the Italian landscape.

Both Simon and I were surprised to see the area so full of mountains. For some reason we thought the south of Italy was more flat. That being said, I had no idea that Italy had so many volcanoes before touring the beautiful country, so what did we know?

Eventually, we could see Salerno and I could taste Pompeii. As we entered the harbor there were black clouds, thunder, lightning and gusting winds.

I couldn't help but feel scared, nervous and anxious. Needless to say my body felt knotted up. It's not nice to enter a new destination with a monsoon about to hit! Furthermore, we saw ripped sails all over the place so our concern about strong winds was in the forefront of our mind.

To make matters worse, we couldn't get in touch with anyone at any marina who spoke English. We finally found a new marina that quoted us $200/night but we wanted something less expensive knowing we'd be staying a few days.

Simon called someone else (by mobile as no one would answer the VHF) and it was the most ridiculous conversation. Simon was speaking English, terrible Italian and then threw some German in for the heck of it. Nether parties could understand each other but in the end Simon said, it's $150 and we're going to here (pointing to the marina on the map).

We made it into the harbor, the storm quickly passed over us and we moored up with very minimal effort. Again, someone jumped on our boat and tied up the bow while I simply threw the ropes over to the jetty. It was so easy.

After so many hours of sailing and being at anchor the night before, I was eager to get off the boat and explore. After a small walk we entered the Salerno old town and were amazed with the sights. The whole city is carved into the side of a hill. The old town has narrow cobbled streets darkened by the beautiful buildings stretching high on either side. There are Mother Mary and Saints alters installed into the sides of homes, elaborate fountains and loads of old stuff. Did you know that the Apostle Mathew was buried in Salerno?

The city felt like yet another dark, dirty yet mysterious place.

I feel terrible to say dark and dirty, but Italy is not a clean place. There's graffiti everywhere, rubbish pushed into corners and very creepy abandoned properties.

Many areas of improvement never became improved so there are old work sites and you wouldn't believe how many "new" roads I've seen that are 4 feet from being finished – those projects have been abandoned, too.

If I had to sum up the parts of Italy I've seen, I'd have to say that people seem to have given up on their country. I'm a foreigner and I have no clue what's going on, but I can't help but feel like it's a massive shame to see such a naturally beautiful country scuffed up so badly by its inhabitants. It's as if they don't care or can't care for one reason or another.

Salerno, however, was the best of a bad bunch – the city was much cleaner than the ones I visited in Sicily, but that's not saying much.

The following day was Pompeii Day! We loaded up a backpack of water and goodies and headed to the train station. After a moderate walk down the coast path and up to the station we easily secured tickets directly to Pompeii.

The train ride was fantastic – we climbed to high heights, experienced majestic sea views (including the Amalfi Coast), and got a feel for the rural backcountry towns as we made our way north. While on the train I got my first glimpse of Vesuvius – like seeing dolphins, I think I'll also never tire from seeing volcanoes.

After 45 minutes, we arrived in Pompeii. We left the station and followed the signs to the "Archeological Site." Before reaching the site, we spent a few minutes taking in some of the architecture in the more modern section of Pompeii.

To my surprise I discovered a tribute to America for the 911 bombings. A piece of the twin towers was standing with a dedication plaque. It was the first time my heart sunk that day – the first of many for that day.

Sienna asked me why I felt upset. I wasn't sure if I should tell a 5-year-old about the events that transpired during 9/11 but I did. I explained how upset I was and she yelled out, "Oh mummy, give me a hug."

We then walked down another road and found the entrance to Pompeii.

There was a line for tickets but it went rather quickly. Once we entered the gate, a tour guide offered her services and we agreed to a 1-hour tour for $80. We thought that Sienna wouldn't last for two hours so settled on the 1-hour.

The guide was well worth the money – she showed us all the important spots and then afterwards we were free to explore on our own. The tickets were $30 each for Simon and me but that was for several historical sites – not just Pompeii. Sienna was free.

Overall, seeing Pompeii was a dream come true.

Simon and I were in awe the whole time we walked around. The ruins were so well preserved. For the first time ever I really got a sense of what it was like to live in those times. If you like Roman history, I highly suggest Pompeii is at the top of your list.

A few tips for Pompeii:

- Go early as it gets hotter and hotter as the day progresses. Also – wear a hat or bring an umbrella. There's not a massive amount of shade at Pompeii.

- Use the bathroom before you enter as there's only one at the entrance (and I mean one toilet) and then there's one at a snack bar on the other side of the site.

- Bring water. You only need one bottle as there are water fountains throughout the site that you can fill it up with.

- Bring snacks/food with you unless you want to pay a fortune at the one and only snack bar. Wear sneakers/trainers/good walking shoes.
- Get a guide – the site is so massive that unless you have a guide you'll probably waste your time walking around missing things.
- Expect herds of people. Eventually our legs couldn't walk anymore and Sienna wanted to move on. We left Pompeii, headed to the station and found a seat next to the rails while waiting for the train. An elderly Italian gentleman sat on the seat and encouraged Simon to have a chat with him. His English was great and his stories were captivating. He spoke of wars, the land and Italy in general.

Before we left the station we realized that the gentleman sat there every day speaking to travelers. He never took a train anywhere...he just sat at the station for social engagement. Kind of cool – isn't it?

Once we were back in Salerno, we grabbed a bite to eat, headed to the boat and slept like logs.

The following day, walked to the train station and this time we headed for Erocolano – another archeological site.

When Mount Vesuvius erupted, it destroyed Pompeii with falling volcanic stones and dust. The whole city was quickly covered and the inhabitants (that didn't escape) died from asphyxiation. Erocolano was different – those who failed to flee died from being burnt up. A volcanic cloud descended on the city and burnt everything it touched.

Interestingly, Erocolano is buried very deep – too deep for archeologists to get to. They've excavated 20 percent of the city but the remainder is under the new city and impossible to dig up. Furthermore, the cost associated to digging so deep is massive. Scientist found

Erocolano first, but once Pompeii was discovered, all attention went to Pompeii. It was more practical and feasible to dig up Pompeii.

If I were an archeologist I'd be so annoyed about Erocolano – there's a whole city there waiting to be discovered but it can't be touched!

Soooo... Erocolano.

You take the same train from Salerno that you do for Pompeii but you go further toward Naples. Once you exit the station there's nothing around to help you figure out how to get to Erocolano. We crossed the street and saw a bus sign so thought that might be a good place to stop. A couple of Italians were there and we said, 'Erocolano?' The husband and wife started pointing, talking and more pointing.

Regardless to our efforts to say "we don't speak Italian," they kept speaking to us in Italian, but louder. Hehehehe.

Within a couple minutes a white van came along. The Italian couple asked the driver something and before we knew it, we were pushed into the van and on our way to somewhere. The roads were the bumpiest we've ever been on. The town was extremely poor.

After 10 to 15 minutes we arrived at the entrance to Erocolano. Unlike Pompeii, you can see the sea from Erocolano.

We walked under the entrance arches, covered in graffiti (as usual), and were absolutely blown away with the view below us.

The city was covered by 60′ or 20m of debris, therefore the archeologists had to dig that deep to uncover it.

We walked along a walkway with Erocolano below us – it was amazing.

Full homes, baths and shops were still intact. The paintings on the walls and ceilings were still there! Even one home still had a wooden sliding door. Pompeii was amazing for its size. Erocolano was incredible for the amount of items preserved. Within the home walls you could still see the timber.

We walked around taking in the sights, listening to the audio tour and commenting to each other about what we learned. I was surprised to see Sienna so interested in the audio. By the time we finished – three hours later– both Sienna and I gave up on the audio and searched for shade.

Simon could have stayed there all night!

Everyone says that you have to see both Pompeii and Erocolano as they're so different. Do I agree?

Yes. We thoroughly enjoyed the two archeological sites and are very pleased we did them rather than, perhaps, seeing another city or going to the Amalfi Coast. That being noted, we live on a boat and we see lots of cities and lots of gorgeous coasts.

If you have limited time while sailing along the south west coast of Italy, I'd recommend doing Pompeii for its size, findings and overall awesomeness.

That evening, we arrived back to Salerno and managed to secure a massive platter of sushi! I know most travel writers talk about the local food but my family and I are so tired of pasta and pizza. We've had enough for a lifetime. And in Italy, it's very hard to find an ethnic restaurant (Chinese, Indian, etc.) unless you're in a city.

When I saw a sushi restaurant I couldn't pass it by.

With tired legs and a full tummy, we all slept like logs and prepared ourselves to start heading west.

There's a Carrefour Express (grocery store) near the marina so Simon got up early, went to get provisions and after his return, we set off to sail along the Amalfi coast to check out the island of Capri.

Once our ropes were pulled in, the fenders were stowed away and our cushions were setup in the cockpit, Simon and I enjoyed the coastal views. Whenever we enter a city we feel excited anticipation. And interestingly, after a couple days, when we leave a city we often feel freedom and relief. It's great to arrive and it's great to leave.

As we washed the city off our boat and bodies, the expanse of the world once again opened up to the big blue Tyrrhenian Sea. Simon and I debated on staying in Capri or making the most of a weather window to get to Sardinia.

We decided to anchor in Capri, eat dinner and then make a decision.

I would have loved to have found a secure mooring and spend time on the incredible island. The next time we sail around Italy, I'll make sure to stop in Capri.

Around 8pm Simon said, "Let's make a move." We cleaned up, pulled up the anchor and set a heading for Sardinia – a 36-hour sail. The first quarter of the journey was motoring. The second quarter was champagne sailing – perfect wind and a level sea. We did 8 to 9 knots and the boat was level.

The second half of our trip from Italy to Sardinia was hell.

We had 30 knots of wind and a 3 meter swell hitting the side of the boat. It was more than being in a washing machine. It felt like one of those contraptions NASA has to prepare astronauts for space flight. The first night I did my night watch. The second night, I had my head to the bed and dreamed of seeing land.

The motion was so bad that although I could lie in a starfish position, my skin moved around my bones at such a high rate, it was impossible to sleep. I wanted to find our hammock to hook it up to the ceiling to reduce the movement between my body and the boat below my body. Life sucked.

In the back of my head I thought, "If the Atlantic crossing is like this, I'll never survive."

But then we arrived in Sardinia with the sun coming up and I immediately liked living on a sailboat again. For me, sailing in bad weather is like giving birth; somehow you manage to forget how bad it really is.

Sardinia was an interesting island. We spent a couple of weeks hanging out with new friends, and then headed to Bonifacio.

[See Appendix A, 'V9. Southwest coast of Italy' for a couple videos]

Chapter 39: Sailing into Bonifacio, Corsica

While sailing around the Mediterranean Simon and I often rely on word-of-mouth recommendations for everything, including anchorages, restaurants, grocery stores, chandleries, things to do, marinas and even sailing passages. Some people resort to bloggers or Trip Advisor, others survey the Internet, but we rely on our newest neighbors for recommendations.

Yes, it can be a bit unsettling because I never know where we'll be from one day to the next. And taking advice from someone we don't know is a bit different from the way we did things in the past, but it's also exciting, very spontaneous and mostly offers exceptional results.

Our decision to leave Sardinia and head for Bonifacio, Corsica, which is a French island, was based on the recommendation of two neighbors we met while anchored in Portisco, Sardinia.

Ken from sailing vessel *Orinoco* and the family from *Crackerjack* both highly recommended Bonifacio, so prior to heading west we decided to sail north to Corsica.

When we left Sardinia, we sailed past boats in the Perini Navi Cup. It was amazing to see the USA boat *Comanche*. Simon counted 21 crew and I videoed them gracefully sailing along. From our viewpoint it looked as if no effort was being used to speed along.

It wasn't long before we pulled down our Italian flag and raised the French flag.

It was the first time that *Britican* flew the French courtesy flag!

After a six-hour sail/motor we eventually reached the lovely sandstone cliffs of southern Corsica. The entrance to Bonifacio is one of those that you can't easily spot by the naked eye. You have to rely on maps or your plotter to find the green and red channel markers. And once you find them, you're led into a narrow cavern with cliffs reaching high on either side.

BIG TIP: Get the boat ready before you enter the channel. In other words, fasten your stern warps (ropes at the back of the boat) and get your fenders tied on and ready to moor before entering the channel. By doing so you'll be able to sit back and absorb the beautiful scenery of sandstone cliffs, historical architecture, amazing boats and the lower town of Bonifacio.

Upon arrival we called the marina three or four times without response.

Eventually, someone responded and a dinghy met us to show us our spot. We did call in advance and reserve a spot, but I imagine it's first come, first served in the summer.

Fortunately, we visited the very popular port in September when the season was starting to die down.

That being said, it was still very busy!

We were instructed to go stern to the wall (back the boat up to the wall) and all went well. As usual, I threw the two stern lines to a person on land and then took the lazy line to the front of the bow and tied that down to anchor the front of the boat. The lazy line was small but eventually I pulled up a massive rope attached to the small rope – in the end I had to use our anchor winch to pull it in as I was not strong enough to do it unassisted.

Within the hour, we were off exploring.

Joanne from *Crackerjack* recommended a restaurant, so we went in search of L'Archivolto. I assumed the restaurant was along the port but we later discovered it was up in the old town.

Feeling lazy, we took a taxi to the old town, and eventually found L'Archivolto. To say that I was ecstatic about the food at the restaurant is an understatement. After almost 20 months of Greek food (good but a bit bland) and Italian food (pizza and pasta) it was so wonderful to enjoy French cuisine at its best. And I must say that L'Archivoltois is the best you can get in Bonifacio, Corsica.

Not feeling as if we explored the area enough, we decided to pay the price to stay another evening.

So, for $150 we stayed along the wall below the great fort rising above us.

We walked around the port area, purchased groceries from the Spar to stock up the boat. We then took the tourist train back up to the old town. We walked around absorbing the breathtaking sights. It was great to see the great big expanse of blue water from a height. We're always level with the sea so it was nice to rise above it.

It was also humbling to see each sailboat as a tiny spec against a massive deep blue backdrop.

After a good nose around, we walked back down to the boat. That evening I moo'd like a cow while eating a bucket of mussels. I'd love to tell you what the sauce was but I couldn't speak French and the waiter appeared not to speak English.

The French are funny… They really hate foreigners not speaking French. And I'm not basing this on my trip to Bonifacio. I've been to France many times. Even when I try to speak French, I get a look of distain. During our visit I told one waitress I couldn't speak French and she then spoke to me in English…but every time she returned to me she spoke French until I asked her to speak English!

One guy looked at me like I was insane when I questioned a menu item. He totally acted as if he didn't understand me. I then had to point at something (the amazing mussels I got) and hope for the best. Ironically, I later overheard him speaking in English to another table. WTH (what the heck!?!?). Bonifacio is just as touristy as any other tourist place.

I suppose that I understand the rudeness received when I was in Paris, because it's a city, but when visiting a destination that is full of English speaking people you'd think they'd be a bit more hospitable.

(As a side note, I have loads of French friends and I love them. French people, alone, are great. It's when it's an 'us' and 'them' situation they all seem to band together and decided to revolt against English speakers…and perhaps other languages, too?!)

To our delight we finished the evening all lying on the back of our boat watching a spectacular fireworks display, right above our boat! We had the best seats in the entire area. I had to pinch myself to see if I was dreaming.

That evening, Simon and I put our daughter to sleep and then readied the boat for an early departure.

The plan was to leave Bonifacio to head for the Balearics – first port of call was the Spanish island of Menorca.

At 5am we left the amazing port, said "good bye" and "thank you for having us." Bonifacio will definitely be a remembered port. It wasn't the same view with the same touristy stuff that you get in many destinations…it had character (both positive and negative) in addition to some spectacular views.

Simon, Sienna and I sailed to Menorca and stayed for a couple weeks. After that we raced in an Oyster Regatta in Minorca. Our imminent Atlantic crossing was drawing closer and closer, however, so we increased our pace and made our way over to Gibraltar and then down to Gran Canaria, an island off the west coast of Africa.

[See Appendix A, 'V10. Bonifacio' for a video link]

Chapter 40: Preparing to cross the Atlantic Ocean

The trip to sail across the Atlantic Ocean covered 2,800 miles, and we had a crew of seven (including Sienna).

Two of the crew are friends we met last year while wintering (laying up in a marina for the winter) in Marina di Ragusa, Sicily: Kenny and Murray. My friend Andrew came from my hometown and Eve was a new face looking for a ride across the ocean.

Before leaving Las Palmas, we spent five weeks preparing for the trip. For the first week, Simon and Sienna flew to England and I spent time on *Britican* getting her organized.

Although I was sad to see my family leave, I was also excited to have a whole week on my own to sort out the boat.

I needed to clean out all the cabinets, determine our inventory and create a spare parts list. Preparing to cross the ocean is a massive job. With the two out of the way, I could work uninterrupted.

I took my bicycle to the old town, walked through the shopping district, enjoyed the beach, noted all the chandleries and grocery stores and found a huge shopping mall. For the most part, I just got to grips with where things were so that when Simon and Sienna returned we'd know how to get around and where to go.

I thought I'd feel strange being in a foreign country alone on my boat, but I thoroughly enjoyed the quiet time. I felt so comfortable with all the surrounding boat owners and crew. I knew if I had any issues there was a whole community of people to help me out.

One thing that really felt strange was the high police presence. Everywhere you look there are police in cars, on bikes and at night most of the clubs have around three bouncers outside. The malls all have security guards and everyone locks everything up. After spending almost two years in the Marina di Ragusa never locking our boat, bikes or dinghy, I realized how different it felt to be in a region where crime must be high. Never in my life have I been on an island and felt unsafe – I always assumed all islands had low crime due to the fact that criminals had nowhere to hide. I was wrong.

While locking up my bike at the end of our pontoon, some sort of engineer or technician working on a nearby boat came to me and in Spanish indicated I was locking my bike up wrong. He pulled out my chain and put it through my front gear plate rather than around the wheel.

That being noted, not once did I personally feel unsafe. I'd be happy to walk around the city at any time, day or night.

After three days of alone time I was super excited at the arrival of my friends Kent, Anya and her two children, Maya and Max. Anya and the kids flew in from Italy, but she's originally from Poland. Her husband, Kent, originally from New Zealand, is the skipper of a lovely 80+ yacht and arrived from Madera, Spain.

With my friends on the pontoon next to me I was able to enjoy some dinners out, go for long walks and enjoy coffees, chats and chilling out. I couldn't help but think over and over again that I'm a couple hundred miles off the north coast of Africa on a tiny island in the Atlantic yet I feel completely at home. How often do you find yourself on foreign ground and feel completely at ease AND have old and new friends around you?!

After a week, Simon and Sienna returned in time to spend 10 days with Anya and the children before they headed back to Italy. The kids would start off on our boat in the morning, go to the beach during the day and in the evening we'd all go out to dinner or enjoy a meal cooked in. Simon and I looked after the children so Kent and Anya could go out and vice versa – we went to a potluck meal three boats down and it was great to enjoy adult time.

On our pontoon alone there must have been at least 15 children (babies to teenagers) from all sorts of nationalities.

Choosing what to stock on board.

For the most part our decisions came down to money. You can stock every possible spare part if you have the cash and the room. For us, we had neither. We decided to get a spare alternator, as losing one could be disastrous to charging our batteries. We also opted for a starter motor (not cheap) thinking that if that goes we can't start the engine.

Aside from those two big items, we ordered spare pumps, service kits, anodes, filters, safety equipment required by Atlantic Rally for Cruisers (ARC), which we were required to participate in for our journey across the Atlantic, and some spare davit cables. We hoped we wouldn't need to use the major spares for a very long time. Once you get into the Caribbean we've been told that you can have things shipped there, but often you have to pay or bribe the locals to get the parts out of customs.

In fact, we've been told it's cheaper to ask a friend to fly out to the boat carrying the part for you!

Considering we'd be leaving our home turf (Europe) we felt it necessary to get everything we knew we might need in the next couple of years. Furthermore, our engine is a Perkins – not the typical Yanmar or Volvo Penta, so parts are not easy to find in a chandlery.

The other big item on my list to start preparing for was FOOD!

I love food. While we're sailing food is all I think about and talk about…it's my savings grace. When I'm not feeling great, I just lie in the cockpit thinking about what we can have for dinner.

Considering my love of food and my unfortunate issue with seasickness, I've decided to cook the bulk of our dinners before we leave. The plan is to make around 20 frozen meals that can easily be defrosted, heated and served. Thus far I've made savory ground beef and mash, cooked meatballs, chicken Jambalaya, mild curry, dhal (lentils), burrito pie and cabbage and sausage stew.

So those were my first biggie items – inventory/stock and food. Other things on the list include fixing leaks, servicing the generator, engine and outboard, servicing the winches, preparing space for the crew, figuring out our homeschooling plan and materials for the trip, ensuring our boat has all the safety requirements laid down by ARC, updating our First Aid bag, buying Christmas presents and attending seminars, dinners and parties that ARC organized!

I always thought that crossing the Atlantic Ocean was a big thing, but I didn't realize how big the planning part of it would be. I didn't realize that you have to consider what you'll do if your water maker breaks. I didn't even think of it breaking! But if it does, you'll need a back-up water supply. For everything on the boat, you need a backup. So, if your fridge or freezer goes down, you need enough food in cans/jars as backup. If your oven fails, you need another way to cook. And if you have to abandon ship it's not likely that anyone will find you for hours, days and possibly weeks, so you need a "Ditch" or "Grab" bag filled with water, food, medication, flares, fishing line - and on and on.

My thoughts at that time: We're going to work with nature to move thousands of miles. We'll be out of contact with the rest of the world for around 20 days. We'll have highs and we'll have lows, but in the end I'm certain that we'll look back upon this adventure as a trip of a lifetime. How often do you throw seven people together in a small space to spend 20 days together working with nature to get somewhere? What an opportunity for all of us.

Chapter 41: Sailing across the Atlantic with the World Cruising Club

The World Cruising Club, organizers of the ARC, is a group of amazing people. For over 200 boatloads of people, they set up parties for weeks before the event and weeks after the event. For three weeks I went to a party or event every day or night. We planted trees (my family and crew helped to plant 1,000 trees in both Gran Canaria and St. Lucia), enjoyed educational seminars, had meals, experienced local entertainment and more. Sienna went to a kids' club every day enjoying dinghy sailing, a trip to the beach, science museum, the pool and many other activities.

Many people choose to cross the Atlantic (2,800+ miles) before or after the ARC rally instead of with it. Some people aren't interested in the social aspect and many feel the rally price is prohibitive. I have to say that the money we spent to cross with ARC was well worth every penny. The ARC helped to provide us with valuable information, enabled us to meet new friends, assisted with safety and security checks and provided an amazing variety of events to mix and mingle with hundreds of like-minded people. Our experience of the World Cruising Club was nothing short of fantastic – a 10 out of 10.

And the race has begun!

At the beginning of the trip I made notes on my phone to remind me about what we did each day. My notes were mainly in bullet form. As the trip progressed I started to write more and more about our experiences.

So... from this point on you'll read what I thought and noted exactly as I noted it.

Atlantic crossing day 1 – 22nd November 2015

The rally started off with *Britican* alongside many other boats at the start line. Thankfully, many of the 200+ boats held back. We were right up on the line before the starting cannon went off for this friendly race, and I felt there were too many boats in one spot for my comfort.

The swell was so large that it took extreme concentration to make sure we didn't hit another boat. We were all yelling to Simon, at the helm, as to what boats were where. Talk about stress city!

After a couple of hours the boats started spreading out more and more. We spent a few hours neck and neck with one particular boat, so time seemed to go quickly. Eventually, however, by nightfall I was amazed at how quickly we lost sight of most contenders.

From the start, we had high seas and high winds with a very a substantial swell. The wind was blowing over 40 knots and at times we were sailing at over 10 knots. We were all happy that the journey started, but the first day was not relaxing.

We were being tossed all over the place and all sorts of problems came flying at us! We had an accidental jibe, sometimes referred to as a crash jibe, that pulled one of our safety rail stanchions over (bent). An accidental jibe is when the boom swings violently from one side of the boat to the other. When sailing with the wind behind you, if the boat is incorrectly positioned, wind can get on the wrong side of the sail, or a swell can cause the boom to shift. If the wind hits the main sail from the wrong direction, BAM, the whole boom shifts sides and there's a terrible crash sound while the boat shudders in dismay. Although we had a rope fastened to prevent the jibe, it couldn't contend with the power of too much wind hitting the sail. The boom pulled the jibe preventer so hard that it bent our stanchion.

Then we discovered that our compass was off by 50 degrees. Fortunately we had our backup navigation system on an iPad and noticed that we were heading for Africa instead of the Caribbean. After thinking things over during our sleep, we woke the next day and decided to look at the compass control. We realized our new camping gas grill was leaned up next to it causing magnetic errors. At the last moment the grill had been tucked away without consideration to the compass. (Later on during the trip we laughed about our compass issue but at the time it wasn't funny.)

TIP: If your compass gets out of whack it can often be down to something metal that's too close to the compass control box. Our box is located under the aft bed. I've heard stories of knitting needles causing compass issues, so start with a good look around before doing anything else.

Our AIS went down, leaving us blind to seeing boats on the plotter (other than using the naked eye)! Of course, we always use our eyes to navigate, but AIS comes in hand by giving information about when another boat will cross our path and how close we'll get to it.

There were so many issues that I couldn't even consider how I thought or felt – we were just working together to get the boat going in the correct direction as safely as possible.

Fortunately for us, we heeded the advice from one of the ARC seminars on provisioning to make our lunch and dinner ahead of time for day one. If we didn't have quick food to grab, I'm not sure if we would have eaten.

During the evening on day one, Eve fell out of bed and ended up in the hallway. Kenny helped her get off the floor and put her lay cloth up. It took Eve a while to figure out what happened – she lifted her head up in a daze wondering why she was on the floor. We all laughed about it the next day.

Unfortunately, I had a fall too. During my night watch I fell out of the cockpit seat and hit my head on the corner of the companionway. It happened so fast – one moment I was sitting on the seat with my legs stretched out and the next I was on the floor. Afterwards, I couldn't help but wonder if I was going to die of a brain clot...I found it hard to be positive in such strong conditions. We were being tossed all over the place and my mind was spiraling more to the negative side.

But...after all was said and done, we survived day one!

Atlantic crossing day 2 – 23rd November 2015

A large part of the day was spent with Kenny and Andrew working on our AIS system. We had our first dolphin visit. As always, my whole body smiled when I saw them. I yelled out my regards and watched them until they decided to head a different way.

Everyone had a nap to get enough sleep to make it through night watches. We had a rolling schedule so that everyone did every shift (9pm to 12pm, 12am to 3am, 3am to 6am, 6am to 9am) and each watch had an overlap of people. So, if I started off at the 9pm to 12pm watch with Kenny, Kenny would go to bed at 11pm and wake up Simon to do one hour with me and then I would go down and wake the next person up to do two hours with Simon. For most nights we all did two night watches.

It might sound confusing, but by keeping someone on during a watch change reduces the amount of sail/navigational fiddling that happens when a whole set of new crew come on. It also breaks the night watches up – you know that you'll have an hour with one person and two hours with another.

Obviously, this kind of system only works if you have several people. At all times we had one experienced member of crew with one inexperienced crewmember. During the day we were relaxed on watches – usually the majority of us were in the cockpit playing games or relaxing anyway.

We all lazed around quite a bit and since there were so many of us we only ever had one task each day. The task schedule included vacuuming, cleaning the heads (bathroom), general cleanup and trash duty, engine/generator checks (when necessary), lunch and lunch cleanup, dinner and dinner cleanup, and rigging checks.

With AIS working intermittently we knew that there were a few boats around us – over the VHF radio we called *El Mundo*, another 56' Oyster, for a chat. It was nice to touch base with other people. In fact, throughout the entire crossing, whenever we came within VHF range of any boat, we called them to say "hi."

After the rocky start, Sienna kept all her food down and seemed to come back to life. Aside from watching movies, she did a Thanksgiving decoration, played with the others and snacked. (Crewmember Andrew had flown in from America so he was able to pick up some fun Thanksgiving crafts to occupy Sienna.)

The swell was still very large but we were able to run with it hitting us from behind the boat, so the side-to-side motion didn't cause everything to crash as much.

I noted in my diary:

> "I don't feel strong enough to move much so am lying in bed – I'm not sick, it's just so hard to move due to the severe side-to-side motion of the boat. I did my first watch with Kenny from 7 to 10 (having Simon for the first hour). We had a nice chat.

There was a bit of rain, a couple boats on the horizon and that was it. Haven't had a clear night for stars yet – been cloudy with the moon appearing occasionally. The sea doesn't smell like anything – no strong smell. There's a hint of the Caribbean in the air but that might just be wishful thinking. Still in full waterproofs and using my hot water bottle to stay cozy. I don't feel any urgency to get to the other side. I feel rather complacent."

Atlantic crossing day 3 – 24th November 2015

After doing my second night watch (during the same night) with Kenny from 4am to 7am, I slept until 10am. I wasn't feeling well – a bit bunged up and head still hurting from my fall. I didn't die from a brain clot so that was good news.

Kenny and I worked together to successfully receive email reports regarding weather, ARC updates and personal messages. For communications, we purchased a Red Box router from Mailasail that had a port for our Iridium satellite phone. Wirelessly, I'd connect to the Red Box from my MacBook Air and tell the phone to dial up a connection. Once connected, we'd request the weather reports via an automated email system. By placing the name of the report we wanted in the subject line we'd simply need to send the email and a report would come back within seconds.

For our first attempt at sea, we received a weather report, an email from my brother, Bryan, and another little note from my dear friend, Becks. Bryan wrote a message to me in Morse code thinking I'd find it funny… I didn't even attempt to figure it out. If I had access to the Internet, I would have Googled it. That wasn't the first time I wanted to Google something but realized that wasn't going to happen. Using a satellite phone is like using the Internet back in 1980. It's slow and you have to do everything with the smallest file size possible. Sending or receiving a large image file would be fatal.

During our email hook up, Kenny and I also received a position report on all other boats. This report came out every day around noon UTC, or Las Palmas time. We could also request a position report as a one off. I think the report was updated every four hours.

Little did I know that the position report would become the main discussion topic every day. It's funny because I assumed that we'd spend most of our time on the weather, but we rarely spent more than five minutes looking at the forecast. For the most part we'd look at the GRIB file (an image that shows where the wind is and how strong it is) and aim for wind.

Regarding the position report... Simon and Murray started off by plotting the longitude and latitude of our main rivals on a map. Later Kenny developed an insane Excel spreadsheet to allow deep analysis! We noticed that some boats went north and others went south. The suggested route was to go south until the butter melts and then head west to get the trade winds. The north route is most direct, however there's a higher chance of missing the winds and becoming becalmed.

Looking back over the whole trip, our main points of discussion included how we were doing against our main rivals, whether or not we should change sails and what's for our next meal.

Day three also included a lesson on map positions from Murray. He showed our newbie guests how to find and plot a position on the map. Eve and Sienna later made Thanksgiving decorations and I defrosted beef stew I made a few weeks ago. Simon, Sienna and I all went to bed and watched a movie.

Atlantic crossing day 4 – 25th November 2015

Day four started with more dolphins. We were so fortunate to have several greetings from them.

Around midday, all of our bowls slid out of a cupboard and smashed to little pieces – thankfully we had plastic bowls as a backup. I regretted not securing things in cupboards better – everything was clunking and banging. And the time and effort to clean up the smashed bowls was crazy.

In the previous 24 hours we did 190 miles making it our best 24 hours to date. Every day, throughout the whole trip, we bet on the distance traveled in 24 hours. By day four, Eve was in the lead. Aside from discussing our distance, we also played our first match of Rummikub, a game that's similar to Rummy.

For the first several days none of us made quite enough food. We were all accustomed to cooking for two people rather than seven. Eventually, we started making enough rice or pasta to bulk out the meals.

Sienna, Simon and I had our first shower and it felt great! Standing in the shower while moving side to side was such a difficult feat! I had all the soap bottles sliding around my feet while I wedged myself into the most comfortable corner. I couldn't help but think, can't I get five minutes of stability!?

We also watched BBC Blue Planet Part One – I thought it would be educational for all of us to learn about the seas while sailing across one of them – especially for Sienna's benefit. Previous to the trip I downloaded the whole series. Unfortunately, we only made it half-way through the second part. I think Sienna was so immersed in sea life that she didn't have the tolerance to learn about coastal erosion, global warming or anything too heavy.

I wrote in my journal:

"I feel like I can't stop eating. All day long I've been munching on stuff. So far everything has been fine – been going with the flow and the whole day seems to progress without me forcing anything. I thought I would be bored but I haven't been once yet. My night watch was uneventful. Not one ship or boat did we see. Simon put up the American flag in honor of Thanksgiving. I had one hour with Simon and two with Kenny. Kenny immediately noticed the flag. With Simon I read my book and with Kenny we chatted about religion, Atheists and our thoughts on how the world works. We also discussed our Thanksgiving Day plans."

Atlantic crossing day 5 – 26th November 2015, Thanksgiving Day!

The day started with American pancakes and a discussion on whether or not to change sails.

The sail configuration was set to a genoa (head sail) and staysail (also a sail on the forward part of the deck) poled out on either side. We were heading a bit more north than we wanted. I pulled off a GRIB file so the team could look for wind.

The most pressing discussion topic was about time zones. We didn't know what to do with our clocks. Should we put them back as we go, or keep boat time? We assumed the total difference between The Canaries and St. Lucia was five hours, but we later discovered it was only a four-hour time difference.

The guys discussed weather and I rested in bed. The pace had slowed so I was able to have the hatch window open – the fresh air was incredible. Until then all the windows on the boat had to be kept closed, so it was nice to air out the boat.

We received an email from our friend Kent, skipper of *El Oro*, who was also sailing across. He indicated a lack of wind until now…I responded that we've had excellent wind and are thinking of heading south. We all then had a discussion as to whether Kent was being sarcastic as we did, indeed, have wind. Later we found out that the crewmembers on *El Oro* wondered if we were telling the truth about the wind, too! It's funny to consider how small things turn into big discussions when there's no TV, news or other interruptions around.

Based on the wind and our weather reports, we decided to change our sail configuration.

Just as the sails were all pulled in, one of our fishing reels started to spin! It was the first day that we put our poles out.

Kenny rushed to the back of the boat and started reeling in. Everyone was so excited. Andrew assisted with the catch and eventually we pulled up a Mahi Mahi using a gaff. The fish was amazingly colorful.

Before Kenny killed the fish I expressed our gratitude – especially on Thanksgiving. Kenny filleted the fish, used half for ceviche and we decided to bake the other half for dinner on the following day. The wind died and our progress went from 8 to 9 knots down to 2 to 3 all through the night. The temperature of the air started to warm up, but at night were all still wearing our waterproof sailing gear.

Thanksgiving dinner was outstanding!

Turkey breast steaks with homemade stuffing, mashed potatoes, bean casserole, cranberries and gravy! There were barely any leftovers, and what was left I ate during my night watch. During the night I spent two hours with Simon and accidentally spent two hours with Kenny (should have been only one hour with Kenny). Kenny and I got into a deep discussion about the meaning of life and time flew by. Simon didn't wake me for my early morning watch and let me sleep in – it was lovely.

Atlantic crossing day 6 – 27th November 2015:

I am sitting on my beanbag on the forward deck shaded by the genoa (poled out) and the gennaker blue and white sail (also poled out). Our main is down and I'd like to keep it that way – those accidental jibes are terrible. We're going around 3 knots and the larger sail is flapping quite a bit (not enough wind).

Kenny and Andrew are doing the rubbish – cutting plastics into tiny pieces and cramming the scraps into used plastic water bottles. They push the trash into the bottles with the end of a spoon. Last night I saw no boats. Today I can see two with cruising sails out. This morning I played with Sienna for a while, cleaned the saloon, and managed a load of laundry (hand towels and sticky matts) while the water maker was going.

I might even shower today as it's so calm. The boat is still rocking side to side but not as drastic. It's day six and I have to say that my expectations have seriously been surpassed...I'm enjoying every moment of this experience. The 360 view of different shades of blue, the smells of fresh air, the sounds of wind, sails, waves, the bubbling wake, conversation in the background, THE FOOD, interacting with all my crew mates, homeschooling with Sienna... Do I miss not having Internet, news or contact with other people?! No. When Kenny caught the fish I wanted to post a picture on FB but otherwise I haven't even had the urge to use the Internet!

Just noticed... For days now I have not seen a plane or the trail of a plane. I have however, seen loads of flying fish.

We were going 8 to 9 knots and now we're down to 2 to 4 knots. Morale has slightly dipped. Everyone had hoped that we'd fly across. For me, however, I feel indifferent. Getting to land a day or two sooner doesn't seem a worthy focus.

Andrew and Kenny are working AIS again trying to get both plotters working. Currently there is only the downstairs one. We saw a boat on the horizon, looked them up on AIS and discovered it was s/v *Skylark*, an ARC participant. Simon gave them a call on the VHF and we enjoyed listening to the skippers from both boats discuss weather, sail configuration, general wellbeing of the crews and of course, the menu for the day. It was great to hear that both boats were enjoying fresh fish!

Atlantic crossing day 7 – 28th November 2015

I'm sitting on my beanbag on the foredeck. It's so peaceful here. I keep looking for spray coming from a whale's waterspout but nothing seen yet. I have the ability to stare out over the water for ages. And while I'm staring, my thinking slows. I have the capacity to watch my thoughts rather than get involved with them.

I pay attention to the sights, sounds, smells and sensations of the moment rather than being lost in a thought of the past or future. I find it remarkable that I'm on a boat in the middle of the Atlantic and I have absolutely no urge to get anywhere.

After seven days I'm feeling great. I wondered how I'd cope with a lack of Internet connection, constant swells, seasickness, living in close proximity to six other people, ensuring my daughter was entertained and all those things you think about when you're on a voyage like this. All my worries have thus far been completely unfounded.

I enjoy keeping in touch with friends/family over the Internet – social media, blogging, emails, but I also enjoy not having it. The back and forth side-to-side swell motion has only caused me a bit of angst during the night when I can't fall asleep. I've learned that the best position to combat the movement is to put a pillow between my legs, hug another pillow, go into a fetal position and angle myself so that my head and feet are swaying back and forth rather than my body going side to side.

I've had a strange side effect to something – perhaps my seasick pills? My tongue has swelled and feels like it's got cracks all around it. When I eat anything my tongue burns and I can't use it to scrape food from the area around my teeth. Simon told me to try taking an allergy pill so I gave it a go. So far it seems to have reduced the swelling. For a food lover this condition is not ideal, but it's not a deal breaker.

Last night I didn't do any night watch – Simon knew I wasn't feeling well so he didn't wake me up. He didn't ask me if I wanted time off so I feel like I've let the team down a bit. On the flip side, I'm grateful that Sim was looking after me.

The sea doesn't feel overwhelming like I thought it would. Perhaps it's easy to feel this way in calm conditions. Maybe I'd feel differently in a F10 storm? I feel so relaxed and peaceful. I'm not harboring any fears.

Even when I'm lying in bed getting ready to sleep I don't have my usual pre-sleep worries. Previous to this trip I'd worry on overnight sails about hitting something, taking on water, the night watch person falling overboard, or the boat tipping over. I can only assume that sailing for seven days has allowed me the ability to normalize night sails.

When speculating about this trip I had no feel for how I'd react to such a long voyage. Becoming seasick and incapacitated was a worry. I just didn't have a clue as to how I'd feel. The pills have worked exceptionally well, and if I'm overwhelmed by anything it's my unexpected love of this experience. I'm not in a constant state of bliss nor am I enlightened by the journey. I am, however, a different Kim. I often write about how sailing forces me to be present. This journey is thus forcing me to be present for a duration that's longer than anything I've experienced thus far.

There's nothing around to trigger thoughts of my past, and for some reason my future isn't in my focus at all. I have no idea where will go after the ARC festivities finish in St. Lucia. I have no idea where I'll be in a few weeks, nor do I know who I'll be around. Heck, I have no idea who might be sailing with us! Because my future is so unplanned, I don't feel the need to ponder anything further than my next meal.

Atlantic crossing day 8 – 29th November 2015

Our first week was now behind us. My night watch was easy going. I spent an hour with Kenny and then two hours with Andrew. It's the first time I was with Andrew.

The first week we made sure Eve and Andrew, the least experienced crew, were matched with the most experienced crew. The second week we mixed everyone up. During the watch we used my night sky app to name stars, planets and constellations. Kenny and I talked about random things and Andrew and I discussed the American economy. Time goes so fast with two people.

I went to bed around 2am – climbed in with Simon and Sienna. A few hours later I heard the engine turn on. We motored south for four hours due to a complete lack of wind.

I love sitting on the foredeck. I'm alone with the sounds and sights of *Britican* and the sea. It's pure bliss. There's nothing to do, nothing to think, and nothing to be. I simply am.

We had quite a few laughs about what others do when we wake them for their night watch. Kenny jumps up as if someone is about to tackle him (he has older brothers), Murray puts his head up quickly and yells "okay – I'm up," and apparently Eve has to call my name 15+ times and rock my leg to get me up. We laughed through dinner. I then put a movie on and Andrew and Sienna watched it. The next I knew Kenny woke me up saying, "I let you sleep – you only have an hour shift to do with Andrew." I was very thankful. I did my hour shift and then went back to bed.

Atlantic crossing day 9 – 30th November 2015

We have more wind today! Finally out of the 3 to 4 knots and into the 5 to 6 knots. And more wind should be coming tomorrow. At this rate we'll hit St. Lucia in 11 days. I think we'll get more wind and be in sooner.

In the morning I did some homeschooling with Sienna – we did a cutout exercise on Where is the Atlantic Ocean? Not only did we find the ocean but we plotted our exact latitude and longitude on it! How many kids get to do that?!

Just as we were working on the letter F I heard the fishing pole go. I leapt out of the saloon and up through the cockpit to the starboard aft pole. Murray helped me pull the pole out of the holder and gave me instruction. I let the fish run and run and run. Eventually I could reel it in. I saw it jump from far away and thought it was a Mahi Mahi. After 25 to 30 minutes I finally got the fish in. Both Kenny and Murray were telling me what to do. Murray used the gaff and pulled the fish up. My arms were aching – mostly my biceps. And I had the pole jammed into a towel over my stomach.

I was a bit worried that the fish would be a tiny thing when it arrived and I would look like a wimp.

Fortunately, it was a really nice sized fish, 92cm – around 3 feet. It may not sound like much but it will feed all of us for dinner. I'm thinking of doing a fish fry with coleslaw and perhaps some potatoes.

Once the fish was aboard we took a picture and then Kenny instructed Simon on how to fillet the fish. It's great to think that I caught the fish, hubby filleted it and I'll cook it. The fish doesn't have a strong flavor…it's so neutral – it's so fresh. There's absolutely no fishy smell or taste to it. Sienna loved it.

The great thing about catching fish is that we're not doing much to get them. When you go out on a fishing trip you sit and wait for ages. For us, we're living life, sailing, and only when a fish is on the line do we have to put our fishing hats on.

I hope we get a tuna. Andrew is the only one left to pull a fish in, so the next one that goes has his name on it.

Around 1am Simon woke me up and I had an hour with Kenny and two hours with Andrew. At 4am I woke Murray and went to bed. The morning started out as usual. I got up, poured myself some corn flakes, got cuddles from Sienna and entered the discussion about our position, how far we've come overnight and where the other boats are located.

From what I gathered it seemed that we have dropped more south than most other boats, however we had more wind and were therefore gaining on everyone. For the past two days we had very little wind – down to 2 knots at times. When looking at the positions of other boats we had to assume that many boats decided to use their engines (allowed in the race but must be declared) due to their progress.

We used our engine for four hours in the wee hours of the morning due to getting no wind at all. So...it's hard to say where everyone is positioned. We have a feeling that we might pass a lot of boats now as we're south enough to get the winds. Boats that are north of us seem to be making very little progress.

Anyway, Kenny set up the poles, I sat around for a bit and played with Sienna. Suddenly the fishing reel went crazy! At 10:45 the reel started and by 11:20 three grown men got the fish reeled in. Andrew started off and then it became a combined effort.

We furled the gennaker in and the genoa to slow the boat down. During the gennaker furl the top half of the sail doubled over and furled over itself – disaster. And I mean disaster. That sail will have to be retired for the rest of the race.

I'm not sure how we fix it – perhaps on land we can unroll it and furl it properly. So – half the team was holding down the gennaker (we lowered it to the deck) and the rest were preparing for the fish.

In the end, Simon, Andrew and Kenny took turns reeling it in. Kenny gaffes it, and lo and behold it was a great big tuna. I couldn't believe it! A tuna – just what I ordered.

Once the tuna was put to sleep we put it in a bag and all helped to bring the gennaker in and put out our staysail. Once we were back up to 7 knots, Kenny filleted and cleaned the tuna.

I was feeling a bit nauseous so I took my seasick pills at bedtime. An hour later I woke in excruciating pain – my left ear was blocked, ringing and full of pressure. I couldn't put my head down. I tried everything to clear the blockage. Nothing worked. I was up until 3 or 4 pm. After taking some ibuprofen I must have passed out. The guys sorted out my night shift. When I woke, the pressure was gone but the blockage remained.

Atlantic crossing day 10 – 1st December 2015

In bed all day.

Atlantic crossing day 11 – 2nd December 2015

I was in bed most of the day. I got up for our half-way party. Each crewmember purchased something special before we left the Canaries to share when we made it to the halfway point of the trip. We had fruitcake, jamon (cured Spanish ham), Canary Island cookies, tuna sashimi (a bonus), special pate, homemade chutney (from our lovely friend Karen), aloe drink and pirate party favors. There were lots of laughs, and despite my ear issue, I managed to have a great time.

Atlantic crossing days 12 and 13 – 3rd and 4th December 2015

I haven't been able to lift my head. Blockage remains. Simon found eardrops for an ear infection in our first aid bag. I've been putting them in and living off ibuprofen.

I've dropped out of doing everything – night shifts, cooking, cleaning. The only time I get up is when I go to the bathroom. The team got the gennaker fixed and up again!

We're doing over 8 knots, which is great to see. I think everyone wants to get to land sooner rather than later.

These past couple days I've wanted to die. The seasickness pills I was taking called Phaia Bombers were my ticket to sane sailing. Unfortunately I didn't consider that I'd have a bad reaction to them after prolonged use. I must take this as the final sign. I cannot put myself through this agony again. Here I am 1000 miles from land and I can't hear, lift my head up or contribute.

Furthermore, I feel very unwell. To make matters worse, it's getting hotter by the day and I'm sweating. I can't stand long enough to shower and the sea teases me with its dark blue coolness. Maybe I can lie on the back deck and Simon can run the hose over me.

Boy do I feel pathetic.

After talking to Kenny a bit, it seems like everyone has a bit of the blues. Kenny said that yesterday was a good day to sleep through – the sky was overcast, there were squalls and everyone was a bit down after the climax of the half-way party.

Now that I look at things it is a bit depressing – once the half-way party is enjoyed there's not much until our arrival in 7 to 10 days. We've broken all there is to break, we've all caught a fish, we've all done our jobs. I hate to admit it, but the newness of the voyage has worn off and the excitement has dampened.

Considering my condition, if I had the choice to moor up in St. Lucia tonight, I would. I am, however, feeling better. Just being on deck watching all the flying fish pop up and down has a therapeutic effect.

It feels weird preparing for Christmas while crossing the Atlantic. It is hot out. Ironically, this will be Sienna's second Christmas in St. Lucia. We celebrated the holiday with my brother's family and our mom and step-dad four years ago. Back then I had no idea I would become a live-aboard sailor, let alone cross the Atlantic Ocean.

Atlantic crossing day 14 – 5th December 2015

Woke up and wanted to die again. An ibuprofen helped a little. My head felt like would burst – liquid mucus sloshing back and forth at every swell. My left ear is once again fully clogged. And I'm constantly fighting bouts of feeling nauseous.

I managed to get up in the cockpit. After eating a bit of food I had Simon put a seasickness patch on my back. Perhaps it won't burn my skin there. Previous attempts with wearing the Scopolamine patch have burned my skin. So far I feel like I'm on another planet. I can't stand for long or keep my head up.

Lately I've been thinking that nothing seems to matter anymore. Not in a bad way. I used to be so caught up in my old life about who I was, what I did, what my purpose was and on and on. I was so full of thoughts, opinions, goals and plans.

Right now I feel like a simpleton. I don't have any strong thoughts, my opinions are more like slight preferences that can easily be changed, and I have not one goal (other than get across this ocean, but that's more of a matter of time than something I have to work to achieve). I have no plans for the future. Nothing. I have no idea where I'll be this time next month.

Is this a good thing?! I don't know. It feels normal now but I'm not sure if I'm a better or worse person for it. I suppose it is what it is and ultimately it doesn't matter. I'm in the middle of the ocean and nothing matters. No drive, no future (other than sailing), no purpose. The only thing I feel strong about is helping my little girl to learn to read, write, do math and understand how to make the best out of life...or at least impart anything I feel that's transferable.

I just looked aft at the slate blue sun-soaked rolling Atlantic and overheard myself think, "I love you... I love this.'"

What is wrong with me? How can a person endure such miserable seasickness and yet look at the disruptive source with loving eyes? Am I like a battered woman who goes back for more, or a prisoner who falls for her captor? It couldn't be the same, could it?

Perhaps in a past life (not that I'm necessarily a believer) I was a sailor and in this life I'm drawn to the sea despite my allergy to swells. It's just that I look out to the sea and I become mesmerized. I watch the white crests powerfully break into being and then quickly disappear. I look through the turquoise transparent swell tops that reach to heights above the back of the boat. And all those peaks and troughs effortlessly dance to nature's tune. I'll have to ask someone if wave movements/patterns are fractals. I bet they are, hence the attraction.

I got a kick out of Sienna as we were approaching the end of our Atlantic crossing. She said, "We only have four days left?! Why did everyone tell me it was going to take ages to cross the Atlantic?" I explained that we've been on the sea for two weeks – did she think it went fast? Sienna's response was, "yes!"

So there you have it – people were worried about us bringing a five-year-old across the pond, and from the looks of it she's faring much better than her mother, so there are no worries about Sienna.

This is a once in a lifetime event and it would be nice to finish with a top score. Boat owners are allowed to use their engines as long as the time/mileage is noted. So just because other boats cross the line before us doesn't necessarily mean they were faster. Many used their engines during our couple days of light wind. We've used our engine for a total of four hours. The boats in the racing division, however, are not allowed to use engines at all.

We broke 200 miles in 24 hours!

Atlantic crossing day 15 – 6th December 2015

Only four more days to go! I woke with an unblocked ear. Unfortunately, as soon as I lifted my body up it blocked again. That aside, I felt like I could move about without getting sick. The Scopolamine patch must be having a positive effect.

We attempted to get the gennaker up despite the fact that the last furling didn't go well. As we made a human chain to guide the sail up, the lower furling unit (attached to the sail) came loose, went flying out of our hands and the wind took it out to sea. Imagine a sail attached to the top of the mast but nothing holding it to the boat.

What's worse is that at the bottom lose end there was a big metal furling unit – essentially a large heavy metal box.

The unattached slightly furled sail became a wrecking ball as it flew back and forth around and in front of the bow.

After a few flights Kenny grabbed the rope trailing from the sail only to have it pull right back out of his hands. Like an angry monster, the sail was twisting and flung its heaviest point all over. Eventually a dangling rope was retrieved and tied to the boat.

Within seconds the sail dropped into the sea and went under the boat.

Then came a "bing, rip, rip, rip, rip, whoosh" sound.

The sail ripped apart and was lodged under the forward part of the boat. We secured as much sail as we could, furled in the genoa and turned the boat to relieve the pressure of the sail under the boat.

Within a few minutes we retrieved everything. What a nightmare. Thankfully no one was hurt and the furling unit didn't bang into (and hole) the boat. Or worse, take someone's head off.

So there goes our gennaker. I don't want to know what the replacement cost of that one is…In fact, I don't want to think about the gennaker or what could have happened. Aside from that entertainment we were hit by one squall – lots of rain but no heavy winds.

I'm okay with still being at sea. I'm a bit tired of the ceaseless rocking motion during sleep time and I'm annoyed that I can't play with Sienna more. Otherwise I'm okay. There are enough people around for entertainment and I love to simply sit in the cockpit and watch the sea dance. I really love the feeling of being high on the crest of a swell looking back down the navy blue and white frothed slope and then gently easing into the valley. And then repeating over and over. Every so often we catch the swell at an angle and the boat slides over to its side quite harshly. I feel these swells are here to keep us awake!

Atlantic crossing day 16 – 7th December 2015

I was on night watch alone and after getting up to survey the horizon for boats I turned around to see a large line of orange where the sea meets the sky.

When such a splash of color makes an appearance in an otherwise black backdrop, one takes notice.

In fact, any time something out of the ordinary happens at sea I seem to get a little surge of adrenalin. In this particular case, it was the moon coming up.

I wish I could have taken a picture. Venus was just above it and it looked as if the crescent shape of the moon was chasing the planet so it can eat it. The planet was big, bold and solid. The moon was soft, small and yellow-orange.

The air was humid, the breeze perfect. We were sailing at 6 knots with our genoa and staysail poled out. The sea was so calm.

Atlantic crossing day 17 – 8th December 2015

We got our spinnaker up today!

It was, however, all over the place so we only flew it for five minutes. Conditions need to be perfect to fly that kite. We had to run the engine to keep the boat steady while hoisting the sail.

There's a weird feeling in the boat today. I think there is a desire to get to land but also a sadness that the adventure is coming to an end. We're all such a strong team now – a family unit. It's sad to think that we'll be parting ways soon not knowing if or when we'll see each other again. And none of us knows what's in store for our future. None of us have jobs or set plans on what's coming next.

Atlantic crossing day 18 – 9th December 2015

If the wind keeps steady or increases we'd be in St. Lucia the next day! Wow.

As I sat there on what might be the last full day of the regatta, I felt relaxed, grateful and full of peace. The sense of nothingness that had been pervading my spirits most of this trip is …. I cannot find a word for it. It's not a bad or good feeling. It's beyond bad and good. Perhaps peacefulness gets close to how I feel. I feel nothing, yet at the same time I feel everything.

Never in my life have I been able to simply *be* rather than *do*. Never have I felt what it's like to be devoid of past and future thoughts. I read "The Power of Now" by Eckhart Tolle several years ago and was inspired by the concept of living in the present more often than not. But until I started sailing I just didn't get it. Now I do.

I feel fleeting moments of bliss that come over me again and again. I think that what happens is I have a thought, momentarily get caught up in it and then I am able to drop the thought and just be for a few seconds – that's when the blissful nothingness comes in. I stare at the waves, move my body to the undulation of the ocean, listen to the water hit the hull and feel a tingling bliss.

Even when I'm seasick I can still find peace at sea. Amazing, isn't it?

Many people think sailing is about freedom, and in many respects they're right. After a long voyage, however, freedom can often be the act of getting off the boat!

Atlantic crossing day 19 – 10th December 2015

Around 6am I overheard Simon and Murray shout, "Land Ahoy!"

All of us jumped up into the cockpit and took our first gaze upon a hazy green mass of land off our portside bow. We all yelled, "woo-hood" and felt the excitement in the air.

After enjoying a cup of tea I decided to start cleaning in preparation for our arrival. I was so excited I needed something to distract me from watching the ETA (estimated time of arrival). I couldn't believe that we had only hours to go.

Sienna became overexcited and started driving us all nuts. It was a case of too much energy and no way to allow it to flow. Fortunately, Eve offered to watch a movie with her, and that allowed both girls to bide time until arrival.

I cleaned our bathroom, started to work on the mess between our bed and the sofa – over the course of our journey the area filled in like a skip/dumpster. Anyone viewing our room for the first time wouldn't realize that there was a walkway along the side of the bed nor would they see a sofa!

Once our room was tidy I started on the kitchen. With so many people cooking and cleaning, all the pots, pans and kitchen accessories were in the wrong place. We had one cupboard that, when opened, the question wasn't whether something would fall out or not – it was more of a question as to how much would fall!

While sailing along St. Lucia heading for our Rodney Bay Marina destination, we heard boats in front of us call the ARC finish line on the VHF. Our excitement grew and grew as we knew our VHF call was imminent. We rounded the top of St. Lucia, called the finish line and prepared our sails for a change. We had to bring the staysail down, remove the pole, bring the genoa in, remove the pole and then put the genoa back out and raise the main. Our sail change went without a hitch.

I couldn't help but think, "It's official, we finally know what we're doing to a competent level and we're quick." I also thought that it was a shame the trip was ending.

With the finish line in sight, we did the sail change while posing for a photographer. Most of the crew had beers in their hand and stood on the foredeck as we crossed the line. I could finally say, "WE MADE IT ACROSS THE ATLANTIC OCEAN!"

For the past several years I had found it difficult to get excited about anything. I was excited about getting the boat and all our adventures but I didn't have any particular moment that brought absolute excitement…until we crossed that finish line. With my stomach full of butterflies and tingles we prepared the boat and made ready to enter the marina.

Waiting for us was rum punch, a fruit basket and many of the friends we met in Las Palmas.

Simon backed the boat in perfectly while friends applauded our arrival – we had lines going astern to the jetty and along the port side. No more slime lines now that we're in the Caribbean.

We immediately received our rum punch (Sienna got a juice) and fruit basket. And many of our friends came up to greet us and ask us how things went. The buzz was incredible. We all swapped stories – did you break anything? How did your seasickness go? How did your child/children get on? How many fish did you catch? Did you use your engine? And on and on it went.

After an hour of socializing we started to clean and get rid of the rubbish. As the day progressed more boats came in and everyone cheered.

So...how do I rate my Atlantic Rally for Cruisers (ARC) Atlantic Ocean crossing? Although I was down for several days, I have to give it a 10 out of 10. The easiest way to equate my experience regarding my sickness is to say what I mentioned before, it's like childbirth - once it's over you seem to forget how bad it was.

The ARC people were amazing. The crew was exceptional. The journey was monumental and, looking back, I wouldn't change a thing. I keep saying this often – this journey will definitely go in my top 100 of life experiences. I'm so proud of my family, crew and me for making it happen.

Now it was time to recover, enjoy some rum and figure out what's next...

[See Appendix A, 'V11. Crossing the Atlantic Ocean' for a few videos]

Chapter 42: From Mediterranean to Caribbean

After sailing around the Mediterranean for two years, spending 18 days crossing the Atlantic Ocean and arriving at the Caribbean Island of St. Lucia, I felt shell-shocked.

Every effort up until our arrival in St. Lucia was spent on planning, preparing, organization and actually getting across the Atlantic Ocean. Not one moment was spent considering the climate, culture and differences that we were about to encounter.

Although sailing around the Caribbean is not new to me, I felt as if I entered a totally new world. Having vacations in the Caribbean on a boat is definitely different than bringing your European-based home across the pond to stay for a while.

The Caribbean is nothing like the Mediterranean. Everything is different – the air, sea, people, food, scenery, wind, fish and…just everything.

With such a difference I felt slightly lost yet extremely revitalized.

In the Mediterranean I knew the layout. I understood who I was and where I was located in the world. I became accustomed to reviewing the language of the country and I knew it was up to me to be proactive when ordering something at a restaurant or finding a new location. I felt comfortable in the fact that I could name the countries and/or islands around me. I felt at home.

In the Caribbean I felt as if we were in the same house, yet it had been turned upside down. Like Dorothy in the Wizard of Oz, our house was lifted out of Kansas and planted in a totally new world.

For two years I struggled with my Italian, Greek, Turkish, French and Spanish. Here in St. Lucia I could simply speak English and get

English in return! For the first week or two I found myself requesting things slowly in a simple manner thinking the person I was speaking to didn't know English well. (I'm sure many of the locals thought I have issues...)

Aside from speaking English, I could visit any of the grocery stores and find products I knew. I devoured cinnamon raisin bagels, American Italian sausages, jerk chicken, and on and on (I've lived in Europe for almost 20 years but being American, it's always nice to find American food that I grew up with).

It was WINTER and I enjoyed sun soaked days and perfect breezy evenings IN MY T-SHIRT.

Not once did I have to put a sweater on or add layers as the evening drew closer. It was balmy in January. Summer in the Mediterranean got hot, but a different hot. And in the winter, the Med is cold, damp and rainy.

The water here was perfect...and I mean perfect. In the Med I couldn't last very long as the sea would have patches of warmth and patches of coldness. In two years of swimming and snorkeling in the Med I can count the amount of fish I saw. In the few weeks of being in the Caribbean, I've already seen thousands of creatures. The water is clear, the fish are bright and colorful and the temperature was perfect.

But let me stop there – I'm not bashing the Mediterranean. Heck, nothing can beat the variety of cultures, amazing anchorages, diversity of food and the history of Europe. I won't be able to find anything comparable in the Caribbean to the Parthenon, Olympia, Delphi, the Palace of Knossos (Crete), Pompeii, the Coliseum and on and on. And although the pizza is great in St. Lucia, there's something far more gratifying about eating a pie in Italy.

Isn't it interesting how we as humans normalize things? Toward the end of our two-year stay in the Med I definitely tired of seeing ancient amphitheaters. Yes, I'm at fault for trying to hit every historical archeological finding, but I just couldn't help it. If you have Pompeii within your reach you're not going to pass it by!

I have to admit that I also struggled with having to fail (over and over) at speaking a foreign language or dealing with the repercussions of buying baking powder instead of baking soda (I often couldn't understand the packaging and purchased the wrong ingredients).

Furthermore, the Mediterranean is not a great place to actually sail. The wind is either blowing a Force 10 (storm conditions) or it's not blowing at all. When we moved locations we'd either get to our next destination completely disheveled, windblown and seasick OR we'd have to motor for hours using up our diesel.

Hopefully these comments don't make me sound ungrateful. I'm certainly thankful for all of our adventures. I suppose, however, that once one sees quite a few amazing things they eventually become less amazing. And once someone lives in a particular area, after time, life becomes less spontaneous, uncertain and dare I say, exciting.

I think I'll have to scratch the "exciting" bit because since we sold up and sailed away, my life has had more excitement than I ever experienced in my previous 40 years of life.

Sailing around the Mediterranean was amazing. I loved every moment of it. Now that we're in the Caribbean, however, when I look back I can see that life in the Med became somewhat predictable.

What do cruisers panic about?

People who don't live on a boat probably think that the biggest worry for a full time cruiser, commonly referred to as a "live-aboard," is about the boat sinking, getting caught in a hurricane, smashing into a whale, getting lost, dragging into the sea or rocks from a mooring or being gobbled up by a giant sized squid. And let's not forget pirates! Although these worries may exist, they're often temporary and short-lived.

There's another worry that seems common, especially among the women cruisers who I've been privileged to befriend, and it has to do with our basic need to nurture, to provide and to give back. And the kicker: guilt.

Let me tell you about my personal experience. I woke in a panic – an event that happens a few times every month. I opened my eyes; looked at the few stars I could see through my open hatch and felt my stomach gnawing away with... what? Was it dread or guilt or fear? I couldn't quite tell.

The panic attack seemed to have strange timing. Earlier that day I explored an island in the Caribbean called Bequia with friends and family. We enjoyed the colorful pink, blue, orange and green Caribbean houses and shops, took in the sparklingly clear turquoise waters, devoured chicken roti's and ran into good friends we met in Europe (it's a very small world in the cruising community).

After I opened my eyes, I heard water splashing along the hull and felt the perfect breeze sweep past my body. Then all hell broke loose and I could feel my stomach churn and heard my inner voice say, "What the heck am I doing?"

"What am I doing sitting on a boat sailing around the Caribbean after two years of sitting on a boat sailing around the Mediterranean? Who do I think I am being able to constantly enjoy one big vacation? And how can someone actually enjoy being on a permanent vacation – my love for this life can't last forever. THIS can't last forever. When it ends what am

I going to do? And what's my purpose anyway? I go from place to place 'living' but I'm not 'serving'…I'm not contributing to the world."

And then another voice in me pipes up and says, "What's the sense of worrying as it totally tarnishes the whole experience. Why sell up and sail away if you're going to allow your thoughts to overtake your mind and temporarily ruin the fun?"

And just like a program, my mind then goes into overdrive trying to plan, organize or visualize a solution for the future. Unfortunately, however, the gnawing in my stomach is so strong that it drives my thoughts into doom and gloom mode and I envision us sailing until all our money runs out, our daughter is sent to live with relatives and hubby and I end up in a tent alongside a desert road. I can even visualize the two cactuses, a small fire pit and a beat-up harmonica!

My panic attacks are not an everyday occurrence, and for the most part I carry on with life in quite a positive manner; however, I feel that instead of coming to terms with my issues I just keep pushing my fears to the side. For weeks I can ignore the fear but eventually it pops up again.

What is my purpose? Is that the issue?

Back on land, I ran a company and felt a sense of purpose – I contributed to society, gave employment to many people, unleashed my creative mind in a way that made the world a better place (or at least, that's what I told myself…).

That said, even though I had a purpose I felt it wasn't good enough. During my childhood I always thought I'd not only make the world a better place but I'd do it in a certain way. I dreamed that my contribution to the world would be more like Mother Teresa, however I accidently went down the capitalistic Donald Trump road. Financial achievement was my main motivator and it eventually left me feeling very empty.

Hence, my action to sell up and sail away! I figured that life on the sea would help me get back to nature, gain stronger family bonds, learn how to make real friends (instead of making work my family and friend base), provide me the ability to slow down and eat a real meal (not peel off the plastic wrap and microwave), remove myself from over-capitalism…and ultimately lead a simpler life.

Everything I wanted came to fruition except for life becoming simpler, but that's okay.

Being a full time live-aboard is nowhere near simple. It's actually a lot more complicated than I ever envisioned. That aside, I must profess that I have definitely become closer to nature, my family bond is amazing, I have loads of real friends, I have no space to buy anything so money is only needed for food, fuel, insurance and boat repairs, and I've definitely slowed down in terms of how I think and the pace of work I uphold.

The benefits of cruising have been incredible, so why is this need for a sense of purpose still waking me up at night? Where is this drive coming from? Why do I feel like I must be contributing to the world and I'm failing?

As I mentioned earlier, these thoughts are not constant. At least 90 percent of the time I'm having a whale of a time. But out of all the worries I have, aside from my desire to not screw up our daughter, is my lack of purpose, direction, planned future…you get the picture.

Chapter 43: Discovering Bequia

After crossing the Atlantic Ocean and then hanging out in St Lucia for a month, hubby and I started to get itchy feet. We enjoyed St Lucia's lovely Rodney Bay Marina, both on the jetty and when using a mooring ball. We anchored in the popular Margot Bay and a few other places near the town of Soufriere and the famous volcanic Pitons.

The time had come, however, to leave our first Caribbean destination and start exploring the surrounding area. While looking at a map, Simon and I discussed various game plans. The main question was whether to go south to St Vincent and the Grenadines or north to Martinique.

You'd think that we would have spent weeks considering our options but when we decided to make a move, we opened the map, had a 10-minute discussion and then started preparing the boat for departure.

During our stay in St Lucia, however, we received reports from a variety of other sailors about what's good and what isn't. Feedback on Martinique was very positive yet many boaters said to give St Vincent a miss due to high crime. Over the course of our meanderings around St Lucia our thoughts were being formed about our next destination.

I always find it funny how we never truly know where we're going until we actually start sailing somewhere.

After a very rocky seven hours, *Britican* headed into wind, I dropped the mainsail and Simon motored us into Admiralty Bay just outside the capital town of Port Elizabeth on the island of Bequia.

Sailors and contacts on my Sailing Britican FaceBook page espoused amazing reports about the small island – I heard that the area was unspoiled, full of tropical delights and home to very kind locals.

Once we anchored in the bay I looked around and thought that Bequia looked like any other island.

I wondered where all the positive reports were coming from. Sure, there were the typical colored houses on the tropically green hillside painted blue, pink, orange, and green. And the beach looked like it had lovely sand embraced with a backdrop of tall palm trees. But there were two large unsightly cargo ships parked in the bay, loads of sailboats and big ugly barge doing the rounds with, "Water, Laundry and Diesel" written on the side.

Many people make the mistake that it's us boaters who have the best view in town, but that's not always the case.

It wasn't until the following day when Simon took the crew and me to shore that I started to realize just how amazing Bequia really is. When we first took our dinghy to one of the many dinghy pontoons, and I took a few steps onto land, I noticed a very colorful, inviting and relaxed backdrop.

The main strip is filled with natural beauty including the light sandy beach, variety of colorful trees, bushes and shrubs. And the restaurants, bars and shops are not only colorful but each one has distinct character.

The Chameleon Café, situated in the busiest area of the harbor, has a seating area that's hidden behind lovely big palms.

The Gingerbread Hotel has an amazing façade on the building and an open grassy outdoor seating area that's shaded by palm trees. The lower area provides sandwiches, cakes and coffee. Over the course of a week we sampled almost every cake. I loved the carrot cake and the gingerbread was excellent. Next to the coffee shop is a homemade ice-cream parlor – there's no need to describe how amazing that place is.

And the upper area, within the Gingerbread Hotel itself, is a lovely restaurant with a great view of the green grounds and harbor.

For our "Date Night," hubby and I took the dinghy into Port Elizabeth dropping crewmember Eve off so she could get some alone time. Back on the boat, our guests Andrew and Michelle watched Sienna.

Simon and I like to enjoy a couple drinks first, so we sat at Whaleboners, a restaurant that has whales ribs upon the entrance and whale spine bones for the bar seats. With the town being so small, we watched Eve walk past us on a few occasions while she decided where to get dinner.

When Simon and I finally decided to eat we settled on the Gingerbread Hotel and wouldn't you know who was there – it was Eve!

We tell everyone that she crashed our date night but in reality we fizzled her solo evening.

As Eve ate dessert, Simon enjoyed a homemade chicken kiev and I had my first taste of Caribbean lobster. All our meals were very enjoyable.

We also sampled great food from Mac's Pizzeria and the Fig Tree serving authentic local cuisine. I was very impressed with Fig Tree – if you have children this restaurant must not be missed. The back wall is lined with children's books!

Sienna and I spent ages reading through a variety of books. I was delighted to find a book that my grandmother read to me when I was I child. I'm sure that it was my father's book that was read to him when he was a little boy. Until seeing the book, the time spent reading with my grandmother was a lost memory!

The Fig Tree appeared to offer games, books and a reading club for children. When walking along the waterfront, the restaurant can be found at the end of the walkway heading south from the town. When we enjoyed the roti's (local Caribbean dish) the owner introduced herself to us and thanked us for passing all the other inviting restaurants. With just one small conversation you could feel her sincerity and kindness radiate.

Aside from restaurants, there are two dive shops, a few minimarkets, one bank (with ATMs), a bookshop, an art museum, a church and many street vendors selling carvings, jewelry, fruit and a variety of other hand-made offerings.

There's one grocery store that is well worth a visit – Doris's. Located behind the customs house, you'll find a brown cottage that houses all sorts of Northern American and British delights. Whether you want curry paste, Hersey chocolate chips or granola, this is the place to stop. You can also get cold cuts, fresh milk and frozen meat.

There's also a covered fruit and vegetable market that is fantastic. The vendors allow you to try all sorts of local fruits before you buy. I was blown away by the flavor and consistency of a soursop. Make sure to try one when you hit the Caribbean – the fruit simply can't be compared to any other!

There are a scattering of beauty spa offerings.

Eve and I looked at a few of the day spas located along the main strip but none of them took our fancy. Most looked like hairdresser type offerings that also gave massages and did pedicures.

We, however, managed to find a day spa called Serenity Day Spa in the Tradewinds Marina at the north side of the bay. With only one practitioner, the lovely Dorcel, we had to wait our turn, but the wait was well worth it! Both Eve and I signed up for a two-hour package including an hour-long massage, a half-hour facial and a pedicure for $70 USD. Our other guest, Michelle, went for a body scrub, facial and eyelash and brow tinting.

The massage room is set up in such a high standard. You'd think you were in a 5 Star hotel, but it's just a room in the marina!

The treatments received at Serenity Day Spa were the best I've experienced in years (and I often go to spas in London and New York). Furthermore, the value for money is the best I've ever come across.

And what about swimming and snorkeling? Coming from the Mediterranean, where the water is often murky and lacking in fish, we've been blown away with the Caribbean waters. The sandy sea bottom creates pools of beautiful turquoise water and then it leads to intricate coral reef housing the most exquisitely colorful fish that I've ever seen.

While snorkeling in Bequia with Sienna, all I could hear was a muffled "Mom, mom, mom...look at that!" Her squeals of excitement burst out of the snorkel with an intoxicating enthusiasm. Every time we went for a snorkel here excitement grew.

In Admiralty Bay the options for snorkeling over the reef are many. And even while wearing a mask around the boat at our anchorage we had plenty to look at. Just around the boat we've spotted turtles, sea snakes, dogfish, barracuda and a blowfish.

Rumor has it that there are many stingrays in the area too!

On a couple of occasions while we were discovering Bequia we took the dinghy over to the beach, enjoyed the silky sand and fantastically clear waters. None of the beaches ever appeared to be busy, there are no watersport activities and the bars and restaurants are limited.

Aside from the bay hosting lovely waters, the swell was miniscule. For the most part the wind continuously blew us away from land from the northeast to east. On a few occasions the wind died completely and there was barely a movement on the sea. Every once and a while there'd be a slight swell giving the boat a side-to-side motion, but it was barely noticeable. By far, Admiralty Bay was one of the most protected, sheltered and comfortable bays we'd anchored in so far.

How about the community in the bay?

After spending two years in the Mediterranean cruising around we often bumped into friends. My fear about crossing to the Caribbean was that we wouldn't know anyone. To my surprise we knew at least five other boats throughout our entire stay while anchored in Admiralty Bay, with a couple of them being close friends.

At one point there were four other "kid boats," all anchored in a line. We'd call each other on the VHF and the children would move from one boat to another or we'd arrange to meet on the beach. One night all the kid boat families planned to meet up at Jacks, a lovely restaurant on the beach, so the adults could enjoy a few drinks and dinner while the children enjoyed playing in the sand.

Feeling like you're a part of a community even though you're in a foreign territory is such a massive benefit that often gets overlooked by non-cruisers. Wherever we go we have friends – perhaps we haven't met them yet, but when we do there's an instant kinship and connection.

For us, our first adventure away from St Lucia over to the island of Bequia was absolutely perfect, It was relaxing, comfortable and we were able share our experiences with old and new boating friends.

Bequia is quiet, calm and relaxing. There are very few boat vendors and even less beach beggars. Unlike St Lucia where you're bombarded every hour to buy something from a local boat, or asked to purchase a coconut, palm weaved hat, glass turtle or bracelet, Bequia is quiet. In fact, not once did we encounter any noise pollution – no sirens, alarms or even loud ferries.

In the course of a week we witnessed only a few larger commercial boats anchor, and many of them only stayed for a few hours. Never did the town feel jam packed and all the restaurants seemed to have plenty of tables available.

Exploring the rest of the island is well worth the time and money. For a small fee the taxi drivers are happy to help you discover Bequia by road and take you for a scenic tour of the island. The east side is unspoiled – there is a beautiful coast with the sea and islands in the distance. Very few homes are noticeable and the few resort offerings look more like bed and breakfast sized accommodation that blend into the natural surroundings rather than tower above the land.

While touring around, we took our daughter and some of the other boat children to the Old Hegg Turtle Sanctuary. It was great to hear the owner's story of making amends for his past.

The sanctuary is very small but the background is interesting and of course it's always great to see turtles up close!

Another island day trip that we took was a ride out to the Firefly Plantation. Upon arrival we were kindly greeted and asked to take a seat while we waited for a guide to arrive.

We didn't book anything in advance – we simply arrived and hoped we'd get a tour. And boy, what a tour we got. There were three adults and three children and we made our way around the plantation grounds eating a variety of different fruits and nuts. It was great to enjoy some almonds, then drink some coconut water straight from the coconut, followed by some strange apples and some really sour berries!

Our guide must have shown us over 15 different trees bearing fruit.

We also tested out raw sugarcane and had a demonstration on how to extract sugar water.

After our tour, the adults enjoyed a lovely refreshing alcoholic beverage and the children threw back a Shirley Temple. We then dropped down to the lower area and all had a swim in the pool. The children had a blast and we adults got to relax after walking the grounds.

We finished our stay with a $35 USD three-course meal of black bean soup, curry of our choice (fish, chicken, beef, goat, or vegetable) and ice cream and crumble. The Firefly plantation was extremely accommodating with the children – essentially they threw a meal together for all of them.

Unfortunately, however, the final bill at the end of the day was eye watering. We thought the price was in Eastern Caribbean Dollar but it was really in USD. That aside, it was a lovely experience.

By the time our feet started getting itchy again we had spent a full week discovering Bequia.

It was the perfect retreat for a post-Atlantic crossing and the comedown after the Christmas/New Year season.

[See Appendix A, 'V12. Discovering Bequia' for a video link]

Chapter 44: Sailing to Mustique in the Grenadines

Mustique, also known as Billionaire's Island, is a private island owned by the Mustique Company which represents all its clients. The likes of Mick Jagger, Raquel Welch, and the late David Bowie have, or have had, homes in Mustique in addition to Princess Margaret.

Aside from homes for the rich and famous, the island also has a few extremely luxurious, and expensive, resorts. The Cotton Plantation on the north part of the plantation is one such 5 Star hotel.

We headed out of Admiralty Bay in Bequia, headed south and could easily spot the five-square-miles island of Mustique on the horizon.

The sail down to Mustique took a couple hours only using our front sail.

The sail was very enjoyable – Simon helmed, our daughter jumped around the cockpit being a goofball, our crewmember Eve relaxed and I read my book while intermittently staring into the deep blue sea.

The novelty of my ability to stare across the sea while watching my thoughts slow, and even stop, will never wear off (I hope!). When we haven't sailed for a while I feel withdrawal symptoms. I miss the state of bliss I feel off and on throughout the journey.

That is, of course, when I'm not seasick!

Eventually, we furled our headsail, turned our engine on and motored into the mooring field in Mustique. Unlike Bequia, which I thought was just another island, I could instantly appreciate the appeal of Mustique.

The whole island is visible from the bay and as my eyes took in the backdrop I felt them smiling with visual delight. Starting from ground level, the sea was navy blue interspersed with light turquoise patches. I caught sight of light sandy beaches, beautiful maintained palm trees and loads of trees, shrubs and grass. Peppered throughout the island I then noticed mansions owned by the rich and famous in addition to resorts – all constructed in a manor not to upset the natural look and feel of the land.

A small town was visible showcasing small homes, colorful shops, boutiques and right on the water's edge I caught sight of the famous Basil's Bar. The bar is famous for its prominent visitors. For example, Mick Jagger has been known to get up and do a few impromptu singing sessions.

What really made my eyes smile were the rolling waves hitting the reef along the coast.

Not only were the waves of the kind that surfers can surf into, but the color was extraordinary. Never have I experienced such a feel for sea foam green before!

Upon our arrival to an outer mooring buoy, a lovely harbormaster came to the boat to help Eve and me attach two ropes to the buoy. We always put a rope on the port and starboard side, run it through the mooring buoy ring and back to the same side (port rope goes down and back up to the port side).

Incidentally, a boat came in later offering the harbormaster only one line. A discussion ensued and after much commotion one of the crewmembers eventually brought out a second line. I think that mooring buoys are notorious for cutting through rope, so if one line goes you'll want to have another as a backup! It appears that the harbormaster forced the crewmembers to get another line.

Once we were tied down the harbormaster explained the rates.

He said that the cost of the mooring buoy was $200EC for one night or for three. We thought that it seemed like a cunning plan to get sailors to stay longer and perhaps spend more money on the island. The plan worked on us – not only did we stay, but spent a bit of money too (too much)!

The harbormaster then explained the layout of the town, told us to avoid the many turtles that rise up from the weed beds for air and pointed out where the reef was for snorkeling. He also explained that we weren't allowed to fish as it's a protected area.

While the harbormaster was alongside, we asked if he'd be kind enough to reserve the mooring buoy next to us for friends who would be arriving within the hour. Fortunately, he took one of our fenders and tied it onto the next mooring buoy indicating a "reserved" sign.

It didn't take long for us to clean up the boat, get our bathing suits on and jump in the sparkling clean water. Swimming with the backdrop of Mustique is an amazing experience. I couldn't help but feel that I was swimming in heaven.

Our friends eventually arrived; we let them settle in for a bit and had the children over to play with Sienna. We made arrangements to enjoy a drink at Basil's Bar ashore at 5pm.

Eager to explore the island a bit, we all loaded into our dinghies and headed for the dinghy dock. With a short commute, we ungracefully rolled ourselves off the dinghy and walked a short distance to Basil's Bar. I thought the view of the island from the boat was amazing, but the view from land was also incredible!

The children played at the beach collecting conch shells and using them to line the outer area of the entranceway. Baily's Bar is on stilts so the entrance is like a dock with areas for decoration along the edge.

We adults enjoyed one of the many cocktails on offer while discussing the day's sail.

The ambiance of the bar was magical. Considering the rich and famous people who frequented the bar I didn't feel like it was pretentious or out of my league. Often when I go to celebrity hotspots I don't feel comfortable – I feel like I have to sit up straight, use the right spoon and dab the napkin on my face rather than wiping it.

For me, Basil's Bar was just a normal Caribbean Bar offering great drinks, good food and live music.

On another evening we wanted to enjoy the Basil's Bar BBQ and live music night, however the start was too late for the children. I would have loved to have heard the Mustique Blues Band play... perhaps another time?

Early in the morning, my friend Sarah from a neighboring boat and I headed to the dinghy dock. We decided the night before to walk into town early and go for a nose around the island. We enjoyed passing all the closed shops, heading up the hills and gaining views from the top of the island. We walked around the community, saw the Police Office, peered into the Post Office and happened upon several large slow moving tortoises.

Upon finding the other side of the peninsula, we watched lovely rolling waves crash upon the shore. I couldn't help but get caught up watching the waves and listening to the ebb and flow.

By the time we made it back to the little town all the shops were open so we then had a snoop around the grocery store, bakery, boutiques and discussed connectivity options with the Digicel woman (Internet).

Both Sarah and I had run out of Internet credit when we arrived to Mustique. Although we were told that you can top-up online it didn't work. After five visits to the Digicel woman and finding the location of an obscurely hidden "self care" page we finally got a connection again.

Not having Internet on the boat has been the bane of my existence since we started sailing around the world! It's by far the most frustrating part of my life.

We enjoyed a coffee at Basil's Bar and then went to the dinghy dock to grab the tender and head home. I noticed that the tenders were really being tossed around – if I had a choice I wouldn't want to leave a tender for fear that damage could be done.

For dinner we all went up the hill to The View restaurant. There were three options –yellow fin tuna, pork chops or chicken. It was all good! The children enjoyed chicken wings and fries.

And the view was just as great as the food!

Looking out over our boats below, we enjoyed good home-cooked Caribbean food, excellent conversation and great memories.

The View restaurant offers inexpensive authentic cuisine in a very relaxed atmosphere. The tables are plastic, the TV will be on in the background and locals come and go. These are the type of places I like best.

The next day Simon and I went to shore with crewmember Eve and enjoyed a coffee while getting Wi-Fi at Basil's Bar. Upon our return the dinghy we discovered one whole side was deflated.

My earlier premonition about the dinghy dock being dangerous was right. There was a huge hole in the right-hand side of the dinghy and the inflatable part ripped apart from the hard boat element.

Simon and I managed to motor the dinghy back to the boat, lift the outboard off the back dinghy and place it on the sailboat. We then used a halyard to lift the dinghy out of the water and place it on the foredeck for inspection. We did all this before the darn thing sank!

Having a special hoist on the aft deck is so valuable. We simply hooked the clip on from the hoist and Simon and I were able to get the very heavy outboard onto safe grounds. If you ever consider sailing as just a couple, make sure you can lift your outboard – if not, have a system in place to get it off the dinghy when disaster strikes.

We decided to head back up to Bequia to seek out a repair kit from the chandlery and get out of the increasing swell. Luckily for us our friends had repair patches and we had dinghy cement. After a massive patch job and 24 hours I'm happy to announce that our dinghy survived.

So what did I think of Mustique overall? I thought it was okay.

Yes, it was beautiful. Yes, it was awesome to get a glimpse into the surroundings of the rich and famous. Yes, the food was good…however...

It just didn't have an overall nice feel to it.

I'm being all girly now and talking about my feelings here…I just didn't feel all that welcomed. No one was rude but no one seemed happy to see us either. I felt as if we (meaning boaties) were tolerated.

I need all the pieces to fit together to have an overall good time. I thoroughly enjoyed Mustique but I don't feel like I ever want to visit the island again.

Is sailing to Mustique a must-do? I don't think so. I'd give Mustique a miss.

[See Appendix A, 'V13. Mustique' for a link to a video]

Chapter 45: Tobago Cays – A visit to an uninhabited tropical paradise

After Bequia, Simon and I decided to head south to St. Vincent and the Grenadines (group of islands) with the idea that we'd sail around the south are for a while before turning north and eventually making it to the States to escape the hurricane season.

Prior to visiting St. Vincent and the Grenadines I didn't know they existed, and I was completely blown away by its unspoiled beauty. The first island we went to was Tobago Cays.

Tobago Cays is an area containing several reefs – there's one huge reef contained within another reef, both horseshoe in shape. Within the reefs are small uninhabited islands filled with palm trees, silky white sand, iguanas, tropical birds and of course, loads of palm trees.

There are two main anchorages in Tobago Cays. The first is on the north side of the reef. There are mooring buoys and places to anchor between two tiny islands. It's noted in the pilot book that this spot is the most picturesque, and I'd have to agree.

When we entered the narrow canal between the islands we were met with turquoise water, palm trees hanging over the white sandy beach and a wonderful mix of navy blues and lush greens with a soft blue sky backdrop. Peppered throughout the waterway were catamarans and monohauls flying mostly, to my surprise, French flags.

After scoping out the area and having a bit of assistance from the locals in fishing boats, we dropped our anchor at the very back end of the canal. One of our charts noted a 2 meter depth further up and another chart said 9 meters. Our keel is 2.4 meters so we didn't want to take any chances!

Little did we know that after dropping our anchor we wouldn't lift it for five days!

Considering there's nothing on the island – no shops, no services, no nothing I didn't think we'd want to stay in one area that long. Of course I love solitude, nature and unspoiled beauty, however I also love trying out local cuisine in the restaurants, nosing through boutiques, and being among people!

That being noted, we were not alone nor did we have to forego local cuisine.

As luck would have it, one of the boats we crossed the Atlantic with us (there were 250+ that crossed with ARC and ARC+), anchored next to us. Our friends had two children so our daughter had her play dates arranged. And then over the course of our five day stay another two "kid boats" came in and anchored – all boats that crossed the Atlantic and all containing children.

Tobago Cays became a playground for the children and adults alike! During the day we'd all take our dinghy's to the nearby beach or go for an adventure on one of the other islands. An area is cordoned off to swim with the turtles, however we had turtles all around the boat popping up every few minutes. None of them minded us snorkeling with and around them.

Along the beaches we found living coral (not something to be found off every island anymore), majestic sized stingrays, moray eels, enormous two-foot puffer fish, loads of colorful small fish and a bazillion conchs and conch shells!

To our delight, our daughter happily used a mask and snorkeled, enjoying all the fish without complication or fright! Until recently she wouldn't put her head in the water or use a mask.

Perhaps the older children that she's playing with have caused her to up her game!

Most days we all met on the beach for a while, with the children running around the island looking for shells, playing games and having an enormous amount of fun. The adults would find shade, set up the towels and sit around swapping stories about what islands are good, where to get the best lobster, future cruising plans, incidents concerning pirates below Grenada (a couple of boats were recently held at gunpoint while the boats were completely ransacked and anything of value was taken), difficulties getting parts flown in and so forth.

Although there are no bars or restaurants on the Tobago Cays, locals from Union Island offer a beach BBQ. There are picnic tables and some covered areas with huge drum grills.

For $120 EC (about $45 USD) we got a massive grilled lobster, baked potatoes seasoned with local herbs, a lovely rice mixture, tossed salad and cake for dessert.

The husband and wife team who provided us with dinner, Simon and Aquilla, even created a meal for the children. They did some lovely grilled chicken and the kids ate every bit.

During the lead up to eating the BBQ, the families all watched the locals cut and clean the lobsters. All the inedible parts were thrown in the sea for the puffer fish and stingrays to swim buy and pick up. We had a live aquatic show at our feet.

The whole evening was bliss – the sunset, laughing children, amazing wildlife, great food. Being able to share it with friends made it an incredible experience.

Over the course of five days it was interesting to watch the ebb and flow of boats in the channel. When we first arrived there were a handful of boats. We wondered why we were so lucky to find space, as the pilot book indicated that the area, being the most picturesque, gets crowed quickly. All but one of the days we spent in remote quietness.

And then two catamaran flotillas came in and our peace was shattered.

It wasn't so bad that the channel filled up with every mooring buoy being used and seeing catamarans anchor on top of each other. We were all far enough away from the buoys not to be too close. What was annoying was the constant and incessant use of the VHF radio on channel 69, the cruiser's choice of channels.

No one minds people talking on the channel to get berthing instructions, or discuss where to be at a certain time, but from around 2pm until 8pm these two flotillas were discussing the beauty of the area, the lobster dinner arrangements, what happens if it rains, the location of latecomers, and random inside jokes.

I felt as if the flotillas high jacked channel 69.

But if that was the worst of my issues while anchoring in Tobago Cays it was still a great sailing destination.

Incidentally, it's not just sailboats that anchor in Tobago Cays.

We were fortunate enough to have the late Steve Jobs's motor yacht drop hook off our port side.

Heck, it's not a boat…it's more like a floating palace. The boat is 79 meters long and cost over $100 million to build. Personally I didn't find it attractive.

There were several other smaller motor yachts that also anchored in the area. We were also visited by one of those cruise ships that has sails. The cruise ship only stayed for a few hours and there must have been fewer than 20 people who actually ferried from the ship to the small island.

What I found very interesting was that most boats in the area were French.

Another local explained that many French people charter a boat out of Martinique and sail down to the Tobago Cays. I couldn't believe the lack of Americans in the area – did they not know about this amazing gem? It made me wonder if certain nationalities have particular hot spots that they frequent more so than others.

While anchoring in January we found that most days were sunny with a constant breeze – sometimes gusts would flow through the channel. It rained every night, often with a serious downpour. Only one day did we have long-term rain that lasted from around 3pm to 5pm - usually the showers or squalls came and left quickly.

One day I was able to do laundry but I had to put three clothes pegs on every item I hung out.

The wind can really get up in the Grenadines! The worst feeling is when you look out at your laundry line and there's a gap between two items. In Bequia we noticed something colorful on the seabed and discovered it was one of our towels!

Overall, I thought Tobago Cays was amazing. It's downright beautiful. The sea and land life is great. The local people are kind and helpful. There's really very little negative that I can say about the place. When pressed, my only issues were the, at times, very strong winds and the arrival of flotillas.

My rating, however, is biased. What truly made Tobago Cays an absolutely incredible experience was having so many sailing friends around us. In total, there were four couples, one lovely single guy, two crew (both 20-year-old Kiwis!), and six children. Aged between 3 years to 49 years old with nationalities from Canada, America, Ireland, New Zealand and Britain, four boats all converged in Tobago Cays to make memories.

It doesn't happen all the time, but when sailing communities meet up with each other it's magical.

[See Appendix A, 'V14. Tobago Cays' for a video link]

Chapter 46: Don't fall prey to Marina Creep!

Marina creep is a term I've created to describe the knotting dark feeling that a cruiser gets after day three of being in a marina. By the third morning, a marina moored sailor wakes with a heavy heart and a sense of dread that seems to appear from left field. Let me back up so to explain marina creep more clearly.

Many full time sailing cruisers avoid marinas as much as possible.

Marinas are often busy, noisy, costly and lacking in wind (to keep the mosquitos away). Furthermore, if you've seen one marina, you've seen them all. The 360 degree view is almost always a bunch of sailboat masts. If you're lucky, you might get a volcano or green hillside in the background. If you're not, the backdrop could include a highway, noisy city or industrial port. For the most part, however, marinas are much the same anywhere in the world.

Unlike marinas, cruisers enjoy staying in a no cost mooring that is a quietly protected anchorage away from close neighbors, the sounds of civilization, and those pesky biting mosquitos or egg-laying cockroaches.

Some cruisers anchor for a couple days and others anchor for a couple weeks in one bay. After an indeterminate stay, cruisers lift their anchor and head to the next no cost, safe, picturesque and hopefully bug-free mooring.

Moving from one lovely mooring to the next is the basic agenda for cruisers.

From time to time a swell will come in and a new calmer anchorage is sought out. Or a bay that should be perfect is complicated by a new hotel going up with noisy jackhammers breaking the peace. And of course, there's usually an issue with an Italian or French boat that anchors too closely, causing the afflicted party a conflict that may end in moving. (No offense to Italian or French people – I love them both…they just have this thing about anchoring five feet away from the only boat in a bay!)

On occasions, however, a full-time sailor will have to enter a marina.

Some cruisers need to fill up their potable water tanks, others have to make a repair and some enter a marina to pick up guests.

Regardless of the main reason, there are always marina jobs that are prioritized to make the most of the marina environment. When we stay at a marina, our list usually starts small but then it grows – we will clean the topside of the boat and polish the chrome, send someone up the mast to check the rigging, fill up with water, go shopping to fill the freezer with meat and frozen veggies and on and on.

At first, there's a bit of novelty about being in a marina. Getting on and off the boat takes seconds at a marina whereas at an anchorage it can take up to a half hour to get the dinghy down, motor to a dinghy dock and finally reach land. It really sucks when you return to the boat by dinghy and realize that you forgot the milk!

Knowing that it's easier to get loads of food, often delivered to the back of the boat, makes a marina environment appealing too! Trying to get more than one backpack and two shopping sacks for each person while anchored is impossible. Furthermore, the task of doing a big shop while the boat is out in a bay takes hours, and it's just not fun.

And when moored in a marina, there are usually services that you often won't find in a secluded picturesque bay…I'm talking about shops that sell nail polish, printer cartridges and proper café lattes!

So there is this initial excitement that happens when having the ability to instantly get from boat to land in seconds.

But then something happens that causes a downward spiral towards marina creep.

The list of things to do gets compiled and although it starts out small the list grows.

So, on day one you take seconds to jump off the boat, go for a walk getting a frozen chocolate coffee with whipped cream and dark chocolate drizzle while window shopping for a replacement bikini or Crocks for the little one. You soak in the sights and sounds of civilization and then you start feeling a heavy presence pressing down on you.

You then realize that the stay in the marina needs to be as short as possible so to avoid spending money (knowing that anchoring is free). You rush back to the boat to start a few tasks to alleviate the unproductive morning.

A crewmember who was sent out to get something repaired or buy a replacement part inevitably then returns saying that it's going to take days longer than expected. A discussion ensues about whether to stay in the marina to wait or go outside and anchor. Usually, someone will pipe up and say, "well, if we stay in the marina we can then get XYZ done…"

Then, the list grows even more to compensate for the cost of the marina as the stay gets extended.

If we need to wait three days to get our furling mechanism fixed that means we have time to open out the spinnaker, wash it, dry it and pack it away AND we can even Sicaflex some of the teak deck! AND…I can silicon the bathroom seams as they're starting to disintegrate AND we can do the engine service, AND, AND, AND…

Ultimately, the novelty of being in touch with civilization turns sour and becomes a race to get mounting jobs done.

I've come to the realization that there are two modes to a cruisers life.

Mode one is the typical day-to-day experience of living in various anchorages and enjoying the sails between moorings. The views are spectacular, the swimming is great, there's wildlife all around and life is rather simple. Jobs still need to be done – we do laundry, cook meals, clean the boat (vacuum, dust, bathrooms) and complete homeschooling every day, but the list of jobs isn't overwhelming. In fact, it's rather normal. An evening drink signifies a day well spent. Mode two is life at the marina. The experience starts off on a high and ends in almost deep depression. Expectations of what can get done are never met. The list of projects increases by the day and everyone on board looks forward to the evening drink because it signifies that the hellish work schedule can stop.

For two years I've been living on *Britican*, and it's taken me over 30 short-stay marinas to finally determine what causes my day-three depression syndrome. I simply thought there was something wrong with me. I couldn't figure out why I enjoyed marinas but ultimately felt this strong desire to get out of them. At least I now know what's going on!

So let me expand on my initial introduction to Marina Creep so that you don't have the unfortunate task of:

1. Having it happen to you and not understanding it or having a label for it (We can call it MC for short! We can then see people in marinas and quietly mumble to ourselves that a passerby has MC) OR

2. Starting your cruising life and failing to prepare for it.

Knowing what Marina Creep is can help you prepare for it.

The best thing to do is to realize that if you're entering a marina for a repair it will take at least three times the amount of time that you're told. If you're waiting for a part to arrive, that could take around two weeks to a month more than you expect. In fact, it's much quicker and less expensive to get a family member or friend to buy the item you need and fly with it out to the boat.

As far as the overwhelming list that goes up by the day...you can perhaps force mornings or evenings off to do something fun. Perhaps go out sightseeing, for an excursion or find a movie theater with English movies (or subtitles). We often fall into the trap where we work, work, work and we lose sight as to the reason why we left the rat race in the first place.

Marina Creep is a real thing, so take this information seriously. Having one crewmember afflicted is a problem, but when the whole boat gets the creep it can be disastrous.

So the moral of my story? Keep Marina Creep at bay by staying in the Bay!

And a special note for people who work on a boat and/or kid boats...

Marina Creep is bad enough when you're a couple or a boatful of adults that are simply sailing around. Adding the element of work and/or homeschooling and general entertainment for children can cause arguments, disputes and in extreme cases divorce.

Normally there are other children around for Sienna to play with.

But when there aren't any she becomes very needy. Sienna doesn't like to play alone – she's ultra social. As long as she's with someone else she'll do or play anything. And when there's no one around, it needs to be one of us adults. Thankfully, Sienna will sit and watch a movie or play on the iPad for a little while, but for the most part she's a social bee.

Simon wants to service the engine (rightly so) and I want to upload a video because there's Wi-Fi. And Sienna wants to play Barbie's. All the while we know that time is in short supply. Marina Creep plus extra activities is hell.

Enough said.

[See Appendix A, 'V15. What to do during marina visits' for the link to the video]

Chapter 47: Can you develop a cruising social network?

After two years of sailing around the Mediterranean with our six-month stay in Marina di Ragusa, Sicily we made loads of friends. Between connections made through my website, Twitter, Facebook and simply making new friends at a variety of anchorages AND meeting over 150 people (19 different nationalities) at Marina di Ragusa, we created quite a lovely social network.

During the last year of our travels there wasn't an anchorage that we entered without some sort of reunion or putting a name to a face interaction.

I make it sound like our cruising social network is in the thousands, but that's not the case. The sailing community is a small community that's spread all over the world. I'm not sure how it happens, but you almost always meet someone you know. When the Atlantic crossing came, I worried that we'd be sailing around the Caribbean feeling a bit lost and perhaps miss our somewhat hectic social life. You might think I'm kidding when I say that an opportunity for evening drinks with other boaters is almost always in the cards. I'm not.

I have never had a busier social life than when living on a boat.

So…we've been in the Caribbean for three months now, have travelled to seven islands/five countries, and not one day has passed where we didn't have a friend or several friends anchored next to us.

To have friends next to you makes the anchorage feel homey. I feel connected even though I'm in a completely foreign place.

A very long time ago, when I worked on the island of Cyprus, I often finished my day with a glass of wine while watching the sunset. Most of the time I was alone. I realized that being in beautiful places or experiencing wonderful things is okay when you're alone, but it's much better when it's shared. During my time in Cyprus I felt that I needed my husband to be with me. Knowing what I now know, I'm discovering that the more the merrier.

Crossing the Atlantic with the ARC definitely helped us to create a new social network prior to arrival in the Caribbean. For six weeks we stayed in the Las Palmas Marina with 250+ other boats preparing for the crossing.

We made some great friends, put names to faces (people that have contacted me through my website) and connected with old friends during our ARC preparations.

Once we arrived in St Lucia, we already had at least ten good boat friends and an association with loads more. While sailing around St. Vincent and the Grenadines, we met up with three different kid boats on and off through our month+ long travels.

The moral of my story?

The sailing community is small. If you make friends wherever you go, you'll surely meet up with many of them later on. To increase our ability to have an ever-expanding cruising social network it helps to:

- Have an extended stay in a marina, perhaps while wintering in the Mediterranean or finding a hurricane hole in the Caribbean. Extended stays within marina communities allow for meaningful friendships to form.

- Join a group of people making a long passage. I can't recommend the Atlantic Rally for Cruisers more highly. Not only were we berthed next to all the kid boats in Las Palmas, but ARC set up social activities almost every night for weeks prior to the crossing. We made some good solid friends in Gran Canarias and I'm very grateful for the opportunities we had.

- Meet cruisers online. There are great cruisers groups on Facebook, there are various forums across the Net and there certainly isn't any harm in reaching out to bloggers like me to start a chat. There are a few sailing bloggers who I've been corresponding with for years. Some of them I've met in person and others I know that I'll eventually meet.

- Help other sailors. The awesome thing about the sailing community is that there's always someone who might need a bit of help – perhaps a boater gets their anchor caught or is having issues pulling up a mooring line. So, be on the lookout for situations where you can help someone. When sending a bit of kindness in any direction it's going to come back to you. By default most sailors are eager to help other sailors. Not only does that create a "pay-it-forward" situation but it helps to make new friends.

Many cruisers often comment that if the world knew how amazing the cruising community was, everyone would sell everything, buy a boat and join us.

Chapter 48: Carnival in Martinique

After a week stay in Rodney Bay Marina, St Lucia, we shook off our Marina Creep and headed north for the French island of Martinique.

We anchored in the large bay outside the town of Sainte Anne.

Upon our approach the sight of the bay was littered with sailboat masts. I wondered if there'd be any space! As we approached the bay, the masts spread out and I realized the bay was massive. There was plenty of room.

Once our anchor was down I had a huge mess to clean up!

The three-hour voyage from St. Lucia to Martinique was rough. The swell was the biggest I'd experienced in the Caribbean – heck, I don't think I saw a swell so large in the Mediterranean either. We were averaging around 8 knots and the boat was going way up, way down and side-to-side.

Much to my dismay we heard a massive crash coming from the Captains Cabin. I was hoping that some of the water bottles fell over, but instead it was Sienna's massive arts and crafts box, her homeschooling textbooks, our printer and Simon's project box.

What a mess!

Aptly named the island of flowers, Martinique is full of colors. The flowers, shrubs and trees burst with pinks, oranges, yellows and reds. And it's not just the landscape that is full of life, the people are colorful too!

Fortunately, we hit Martinique during Carnival week.

Every day for four days many of the 400,000+ inhabitants congregate at the capital and smaller towns to parade down the street in costumes. Bands play, dancers dance and massive speakers are tied onto trucks providing heart-pounding beats.

Our plan was to take our dinghy to the village of Sainte Anne, grab a taxi to the capital Fort de France and witness the main Carnival celebration. To our delight we had sailing vessel *Delphinus* with us. Brits Paul, Jane and 13-year-old Lily (three-year veteran cruisers) shared a taxi with Simon, Sienna, crewmember Eve and me.

Before leaving for the town, Eve did makeup and hair for Lily and Sienna. Sienna dressed up as a princess pirate sporting a princess dress, dragon tattoo, hook for a hand and a pirate hat. Lily and Eve went down the subtler makeup and tattoo route.

The themed colors for the Carnival parade were red and black.

Every day the Carnival colors change. We later learned that the following day's colors were black and white. Once you know the colors you can dress any way that you want – you can be scary, dress as the opposite sex or create a costume that's sexy or simple. There are no rules to the costumes!

Unfortunately I don't own any red clothes! Simon grabbed his dark red Sailing Britican t-shirt and Eve wore black. As for the rest of us, we just went as we were.

Getting caught up in the excitement of the day we all piled into the taxi forgetting to ask what the fare would amount to. After twenty minutes of driving and noticing that the fare was over $100 with at least twenty more miles to go, we had an emergency meeting.

Discovering that a round trip taxi ride to Fort de France would cost around $300, we changed plans

So a big tip about Martinique – taxis are not cheap!

Buses are a fraction of the price; however they don't run during Carnival nor are any shops open. And very few restaurants are open.

Fortunate for us, Paul spoke a bit of French. He explained to the taxi driver that we couldn't afford the cost of the trip. Instead, he asked, can we get a little scenic ride back to Sainte Anne's.

The taxi driver must have felt sorry for us.

I caught him looking in his rear-view mirror looking at all our faces. The whole reason we sailed from St. Lucia to Martinique was to see the Carnival!

As luck would have it, the driver indicated that he'd forget the fare clock and take us on a tour around the Pointe du Diamant and deliver us home for $200. We were going to pay around $200 just turning around so we jumped at the offer for a road tour of the point.

Unbelievably, the taxi driver spent the next two hours taking us to points of interest allowing us to get out, take pictures and look around. As we made our way around the point, we stopped at some villages, three scenic picture points and the site of a famous shipwreck.

Along the coast above the shipwreck a memorial of statues was created to remember the people, mainly slaves, who lost their lives when the ship crashed upon rocks.

I couldn't help but feel moved by the statues.

And when I noticed a picture of how the slaves were transported I physically felt sick. The slaves were apparently shipped in coffin type arrangements, forced to remain in a horizontal position chained to their "bed". They were given a tiny bit of food but forced to defecate right where they were. Many died on the journey.

When I expressed my deep feelings of anger and sadness, Sienna asked what slaves were. I was so upset I failed to tell her much of anything. I made a note to myself to teach her about slavery but not yet…

Moving forward from the wreck site, we stopped at a picture-postcard village that had the most gorgeous beach ever. There were palm trees, white and black sparkling smooth sand and the Diamond Island land mass in the background. Our new focal point lightened my dark feelings, and as if my eyes couldn't smile any more, they did.

We went from one scenic view to the next, passing colorful flowers, trees, homes and mountainside. At the viewpoint closest to Diamond Island, we got out of the taxi, went to a viewing station and took more pictures to remind us of the beauty of the island.

Little did we know that we'd be sailing past Diamond Island the very next day.

Curving around the coast heading north, our lovely driver stopped at a village to allow us to get some cold drinks and churros. Never did I expect to get churros on a French island! I thought they were a Mexican treat! Either way, we gobbled them down with Martinique-made chocolate sauce and Orangina (carbonated orange drink).

The surge of sugar was much needed due to the high heat of the day – especially considering all the sugar cane plantations we drove past! Sugar was certainly on our minds.

Once we started to head back our taxi driver received a few phone calls. Paul wasn't certain of the conversation but we think the driver needed to either get somewhere to pick people up or, perhaps, he was late for dinner.

Regardless, our driver proceeded to tailgate every car that was getting in his way. On a couple occasions I thought we were going to get in an accident and once I let out a little scream.

By the time our driver dropped us off the amount on the fare monitor was almost up to $400. Thankfully the cost was capped to the $200.

We paid our fare, thanked the driver and walked into Sainte Anne's to enjoy the localized Carnival procession. It was fantastic. A group of people dressed in red and black walked through the town dancing, playing drums leading several local kids and adults – all dressed for the occasion.

Interestingly there were quite a few men dressed in woman's clothes.

The men seemed to really enjoy wearing dresses, heels, wigs and accessories. They certainly impressed the crowd of onlookers. The parade went around the town a couple times and then a large truck with around 12 speakers joined in blasting super loud music. As it passed I could hear my heart pound to the beat.

Eventually the parade ended and the participants and audience dispersed into one of the many restaurants, cafés or bars. We chose a lovely restaurant on the beach and enjoyed some drinks. Another cruising couple whom we met earlier in the week at St. Lucia walked by, so they pulled up a chair and enjoyed some conversation with us. Before heading back to the boat we all had a meal.

To my surprise none of the restaurants offered typical French food.

I had chicken curry, a few people had steak and fries and Jane, a vegetarian, enjoyed a plate of wonderfully presented vegetables. Where was the brie cheese, baguettes, pate and delightfully French dishes cooked in butter?

The following day we sailed along the coast that the taxi driver so kindly took us around. From the sea we could pick out the statues dedicated to those who lost their lives in the shipwreck. We could also spot the various lookout points. And we had an excellent view of Diamond Island.

During our stay in Martinique we anchored in Sainte Anne's, Anse A L'Ane, Grande Anse D'Arlet and the capital city Fort-de-France. All areas had great holding, little noise and an unnoticeable swell.

The areas outside the capital did have a few restaurants open so we attempted a meal. In Grande Anse D'Arlet, we went to the restaurant recommended in the Pilot Book. Once at the restaurant we were told in French and quite flippantly to go to the next bay. Despite a sign hanging on the restaurant saying they'd handle Customs we were told to go elsewhere.

Before heading to Petite Anse D'Arlet we decided to stay for a drink and get a small bite to eat. The food looked amazing. After 20 minutes of trying to flag over the two waitresses/owners and failing to get noticed, we finally decided that we weren't going to be served. If only I could speak French I would have had a few choice words to say!

Things like that really drive me mad. We spent months in the Caribbean and I couldn't say a bad word about any of the service. We're on a French island for a week and I can count several occasions where we were totally dismissed or waved off.

That being said, we also met some wonderful people – mostly in Fort-de-France. And look at what our taxi driver did! I shouldn't let a few bad apples spoil the bunch now, should I?

All in all it's my issue for not being able to speak French.

So…my overall rating for Martinique is that it was good but not great.

The anchorages had good holding. The views were beautiful. The country seemed to be very, very clean. The roads were fantastic aside from the construction in Fort-de-France, and there were quite sophisticated marine services available.

I suppose it's the service level that let me down. Compared to St Lucia, the islands in the Grenadines and Barbados, many of the people in Martinique seemed to have a dislike for tourists…or perhaps English tourists?! I don't know. I just felt like it was so different coming from the other islands where people bent over backwards to help you.

[See Appendix A, 'V16. Martinique' for a video link]

Chapter 49: Dominica – should you sail past or visit?

Previous to sailing in the Caribbean my knowledge of Dominica was non-existent. Never before had I heard of a friend or relative visiting the country. In fact, when I mentioned Dominica to my mom on Facebook Messenger she responded, "It's funny. I travelled that area and I can't remember Dominica. Was it renamed or something?"

The first thing that sailors do when they meet up is to swap stories about where they've been, what they've liked/disliked, and add any life and death stories (living through a storm, dealing with a Man Over Board or avoiding a sinking situation) and sometimes big fish events make the exchange.

During this particular encounter friends we met in Gran Canaria and then ran into in Bequia, couldn't say enough about Dominica. They explained that Portsmouth was the place to go – that there were mooring buoys, a large area to anchor in, boat men to help out and organize excursions and an island full of raw beauty.

Our friend's spoke with such enthusiasm I decided Dominica was a must-see destination.

Later that evening Simon told me that Dominica had a bad reputation and that most sailors pass it by. Apparently, in the past, the crime rate was high. Many sailors reported thefts of dinghies and break-ins on boats.

What I've discovered for myself is that many islands get a bad reputation. Something bad happens, it hits the news and sailors decide to skip the island or country. Interestingly, however, the same sailors, and I'll include myself in this, often come from a city or live near a city where bad things happen all the time. Heck, in my home city we have over 300 murders a year. Did that stop me from leaving my house? Of course not...it's just the way it is. I know enough to avoid being in certain areas at certain times. I make sure to lock my house and car. If I see a situation that doesn't look good, I move.

Bad stuff happens all over the world, it makes the news and it highjacks our focus that would otherwise be on the 99.9 percent of the good stuff in the world.

If I passed Dominica by, knowing what I now know, I would have missed out on seeing one of the most incredible countries that I've ever experienced. In fact, if someone forced me to pick a place to live right now I'd make it Dominica.

When we arrived in Dominica our first anchorage was in Roseau Bay.

While motoring into the area a boat came to greet us asking if we'd like a mooring buoy. The kind man on the boat labeled *SeaCat* explained that it's $15 USD/night on a mooring buoy but we were welcome to anchor for free. Later we discovered that SeaCat was the name of the boat *and* the name of our tour guide.

We decided to take a buoy.

After explaining that friends were coming behind us (*Delphinus*), the lovely man found two mooring buoys right next to each other. We later learned that *SeaCat* owned the mooring buoys and offered a variety of services.

On some islands, like St. Lucia, you pay the boat boys to help you tie up to a mooring buoy (optional) and then you pay a park official or mooring buoy attendant for the mooring. In Dominica you pay the guys on the boats for the mooring and they help you to fix the warps (ropes) as the whole part of the deal.

Once we were settled in, we took our dinghy to shore and found the Anchorage Hotel to get on stable land, enjoy some drinks, watch the sunset and find Wi-Fi. *Delphinus* joined us for a drink and a discussion ensued about what to do first.

Paul, from *Delphinus*, wanted to do the boiling lake hike.

After climbing the difficult Piton in St. Lucia I was a little wary of saying "yes" to hikes. The man who went by the name of SeaCat arrived at the Anchorage Hotel explaining the details. The hike took an average of three hours to get to the boiling lake and three hours back. A short car drive was required to get to the trail. The cost was $50 USD and included the drive, food and our guide. There was also a very small governmental fee to enter the park.

Jayne from *Delphinus* offered to take her daughter, Lily, and Sienna to Champagne Beach, allowing my husband and me the freedom to do the hike. Jayne and the kids would also be able to meet up with sailing vessel, Honu Kai, a kid boat with three other kids between the ages of 10 and 14.

Having the freedom to do a long hike with my husband doesn't come often.

With Jayne's offer to take our daughter for the day our decision to see a boiling lake was made quickly. Eve also decided to come for the walk.

If I had known what I was getting myself into I'm not sure I would have done the trek. It's a hard hike. A very hard hike.

Unlike the volcanic core I climbed in St. Lucia, the Piton, where we hiked for hours up and then hours back down, the hike to the boiling lake was full of ups and downs.

When I thought I couldn't climb up any more, there was a plateau or a downward section. When I thought I couldn't climb down anymore, there was an upward path. After what felt like hours we eventually asked, "Are we near the lake yet?"

SeaCat responded with, "We're not even half way yet!"

Thankfully, SeaCat broke the hike up with periodic stops to look at a variety of tropical rainforest flora and fauna. We learned about ferns, trees, roots, birds, herbs, rivers and loads about Dominica as a whole. SeaCat provided an amazing amount of interesting and fascinating information about the country.

On our way to the boiling lake the path was easy to follow. A series of old fern trunks led the way. There are also red markers guiding the way.

Some people choose to do the hike without a guide. For me, having SeaCat show us the way allowed me to take in the tropical surroundings without having to question my direction. Furthermore, the education we gained was priceless. How many people get to learn about a tropical rainforest from a local while walking through one?

Before entering the Valley of Desolation, a barren area where the greenery has been killed by the sulphur steam, we stopped for a drink break. SeaCat said it was rum punch but thankfully it was grapefruit juice. If we had rum I think we would have never made it home.

We then descended along a stream/waterfall into the Valley of Desolation.

What an amazing site. There were holes in the earth were steam was pouring out and the wind was sending it up along the mountainside. There were puddles of water and mud all over the place boiling at lesser or higher degrees. Some were boiling so much that they were spitting water high into the sky.

SeaCat found mud – the kind that's used for mud masks – so Eve took advantage of the situation. When I saw her, her face was covered in a gray-greenish hue.

SeaCat then pulled a bag of boiled eggs out of one of the boiling pools of water.

The eggs were black due to the various minerals and nutrients in the water. We all cracked our eggs and enjoyed the solid whites and milky yellow centers. It was one of the best boiled eggs I've ever had!

Walking along the Valley was tricky. One wrong move and we'd have a boiled foot. Eve and I kept close together and slowly progressed back to a more tropical path.

The rain progressively got heavier and heavier. Thankfully I had a visor on my raincoat that kept most of the rain off my glasses.

Eventually, we arrived at the boiling lake.

That's when all the hiking struggles paid off. I looked down into this massive crater and saw the lake boiling. A boiling lake! Yes! We made it!

I stared at the bubbles in awe trying to visualize how much lower the lava must be to have such an effect on the lake. Was the lava or volcanic matter close below or was it miles deep? How was the lake able to boil like that?

The smell of sulphur was strong and when the wind blew in our direction we were covered in a white fog of fart smell. It was brilliant!

Then it dawned on me that we had to now walk back. I wondered if I'd make it. Already my feet and ankles were tired.

As I did on the Piton, I said to myself, "Kim, just take one step at time and don't think any further."

The rain got heavier and heavier. Our path turned into a river itself. Interestingly the fresh cool water felt great on my feet. I actually started to look for deeper pools to refresh my weary toes.

With an hour left we came across an elderly gentleman in a red poncho with one flip-flop.

The man was lost. The fire department called SeaCat while we were descending saying to keep an eye out for the lost man. Apparently he was supposed to go to a waterfall, but missed the falls and carried on walking towards the boiling lake. The man walked an hour further than he should have!

While crossing a river, he lost one of his shoes.

Can you believe that when SeaCat found the man in the red poncho SeaCat immediately took his shoes off, gave them to the lost man and said, "You're found now!"

SeaCat called the Fire Department letting them know that the search was off.

We finally made it to the beginning of the trail. There were picnic tables set up for us to enjoy lunch. The plan was to eat by the boiling lake but the rain was too heavy. We opted to eat at the end of the hike.

SeaCat prepared a lovely fresh salad, salt fish and fried plantains. We all shared some baguettes and savored every bite.

The hike was excellent. The boiling lake was incredible. And our guide was fantastic. Our first experience in Dominica was brilliant!

From there on things got better and better.

Simon and I spent some time walking around Roseau, the capital city. Our main objective was to get an all steel lock, pick up some groceries, and sort out our Digicel SIM card. We had a St. Lucia SIM and had to get it changed to roaming so it would work in Dominica.

Periodically we'd ask some locals where Digicel was or a hardware shop. Every time we asked they'd all get together and discuss the best directions to give us and then one would be a spokesperson.

While walking into the city we found a hardware shop. There was a cute little girl around the age of eight watching over the shop for her mom. She got a bit nervous when we asked how much something was and tried to pay for it. Just as her nerves seemed to hit a high her mom walked back into the shop and she yelled out, "Thank God you're back!"

As we paid for our item we enquired where the Digicel Shop was. The woman looked at us and said "I can do something better than tell you where the shop is…Mr. Digicel is right behind you."

A lovely man by the name of Yoni took a look at our SIM, put it in his phone, tried to get roaming set up and then helped us get to the shop. He was so kind. And when we went to the shop, the woman who helped us call customer care was super lovely too.

From Digicel we wandered around looking at all the unique tiny stores and shacks. I came to the conclusion that everyone in Roseau owned some sort of business, whether it was a tiny bakery, a shed offering barber services, a street stall provider or a taxi driver.

The other thing that really stood out to me was the lack of tourist shops. There were a few located near the cruise ship dock, but otherwise the city looked like a working city. It wasn't set up to cater to tourists.

Finally, I thought, a real city!

The longer I stayed in Dominica the more I fell in love with its authenticity. It is a working country dependent mostly on agriculture.

The coastline is filled with wild palm trees, corrugated shacks, rundown hotels, abandoned homes and the remains of old jetties. The rivers are still a place where the community comes to wash their dishes, clothes, vegetables and to talk about life. The restaurants all look like they've lived through huge storms and perhaps survived several hurricanes.

There are no big hotels, no fancy bars, and no modern architecture. There are no areas for watersports or beach guys trying to sell palm weaved hats.

What there is, however, are local guides who will show visitors, like me, the beauty of their country. They will pick you up at your boat, arrange excursions and spend the whole day educating, guiding and demonstrating the beauty of Dominica.

We left Roseau Bay and headed up to Prince Rupert Bay outside Portsmouth, Dominica's old capital city.

The wind wasn't blowing so we set off with our motor. To our absolute delight we came across two sperm whales.

I totally freaked out. For two years I've been scanning the horizon for whales. And for two years I've seen nothing. Our trip along the Roseau coast finally made a dream come true.

After seeing the two whales we motored closer to them.

A whale sightseeing boat was also looking at the whales. There were people ready to jump into the water with the whales with snorkel, mask and flippers.

The sightseeing boat pointed out another whale to us so that we'd avoid messing up their experience. We drove over to the other whale and before I knew it, Simon jumped into the water and swam with the whale. Sim looked the whale right in the eye! If it wasn't for the whale watching boat offloading people into the water I'm sure Simon wouldn't have had the confidence to get in the water with a whale!

Needless to say I was on a high for the whole afternoon.

We eventually motored into Prince Rupert Bay and anchored next to s/v (sailing vessel) *Delphinus* and s/v *Honu Kai*. Paul from *Delphinus* greeted us and said, "It's Yachty Appreciation Week here in Portsmouth. The community is taking us out to eat for free. We have to be at the dinghy dock at 6 where buses will take us over to Fort Shirley." Free dinner? Bus ride to a Fort? How can life be so amazing!?

We had an hour to get ready. Armed with our videos of the whale experience, we met our friends on the dinghy dock. We all loaded into a small bus and took a ride over to the fort.

We arrived at the Fort Shirley with around 100 other boaties. There were free drinks – rum punch to leave no one standing. After some drinks we were directed upstairs where there was a massive buffet lined up filled with outstanding food.

Three very short speeches were given.

The Tourist Minister spoke in addition to Marin, our contact in the bay, and the lovely American who helped get the mooring buoys set up on the bay.

Each of the speeches thanked us for visiting Dominica and asked us to spread the word about how amazing the country is. Apparently this was the first Yachty Appreciation Week.

The children all had a great time running around the Fort and the adults all enjoyed the rum punch (a little too much enjoyment, as everyone's head hurt a bit the next morning).

The following day, all of the sailors from the three kid boats were taken for a boat trip up the Indian River. Martin, who goes by the name

Providence, picked us up from our boats, motored over to the Indian River and then rowed us along what is called The Mini Amazon.

The trip was magical. Absolutely magical.

Martin pointed out birds, trees, bushes, plants and wildlife. He educated us all about the history of the island and the flag. Martin even sang to us! He elicited questions from the kids and worked hard to teach all of us in a fun way. Our friends, Jayne and Paul, from *Delphinus* enjoyed the trip so much that they went back several months later to get married along the banks of the river.

Traveling up a river in a rainforest while learning about our surroundings was bliss. To see all the children so interested in what Martin had to say was a blessing.

And people have had the nerve to say that I'm depriving my child of education – humbug to them!

After the Indian River trip, we all went home to catch up on homeschooling and nap for a bit. In the evening we went to the P.A.Y.S (Portsmouth Association of Yachting Services) BBQ. P.A.Y.S are the official guides who take care of the moorings and assist all the boaties in the bay.

For $15 each we all ate like kings and queens. There was BBQ chicken, pork and fish. They also served rice and salad. While at the BBQ we met up with other sailors, swapped stories, and some of us did a bit of dancing.

What excursion did we do next? Milton Waterfalls!

Having our five-year-old in tow, we often have to find hikes that are not miles and miles. Martin explained that Milton Waterfalls would be best – we could walk around a plantation, hike through a stream and quickly be at some majestic waterfalls.

For this day out it was only s/v *Delphinus* and us. The seven of us enjoyed learning about coffee trees, cocoa, cinnamon, lemongrass, thyme, bay leaf, plantains, celery, mangos, grapefruit, passion fruit, papaya, and much more.

Amazingly, most of the stuff we saw you couldn't buy at the local market. Things like lemongrass are all over the place so the locals go pick it rather than sell it. I wonder if the locals will one day realize that they could make a 100 percent profit by selling the boaties all the natural stuff growing at the side of their roads!

After learning about all sorts of things that grow in Dominica, we made it to the most beautiful waterfall I've ever seen. Everyone had a good shower in the falls. The guys tried to stay under the heavy dropping water but it was too difficult to keep still. The water pressure was intense.

The crew all dried off and we then went to a lovely fishing village to enjoy some sorrel juice, a local Caribbean drink make from a flower. We witnessed people cleaning their dishes and vegetables in the river, a woman carrying a bag of something on her head, chickens and chicks roaming all over the place and many small little houses made from wood or metal.

On our way home Martin took us to Strawberry Restaurant near the Ross Medical School where we ate like kings and queens for less than $2 a plate.

The food was great and so inexpensive.

For our final excursion on Dominica we took a lovely drive down the west coast seeing the towns of Colihaut, Salisbury, St Joseph, Massacre and Roseau. Our guide, Alec, took us to a lookout point above Roseau so that he could tell us what all the buildings were and some history of the capital.

After our drive we eventually made it to some hot sulphur springs in Wotten Waven. What a treat! For a very small fee we had full access to three hot baths varying in temperature and size.

We spent a good hour in the baths relaxing, enjoying a hot shower and allowing the magical powers of the sulfur springs to heal our bodies.

Previous to the baths our guide also gave us all mud masks.

When Sienna washed her mask off she asked, "'Do I look younger mummy?'"

Alec, one of our guides, taught us all about different herbs that were natural remedies for headaches, prostate health, colic in babies and more. Throughout the whole trip he'd pull over at the side of the road, grab something, and then tell us what it was.

After the falls we all enjoyed a lovely bite to eat at the only French café on the island. Ironically I had pizza – something that's not really French or of Dominica origins. Regardless, it hit the spot.

On the way home Simon, Eve and Sienna all fell asleep.

I enjoyed the quiet ride and looked out at the boats thinking, "I wish I had a boat."' It's funny because sometimes I forget that I have a boat. Sometimes I look out and wish that I could be living on a boat and then I remember that I AM!

That evening Simon and I went on a "Date Night" while Eve and Sienna watched a movie.

We took the tender to the jetty to the right of the P.A.Y.S dinghy dock where the Blue Bay Restaurant is located. At least, I think that's the name of it. Half of the building is a bar, the Sandy Bar, and the other half of the building is a restaurant.

I had lobster with garlic butter, sweet potato mash and a lovely tossed salad with ranch dressing. The lobster was the best I've ever had. Simon had grilled Mahi Mahi and with a lime, ginger sauce and that was excellent too. I highly recommend the restaurant.

So…my overall rating for Dominica?

It might be the fact that my expectations were exceeded or perhaps it's the first time that I've found a Caribbean Island that is authentic (not set up for tourists), but I simply can't say enough about this country.

The people are kind, generous and eager to help out. The anchorages are beautiful, sheltered and mooring buoys provide secure holdings. The excursions and food are inexpensive. The island is full of trails, waterfalls and dense real tropical rainforests. And…I felt 100 percent safe the entire time we were there. The only negative that I can offer is that the country is not set up to help sailors in need of serious repairs, but with Martinique only 25 miles away, any serious parts or services can be had there.

Therefore my rating for Dominica is outstanding!

[See Appendix A, 'V17. Dominica' to get a taste for how awesome it is]

Chapter 50: Racing in the Oyster Antigua Regatta

While in the Mediterranean last year, we entered our first ever sailing regatta. And when I say 'first ever,' I mean it was not only the first time we raced *Britican*, it was the first time we ever raced in a real race.

The only experience we had prior to the regatta was a few fun races when we had a week-long sailing flotilla vacation. When you sign up for a flotilla with a company like Moorings, Neilson's or SunSail you start and end each day with a group of other boats – usually around eight to 15.

Flotillas are a great way to build your sailing confidence because you have help leaving and arriving. Furthermore, many of the outfits offer a little race on the last day to allow participants the opportunity to see how fast they can make the boat go.

Needless to say, our racing experience to date was limited to one official regatta, several flotilla fun races and my husband's incessant need to race any boat that comes within eyesight of us!

We were the newbies on the block, and boy, did I feel intimidated. The instant we arrived I realized that the regatta would be nothing like the friendly flotilla races. There were big boats – over 80 feet – and massive crews. Even similar sized boats like us had up to 15 people crewing. Furthermore, almost all of the crews were professionals meaning that they certainly knew how to race. Many of the big boats sent home their normal crew and brought in special racing crews for the week.

In the Med we were the only boat racing our home.

We were also the only boat that had a child on board. Thankfully, Oyster supplied us with a variety of crewmembers throughout the week and we managed to get a couple of our friends to join in too.

Overall, I think we placed around 8th out of 30 boats, which isn't bad considering our circumstances.

When deciding whether or not we'd enter the Antigua Oyster Regatta both Simon and I were a bit skeptical. Our biggest issue was to ensure our daughter had other children around.

Imagine trying to race all day and then go to cocktail parties that ended late in the evening AND entertaining a five-year-old? It just didn't work very well for our first Oyster regatta. In fact, when the last race day came I took Sienna off the boat and enjoyed a day at a local aquarium.

At the Antigua regatta, however, and to our delight, the organizers at Oyster worked hard to find other kid boats to join. We were also promised that Oyster's CEO, David Tydeman, brought his 13-year-old daughter, Sasha, to help us out. By the time the decision had to be made, two other kid boats, both of which we knew, had signed up and some other kids would be present on one of the larger boats racing.

So our desire to have children around was taken care of.

Our next issue was that we needed crew! To sign up we had to have at least three crewmembers, but based on our experience of racing the previous year, we felt that to be able to possibly compete we'd need five or six other bodies – preferably people who had been on a boat before!

In an ideal situation you need two people on each winch, a helmsperson, someone on the main sail and a couple people to work the foredeck.

While enjoying our time around the country of Dominica we were sailing with our friends on Delphinus. Simon mentioned our crew issue to them and they said, "We'll be crew for you!"

Not only did our friends know how to sail but we acquired another kid, Lilly. Talk about result! I must say that I'm not so sure our friends knew what they were getting themselves into.

As the date to the regatta got closer we also discovered that a good friend of ours, Harry, was due to fly into Antigua the week before Antique Race Week. Harry is a professional Skiff Sailboat competitor so we asked the owner of the classic boat Harry was on if we could borrow him for the Oyster Regatta. One thing led to another and we got Harry!

Can things flow any better than that?

So...the month before the regatta we arrived in Antigua. Unfortunately we located an issue with our gooseneck – the device that attaches the boom to the mast, which could have been a fatal malfunction.

Thankfully the guys at Antigua Rigging Limited sorted us out in time for the regatta. They had to work hard to squeeze us in amongst their already tight schedule.

One thing to note about Antigua is that it's fairly quiet all year round except for April, when the Falmouth Bay and English Harbour are CRAZY. The two main regattas for the Caribbean are hosted in this area – Antigua Classics followed by Antigua Race Week.

While our gooseneck was being mended, Simon and I put Sienna in a local pre-school and started preparing the boat for guests and racing.

We cleaned, organized and serviced everything we could.

Although it was a bit annoying being laid up before the regatta, in hindsight, it was a good thing. The extra time gave us the opportunity to

Sailing Britican

get the boat ready and to relax before all the buzz and activity of the Oyster Regatta.

Finally, the day came to enter English Harbour and moor up in the historic Nelson's Dockyard.

For the previous month we frequented Nelson's Dockyard to enjoy the history, look at the massive yachts and grab a beer or two. It was fantastic to finally enter the dockyard as a regatta contestant – the same dockyard that some of the most famous boats would soon enter for the Classic and Race Week.

The mooring instructions were to drop the anchor, go backwards against the jetty and have two lines aft holding the boat in place.

Due to the wind and current it took Simon several tries to get the boat lined up and backed in. He's very happy to start over if he doesn't feel things are right. Eventually we moored up being the seventh Oyster to arrive.

That evening, our crew from sailboat *Delphinus* arrived: Paul, Jayne and Lilly. While they were sorting themselves out, we were saying "hi" to old friends and introducing ourselves to new friends. There was a lovely buzz on the dock and I instantly recognized that the feel of the Antigua Regatta was going to be way different from the previous year's races.

I felt relaxed and calmly excited rather than a ball of nerves.

For arrivals and check-in Simon and I booked in at the temporary Oyster Race Committee booth. We received our instructions in addition to a really nice SLAM laptop case. I love all the goodies you get at these events! I think it's the adult version of getting toys in my cereal as a kid.

Once booked in, Jayne and I went for a wander to see if she could get her haircut and I could get a pedicure. I usually do my own toenails but considering I had to wait for Jayne I decided to treat myself.

For two hours we chatted with the hairdresser and her daughter. It was such a calming thing to do. I felt so privileged.

In the meantime, Sienna and Lilly played with Legos and Simon and Paul went to the Skippers Meeting. In the meeting, the Oyster Race Committee Team talked about the course, experience of the crews (some had lots – 88.5' *Guardian Angel* was mentioned and some had very little– *Britican* was named), the importance of timings, enjoying the races, the rules, destinations of the places we were sailing to, events and so forth.

Around 6pm, all the boaters made their way over to the historic Admirals Inn to pick up a little boat transporting us over to Boom, a restaurant that used to be the old gunpowder shed.

The children all quickly met each other and set up camp around a table. The adults grabbed a rum punch and started socializing. And soon lovely nibbles came out. We enjoyed tiny hamburgers, grilled chicken on a stick, bruschetta, shrimp balls and other tasty delights. There was certainly plenty to eat and drink.

Unlike the last Regatta, where I felt as if it was a business networking event, this first social element was relaxed and very enjoyable. I was able to chat with friends I already knew and also meet quite a few new people.

I'm not one to enjoy small talk but the evening didn't feel forced.

And it was so relaxing to know that Sienna had loads of friends to play with. Both Lilly and Sasha, David Tydeman daughter, looked after all the children. It was a dream come true for us. Furthermore, it was great to see a new friendship form between Lilly and Sasha.

We all went back to the boat and tried our best to get a good night's sleep.

In the morning we were all up ready for the day to unfold. Everyone grabbed some cereal and Simon made coffees. The first thing to do was to go around the boat explaining how things worked. Simon gave an introduction to the winches, managing the main sail and how to work the poles on the foredeck.

A knock came on the boat and when we peered out we saw Simon from the insurance company Pantaneus, an event sponsor. In the last regatta, Simon had helped us out for a day and we really enjoyed having him. As luck would have it, we managed to get him for a second time!

It didn't take me long to hand out our raspberry colored sailing t-shirts.

While laid up in Catamaran Marina getting our gooseneck fixed I found a t-shirt printing company nearby. We missed the cutoff date for Oyster to arrange t-shirts so it was a good find. Last year we had navy shirts and they didn't feel lively enough. My decision to go for raspberry was to add a bit more energy to the boat!

With everyone in raspberry, we hovered around the VHF waiting for the weather report and race instructions. Paul wrote everything down and Simon plotted on the map the day's course.

The energy on the boat was a bit nervous.

By 10am, we slipped our lines and proceeded to the race line start. I felt fairly calm and looking at Simon, I kept seeing a big grin on his face. He was eager to get going and see how we'd fair against our Class 3 competitors.

The course started us off outside English Harbour going west around a marker to the east of the island and up to Nonsuch Bay for the finish line. We declared white sails rather than colored, or racing sails, as we'd need more people to fly our gennaker or spinnaker.

For the most part, the first half of the race was rather calm. The wind was light and we simply did our best to go as fast as we could. At one point we were able to do the goose-wing configuration where we had our front sail on one side and our main out on the other.

As we passed boats or boats passed us we'd give a big wave.

The kids mainly stayed in the saloon playing games or watching a movie. From time to time they'd pop upstairs and ask how we were doing. Everything seemed to flow very easily.

By the time we got to the finish line there was only one boat in our class next to us.

They had a more advantageous handicap so we knew that they came in first, but we were delighted with a second place position.

We followed the channel up Nonsuch Bay, found a place to drop anchor and recounted our day's sailing. Friends in the bay took a dinghy over to hear how we did and we had some other visitors from other Oyster boats. We enjoyed some nibbles and prepared for the 6pm water taxi pickup.

Us girlies put on our dresses, took the taxi over to the Nonsuch Bay Resort and walked along the beach to a massive tent. Upon arrival a lovely woman introduced herself and explained that they set up a "kids club" for all the children where they'd get pizza, play some games and watch a movie.

Once we made it to the big tent we were handed cocktails and nibbles came out. There was sushi, fried wontons and various other lovely appetizers. Simon, our crew and I chatted with others about our day. Everyone seemed very easy going.

The prize giving ceremony for the day started promptly. Simon was delighted to receive a lovely chrome sailboat for second place. The previous year we were fortunate to win an award for having the youngest crewmember, Sienna, but that wasn't a real prize. It was nice to get something.

We all then sat down at a table, enjoyed a wonderful buffet of lovely food and talked with everyone around us. Around 9pm the children came down to the beach and not long after we headed back to the boat to get some shut-eye before the next day's race.

At 8:30am our friend, Harry, arrived to our boat by water taxi. His flight from Australia to Antigua had come in the night before. Harry helped to get the owner of the classic boat to English Harbor and then took a taxi up to Nonsuch Bay to help us for the rest of the regatta.

Not long after, Declan O'Sullivan, from Pelagos Yachts joined us.

Two new crew – great news!

Harry didn't take longer than a few seconds to get right into things. He pulled out the spinnaker, tested out how the poles worked and became very acquainted with the way the boat was rigged.

As soon as I saw the spinnaker come out I started to get nervous. The first time we tried to fly it, we ripped it. The second time we tested it out, while crossing the Atlantic, it seemed unmanageable. We only flew it for a couple minutes before taking it down.

It's just such a huge sail and it involves quite a few ropes to get it working!

At 9:30, Paul was at the navigation desk ready to write down the weather and race marks. Jayne and I prepared some wraps for lunch and cut up veggies for snacks.

We proceeded out of Nonsuch Bay with eager anticipation.

Having two new crewmembers on board was exciting. But I was also slightly nervous when Harry said, "Kim, you're going to do the foredeck with me." I thought, "What does that entail? Will I be strong enough to do whatever I have to do? Yikes!"'

Secretly I hoped that we wouldn't be able to fly the spinnaker. I'm such a chicken. In the lead, Simon helmed us down the east coast of Antigua and once we rounded the first mark, Harry yelled, "Come with me, Kim!"

Harry attached the spinnaker to the front of the pulpit (above the anchor). After pulling the spinnaker up to the top of the mast and having me guide the spinnaker up, he gave me some ropes and said this one will come down and the other will go up. They were the guide lines to allow the spinnaker shoot to be pulled up over the spinnaker allowing the spinnaker to open and fill with wind.

Harry pulled and pulled and the outer sheath that was supposed to go up easily kept getting tangled. After 20 minutes of going in the wrong direction the spinnaker finally opened completely and off we went.

All the other boats were flying asymmetrical spinnakers and since ours was symmetrical we had a higher range of wind angles we could fly in. Once we got back in the race we ploughed by everyone...and I mean everyone. We flew up to the next mark.

My job was to manage the topping lift on the poles – either pull it up or let it down. I was the one who also used a winch to make the poles go up or come down. It was hard work but I loved it.

Furthermore, because I was busy doing stuff on the foredeck not once did I get seasick!

In the end we beat one of the 82' Oysters across the finish line and won first place for our class and the class above us! Considering Oyster wants to sell new large boats I'm not sure our win went down too well. Hehehehehe.

The prize giving was at Tamarind Tree restaurant in a spectacular resort called Curtain Bluff. We all piled onto some buses and took a 20-minute ride down the coast. It was a lovely resort with amazing surroundings.

And to our delight, the restaurant put a table together for all the children and they seemed to have a fantastic time.

The meal was lovely, the people at our table were great and the live music was brilliant. And winning first place was an absolute dream come true! At first I thought that the pressure was now off.

We won a first place trophy – it was more than we could have ever dreamed of – so now we could chill out and really enjoy the rest of the event.

WRONG.

Now that we won a first place, I wanted to win two more first places and win the whole regatta. I'm sure Simon did too, but I was surprised at my response. That being said, as the days went forward I became more and more anxious.

Fortunately we had a beach day scheduled in for the following day. When I woke up I felt shattered. I felt as if I was run over by a bus. Was it doing the poles? Was it the anxiety of raising the spinnaker? Was it the fact that we won a first place and I wanted to now get a taste of even more glory?

For the beach day at Jackie O's Beach, everyone went except for Paul and me. Paul's boat, *Delphinus*, was at Jolly Harbour so he went home and relaxed. After the first day his back started to act up so he was in quite a bit of discomfort. I just needed a break. I wanted to give the boat a good scrub, make some food for dinner and relax. Going to the beach would have just been more socializing and drinking.

The morning started with a bit of hustle and bustle. The boys pulled our asymmetrical sail out and the plan was to leave early to see if we could get it to fly.

While crossing the Atlantic Ocean, we had that massive disaster with this particular sail. Since it ripped and the furling unit got banged up, we hadn't tested it out again. Simon had the sail fixed in St Lucia but it had been bagged up ever since.

So...Sienna took us out of the Jolly Harbour Marina.

Once we were out to sea, Harry hoisted the asymmetrical sail and after 10 minutes of fiddling with the furler it was decided that it wouldn't work. Down went the sail back into storage.

Thankfully, we wouldn't have used the sail anyway.

We declared "white sails," meaning that we wouldn't sail a spinnaker (symmetrical or asymmetrical). By declaring white sails our handicap would be higher.

The day's race started with all of our class right on the line. We tried hard to be first but we were beaten to the line by our friends on sailing vessel *Crackerjack.*

Harry called the shots, Simon helmed, Paul released the jib sheets (ropes holding the front sail to the winches), I pulled the jib sheets in and helped Harry with the poles, Jayne was on constant watch for the marks and the children helped to blow more wind into the sails!

The feeling on the boat was nervous anticipation. When Harry told us to do something we all jumped to do it. With the whole fleet on our heels I kept willing the wind to keep us in the lead.

For over four hours we were in the lead.

It wasn't until the very last few minutes that the two 88.5' boats, *Guardian Angel* and *Lush*, passed us. In the end we crossed the finish line 4th out of the whole fleet and well before anyone in our class came close the line.

Amazingly, we didn't use a spinnaker and all the big boats did. I wonder how much we would have beaten the big boys if we did fly our colored sail?

After the race we returned to the Jolly Harbour Marina and all collapsed in exhaustion. We cleaned the boat, enjoyed a beer and had some snacks. It wasn't long before we would meet at the Greek Restaurant for the prize giving.

For Day 3 there was no doubt in our minds – we knew we came first in our class.

The only boat we were worried about flew their spinnaker and came in behind us, so it was official that we would win the day's race.

Jayne, Lilly and Sienna went up to receive the price. We won two lovely Darlington crystal glasses engraved with "Oyster Regattas" on them.

The pressure was serious now – we could win the whole regatta!

The next morning I woke feeling like a truck had run over me. There was a lump in my throat and a nervous feeling in my stomach. I kept telling myself that I was excited, but in all honesty I was extremely anxious.

After doing the poles for a couple days my body hurt all over. I was hunched over in an odd position and rotating a winch that didn't really want to move very easily.

Racing for four days probably doesn't seem like much but aside from the physical activity required, the mental side of things is extremely heavy. After we finished racing I often couldn't do simple computations or decide whether or not I wanted a beer!

My appreciation for those massive ocean-going racers has risen drastically.

So, for day 4 the pressure was on. We slipped our lines as early as we could to get out of the marina. After listening to the weather there was talk, at first, about using the spinnaker, but the winds were increasing.

By the time the race started, Harry and I put a reef in the main, reducing the size so that we wouldn't get blown over. In hindsight, it was an excellent decision because the winds got up to 40 knots!

Unbelievably, *Crackerjack* beat us but we soon passed them and then not one boat beat us past the finish line!

We were in the lead the entire day and had line honors. The day was not without a bit of panic, however.

I'm not sure how it happened, but I must have blacked out a bit and reduced the tension I held around the jib sheet that was wound around the winch (the jib sheet is the rope that holds the front sail). I saw my life flash before my eyes as the front sail blew out to sea as the rope holding it to the boat unwound furiously around the winch.

I quickly moved all the rope off of me while Paul did the same. The fear was that a body part might get caught in the furious unfurling of rope. Harry ran over, grabbed the now loose rope. I wrapped it back around the winch and pushed the button to wind it back in.

We barely lost any speed but I felt terrible.

After things were back together I looked at all my fingers to make sure they were still there and working. Later that day my heart actually hurt – I think I got a massive shot of adrenaline and had a bit of shock!

With all the anxiety about winning the final race I was worried that I could have ruined things. There was no need to worry – we annihilated everyone even with my mishap.

For Day 3 and 4 the Oyster Race Committee stopped telling us whether we won on other classes like they did on day 2. I have a feeling that if scores were calculated across the board, based on handicap, we would have won the whole regatta for all classes.

But Oyster can't be shown to have a 13-year-old 56′ boat beating all the brand new 60′ to 88.5′ vessels, now can they?

One thing is for sure, with the right people on our boat, boy can she fly!

Being a part of the Oyster Regatta was a blast and winning first place in our class was better than a dream come true.

At the final prize giving ceremony, Sienna and Lilly went up on stage to get our trophy for winning the day's event. Then all the children went up to receive an award for participating. Finally, all of us we went up again for winning the whole regatta.

We all worked hard and it was brilliant to have the crew we did…but part of me can't help but think a miracle happened this past week. I look back to those scary days of thinking, "Should we actually sell up and sail away?" and think how close we came to playing it safe and not following through on our dreams.

I'm not sure how or why things work the way they do, but I'm positive there's magic in the universe and those who say "screw it, I'm going to do my own thing," do get rewarded.

[See Appendix A, 'V18. Racing in the Oyster Regatta' to get a glimpse into our experience]

Chapter 51: Do I need a vacation from cruising?

I was tired. I never thought I'd say this but I think my mind and body might be missing winter.

For my entire life, I've always had months of down time. Whether I was living in Rochester or London, winter was a time when the weather became cold, the days drew short and the inclination to do stuff was far reduced.

Heck, in Rochester, the snow got so bad that the thought of scraping and brushing the car off was enough to keep me locked indoors for the whole season. The only time I left the house was for school, work and to get food.

In England, the weather wasn't nearly as bad as the States, but daylight ends around 3pm and by 5pm I was ready for my glass of wine, a chick flick and a long night of sleeping.

A similar thing happened to me regarding celery. I didn't hate celery, but I didn't go out of my way to get it either. When a recipe called for it, I'd use it. Celery often goes in soups, salads, and stews. It's one of those things that, if left out, you wouldn't think you'd miss it.

Well...after three months of not being able to buy celery I realized that it's a worthy vegetable. In soups and stews it adds more depth of flavor, and in salads the crunch cannot be replicated with any other vegetable!

I'm sure you see the point that I'm making. You don't know what you don't know. You don't know what you'll miss until you don't have it. We spend our lives thinking about living the dream, and yet when we do live the dream it's not always what we expected it to be.

Yes – I want a vacation from my "living the dream" lifestyle!

How has this happened? Well...having one summer after another for over a year hasn't helped. Being a part of one of the most social communities in the world – the cruising community – hasn't helped.

On a daily basis we usually have to choose between having dinner with some friends in the bay, going to a potluck BBQ, meeting up for a party or joining a group for an adventure to some interesting site on land.

And because the cruising community is so transient, it's almost impossible to say no to the people you know will soon be heading in a direction opposite to you.

We've spent months cruising around with various boats and when it comes time for them to leave or us to go toward a different heading we tend to spend even more time together knowing that we'll soon be parted...perhaps never to see each other again.

And then if you add in the extracurricular activity of doing a regatta, we'll that was, for me, the straw that broke the camel's back.

At the Oyster Antigua Regatta we had six days of activities, four days of racing and a whole heck of a lot of socializing. We won loads of awards and we won the overall regatta. What really made the race amazing is that most of the rest of the contenders had a professional crew and none of them were live aboards. By nature our boat is very heavy because we live on the boat. We totally stole the show. The event was an absolute blast, and part of the total living the dream package, but I must say it came at a price.

The fact that the Classics Regatta took place immediately after the Oyster Regatta didn't help. No – we didn't enter the Classics, but our dear friends on sailing vessel *el Oro* did...and they needed crew! How could we say no to racing a classic boat in one of the oldest classic regattas in the world?

That's the thing – you can't say no because on a daily basis opportunities for new experiences, amazing memories and incredible friendships are up for the taking.

Even if we were in Antigua, what would our chances be to know someone on one of those amazing boats?

With the Oyster Antigua regatta over and some outstanding experience while racing in the Antigua Classics, it was time for Simon, Sienna and me to head north. Our ultimate plan was to make it to the east coast of America by June/July, but more on that later.

After Antigua, we were committed to stopping in Anguilla due to Simon's fathers' history on the island...

Chapter 52: Don't miss Anguilla

If you're looking for white sandy beaches, a diversity of food, wonderfully welcoming people, a history you can grasp and an absence of over-the-top tourist attractions, put Anguilla on your countries to visit list.

Being the most northerly Leeward Island in the Caribbean, Anguilla is the last stop, heading north, before hitting the Virgin Islands.

So...prior to our arrival in the States, we're picking up friends for a 10-day tour of the British Virgin Islands. Both Simon and I have sailed this area through chartering a boat, but this will be our first time in the area with *Britican*. Exciting times!

When choosing where to stop on our dash to the Virgin Islands and then to the States, Simon and I surveyed the map, discussing our options.

For as long as I've known my father-in-law, Keith, he has told us stories about his role in the Anguilla Revolution. Keith was a policeman in the Metropolitan Police Force (London). In 1970 Keith was offered a three month position in Anguilla to help keep the peace. He often recounts stories of playing with the children on the beach, catching lobster and doing lobster grills for everyone around and enjoying his co-workers and the local people. Not once did he experience any adversity during the troubled times.

When Britain decided to decolonize, the government lumped Anguilla in with St. Kitts and Nevis. Anguilla was not happy being lumped together with an old colony – they wanted to be free and independent.

Simon, Sienna, and I toured the Heritage Collection Museum to get a full understanding of the island's turbulent history.

In 1969, Britain sent a gunboat and some assault troops. Fortunately the revolt was bloodless. After a UN intervention, in 1971 Anguilla became and Autonomous Crown Colony and then, in 1980, a British Dependent Territory.

Anguilla now has its own constitution, an elected assembly and an island government.

When Simon asked a historian what he thought of the "British Invasion," he explained that Anguilla was happy that the British were there but they were not happy how they came. Apparently troops invaded Anguilla on boats – there are pictures of paratroopers jumping off the boat and running up the beach with rifles.

Interestingly, before Anguilla became "free" there was no electricity or water running to homes. They had nothing. The revolution caused many changes for the people, providing an opportunity for a much higher quality of life.

I couldn't help but feel terribly sad for the Anguilla people. It seems as if the island has been hit with a wide variety of tragedies. Hurricanes destroyed everything time and time again. A massive drought caused most of the island's people and animals to starve to death. Most of the crops that were used to create an income eventually failed – there was either a lack of demand, the crop simply failed to grow or after the abolishment of slavery the income produced couldn't pay for the labor.

After our trip to the museum, we drove to Shoal Bay on the East End to enjoy a wonderful lunch and a picture perfect beach line, then went to The Valley, or main town, to locate Keith's old Police Office.

Simon found the current Police Office and went inside to inquire where his father was stationed. The old Police Office was literally across the road and up a bit further. It's currently the Chamber of Commerce.

When we knocked on the door a lovely woman answered and gave us a tour of the building. It was great to finally step foot in the office where Keith recounts some of his best memories.

There are multiple points of attraction on Anguilla. The whole island is filled with amazing white sand palm tree lined beaches, top notch resorts, boutique villas and loads of restaurants. Whether you want Mexican, English, Italian, Chinese, Asian, French, seafood, grill or Caribbean cuisine, you'll have an excellent amount of restaurants to choose from.

Just in Sandy Ground, where we anchored, there are around seven cute restaurants.

Additionally, there are local art galleries dotted all over the island. Living on a boat, Simon and I shy away from galleries in case we see something we like. I must spend hours a month trying to offload things – the last thing I want is added weight (it slows us down and clutters the boat)!

Otherwise, there's the miniature golf course we played, a PGA standard golf course, dive centers, horseback riding, a nature exploration, a waterpark, watersports and boat trips to the many tiny islands around Anguilla. There's also a ferry to St. Maartin's. The island has many natural salt lakes, so if you're in need of some sea salt, this is the place to stock up!

That might seem like a lot of offerings, but so far in our journeys this island is the least spoiled by cheesy touristy things.

The anchorage is a bit flat. I prefer a backdrop of lush tropical forest, some mountains, a volcano, perhaps a waterfall, turquoise waters, no other boats and enough breeze to keep the bugs away and my family cool.

Am I spoiled or what?

Road Bay has a lovely white beach lined with beautiful palm trees dotted with restaurants and homes. There's a fantastic dinghy dock that leads right up to the Customs and Immigration Office. Alongside the office are loads of rubbish bins (no recycling). And Wi-Fi is not only available at most restaurants, it comes without a passcode.

Using our Wi-Fi bat, or a booster hooked to a router, we got Wi-Fi on the boat!

From the anchorage you can also take a boat over to Sandy Island to enjoy lunch, snorkeling, diving and kite surfing. It's a lovely little island on a white sandy reef with some palm trees. It's paradise.

The downside to this bay is that there's no store – not even a quickie market – and no vegetable stand. No one comes to the boat offering food. There are simply no services at all.

What about provisioning?

If you do get a car there's an EXCEPTIONAL grocery store called Best Buy, about 15 minutes away. The selection was fantastic and the prices were very good. The grocery store also had a hardware, plumbing and electric side to it. There's also a Best Buy heading toward the East End of the island.

Other interesting notes…

When we hired a car, a lovely woman at Roy's Bayside Grill ordered it for us. When the car came it was left hand drive; however, we had to drive on the left side of the road. Considering that the island only has a few paved roads it wasn't too difficult to deal with. If, however, you're nervous about driving in a foreign country, make sure to request a car that at least puts your body in the correct place (in the middle of the road rather than along the side of the road).

Being the passenger where the steering wheel should have been I kept pushing my foot on an imaginary break!

I found it interesting that there are no signs saying "to the beach" when you drive around. We simply looked on the map for a restaurant near the location we wanted and headed for the restaurant.

Most of the beaches we stopped at have public bathrooms that are really good.

If you go to Roy's Bayside Grill get the Lobster Bisque. After I raved about it to our waitress she responded, "well, that is what this place is known for." Thankfully I ordered it because the menu didn't point that out! The chunks of lobster were plentiful, the soup base was creamy and the extras fit in perfectly.

When you walk around, everyone who passes you in a car waves at you. Be prepared to wave back.

When you enter the bay there are two large shipwrecks on the beach – don't let that scare you. The holding is excellent in the bay – it's sand and weeds. Just make sure to drop your anchor on the sand patches.

All the tourists we met have been coming to this island for years. Many come year after year and stay in the same villa or apartments. One couple we met were married here 24 years ago, visited the island six years ago and revisited while we were there. They explained that it's their favorite Caribbean island.

After Anguilla we travelled up to the British and American Virgin Islands. My girlfriend flew in with her boyfriend and we had an excellent 10 days of sightseeing. Fortunately, Simon and I have sailed the area several times while doing week long flotilla holidays. We were effectively visiting old haunts. Interestingly, I discovered that my love of the British Virgin Islands has, however, changed…

Chapter 53: Top 16 reasons why sailing the BVI is bittersweet

After spending two weeks visiting old and new anchorages our time in the British Virgin Islands (BVI) provided a bittersweet feel.

Some aspects I loved, yet others made me want to move on, never looking back. Overall, the region is set up to cater to weeklong boat charters providing tourist offerings and tourist rates.

Sure, there are a few places off the beaten path but they're few and far between. If you sail around the BVI expect busy waterways, inexperienced sailors, and expensive food all, however, surrounded with some of the most picturesque backgrounds in the Caribbean (it's bittersweet).

These are the qualities that make the BVI sweet:

1. The views are some of the best in the Caribbean – some of the anchorages and restaurants/resorts are truly set up to offer a view of paradise. The beaches are white sand and the sea floor is navy with stunning turquoise and sea green patches. There's an abundance of well-kept palm trees and shrubs offering bursting pinks, purples, yellows and whites. There's no litter and the tourist areas are sparkling clean.

2. There's an abundance of beautiful bays with well-maintained and easy to use mooring buoys. If you're new to sailing and worried about the strong trade winds, the BVI is a perfect place to sail. Almost every popular bay has mooring buoys. (Note: A mooring buoy is made up of a concrete block seated on the bottom of the sea with a rope attached and floated on the surface by a large floating ball. A mooring buoy, also called a mooring ball, acts as a replacement to your anchor. To attach the buoy you simply pull up the end with a hook and feed warps or ropes through an eyelet and fix back on the boat).

3. There's entertainment to be had at every mooring – watching the charter boats mess up can provide hours of amusement. Over the past week we enjoyed watching:

- a boat made 14 attempts to pick up a mooring ball;
- a husband/wife team attempted to grab a mooring ball while the main sail was still up (the boat flew right by the ball);
- a couple of boats sailed over the top of the mooring buoy and then they couldn't find it;
- several charter boats attempted to anchor, drag over and over and then eventually leave the anchorage. In most cases the crew was not putting out enough chain for the anchor to even hit the bottom of the sea, let alone dig into the floor;
- several people on a Moorings charter boat (Moorings is a company that offers sailing vacations) turned on their engine, raised the main, detached from the mooring ball and then put the boat in reverse at maximum revs to get out of a mooring field. (We're thinking that perhaps Moorings is teaching their clients to perform this task as it prepares the helmsperson to sail out of danger if there's engine failure! It's the only thing we could think of...);
- many catamarans motor everywhere without putting their sails up;
- many mono hauls and catamarans had full sails and their engines running;
- a few boats attempted to put their main up with the wind behind them rather than pointing the boat into the wind.

4. The wind is plentiful – there is great sailing and nice breezes at anchor. After sailing the Med for two years and having either too much

wind or no wind at all, the Caribbean seems to be a dream come true for sailors. There's almost always a wonderful 15 to 20 knot wind. The wind allows for great sails, cool breezes and a lack of mosquitos.

5. The snorkeling/diving is very good. I'd like to say it's great but like many other Caribbean islands some of the reef is dead or dying. It's terrible to see. Otherwise, there's a fantastic amount of small and large fish. It's always great to see stingrays, moray ells, barracuda and the massive tarpons. Off Norman Island Simon and I spotted a 6-foot nurse shark and it made our day! Diving the RMS Rohn shipwreck is well work the time, money and effort.

6. You can sail for one hour or several – every island is very close. The longest passage we had was four hours and that was going from one end of the BVI to the other.

7. Picking up/dropping off friends, family or crew at the airport is super easy. If you pick up a mooring ball in Trellis Bay it will take you five minutes to take your dinghy to a dinghy dock and five minutes to walk to the airport – that's it! If you have guests interested in visiting you this is an excellent region of the Caribbean to make the airport transfer painless.

8. Marinas are expensive but good quality. Generally, the facilities are nice, many have WI-FI and there are various restaurants and grocery offerings. If you have to pick one marina to visit, I recommend Nanny Cay Marina. You'll find the best chandlery around (Budget Marine), there's a tiny but good supermarket, the pool is lovely and free to use for berth holders and there's a nice little beach, restaurant and bar. For our 56' mono hull we paid $95 USD/night plus water and electric.

9. Many bars/restaurants/resorts offer use of the beach, beach chairs, pool and the various facilities. I enjoyed Saba Rock in the Gorda Sound

in Virgin Gorda, Marina Cay in Tortola and The Bight on Norman Island. On Saba Rock you'll find a restaurant with some rooms to rent. Dotted around the area are double cushion beach chairs, hammocks, sofas and restaurant seating. The views are breathtaking. After a snorkel, you can enjoy a tasty (but pricey) lunch and then find a shaded or sunny area to relax.

And now for the things that are bitter...

1. It's very busy. We enjoyed the BVI during May, one of the "quiet months", yet it was still very hectic. I got the feeling that many charter boats woke up in the morning and raced to the next anchorage to ensure they got a mooring buoy. It seemed that by 9am everyone in a mooring field would be gone and by 3pm the fields were jam-packed. We never failed to secure an anchorage but I imagine that during the high season it would probably be prudent to get to anchorages early or have a few alternatives ready if you can't find space. Fortunately, nothing is far away in the BVI – within an hour there are surely several places to get a buoy or put a hook down.

2. Anchoring is often not an option. We found this very annoying. In our pilot book the maps show several bays with both mooring buoys and space for boats that want to anchor. In almost every bay we entered the space for anchoring was full of mooring balls. You can't anchor near a mooring ball due to the difference in scope. In other words, a boat that's anchored will have a much larger swing circumference than a boat on a buoy. If you're going to anchor near buoys you have to provide enough room to be far enough to swing and often the depths were too deep to do that. All the mooring buoys seem to be priced at $30/night and have a limit of 60' maximum sized boat.

3. Authenticity is hard to find. We're in the Western Caribbean now – leaving the Eastern Caribbean under our belt. In the east we experienced amazing local foods, great reggae and steel drum music and even learned a bit of the slang language. In the Grenadines, St Lucia, Martinique, Guadeloupe, Dominica, Antigua and Anguilla there was a sense of Caribbean culture. In the BVI, I feel as if I could be anywhere. While enjoying a Western Caribbean Beach BBQ at the Bitter End Yacht Club we listened to a band dressed in Hawaiian shirts singing cover songs by Lionel Richie, Phil Collins and Madonna! The BBQ was near the beach but it wasn't on it. And the food...well, it was okay. There were rice and beans in addition to roti's, a Caribbean wrap, but I have to say I was disappointed. The food wasn't like the local dishes we got in the eastern Caribbean. It was food I could get anywhere. But that's me – I like to feel a culture whereas other people are looking for warm weather, good sailing and food they're accustomed to eating.

4. Food is expensive – groceries and restaurants. The BVI is certainly not a place to visit on a budget. It's hard to find a cheap burger place...there are a lot of froofy (a Kim word) restaurants that provide lovely plated food at a high price. There are also several mediocre restaurants that provide normal food at a high price. If I didn't experience places like Dominica where eight of us had a lovely lunch with a variety of local dishes for $50 USD TOTAL I probably wouldn't complain. For a week-long charter or a short stay in the area the prices are okay, but if you're living on a budget and have been to surrounding areas you'll balk at the cost.

5. Defensive sailing is a must. You have to sail as if everyone else on the water is an idiot and doesn't see you. Understanding the rules of the sea can often be confusing. Generally, boaters under sail give way to any

other boat on a starboard tack (the wind is following over the starboard or right side of the boat). If two boats are both on a starboard tack the boat closest to the wind generally has to give way. Of course, no boat officially has right of way…all boats must be vigilant and prepare to move off course when necessary. In the BVI, it's best to assume that every boat around you will think they have right of way – whether they are sailing or motoring. On one occasion we were on a collision course with a catamaran. We noticed that the group of four on deck were not paying much attention. To be fair, the sun was in their eyes. We were prepared to make a quick tack to avoid them and that's what we had to do. When the people on the cat saw us they all jumped in the air thinking, "where did they come from?!" Heck, I suppose a 56′ sailboat can be difficult to spot?! (Gosh – am I growing cynical in my older age?!)

Side note: I've made more sailing mistakes than most. Everyone has to learn and the best way to learn is to fail. Having to approach a mooring ball 10 times when you first start is normal and I totally respect people who are brave enough to get out there and fail over and over again. It's not fun to fail publically, but that's life. That's how you ultimately find fulfillment… What troubles me is when people are reckless and that leads me to my next point…

6. People on the charter boats can come across as reckless or irresponsible. It's not cool to drink (loads) and sail. Having a couple beers is fine but arriving in a mooring field drunk and leery is not cool. In the BVI we saw quite a few reckless people.

7. Wi-Fi is available almost everywhere but it's only good enough to do very light surfing – definitely not good enough to upload good pictures or video. If you're looking to work while you're cruising and need a reliable Internet connection, I can't say the BVI is a good spot.

Saying that, however, I didn't get a SIM card. Digicel, and other carriers, are in the BVI so assuming you get a SIM card there might be hope.

My overall British Virgin Island rating?!

If you're not a seasoned sailor and are looking for a great place to learn to sail or are in need of a fantastic sailing holiday I'm not sure there's any place better than the BVI. It's a holiday or vacation paradise for sailors. The sailing, snorkeling, diving, beaches and food are great – it's a full sun, sea and sail package.

If, however, you're a full time cruiser... as long as you know what to expect, it's still a great place.

What I would suggest is that you stock up on your food and drinks in Antigua or Anguilla if coming from the south, or Puerto Rico if coming from the North. Research the bays that have anchoring only; for the most part they're a lot quieter than the bays with mooring balls. And it's definitely worth seeing some of the sights.

The Baths on Virgin Gorda are a must-see, snorkeling or diving the RMS Rhone shipwreck off Salt Island is worth the time and effort and some of the beaches are downright spectacular.

My rating for the BVI is great but not outstanding.

Although our visit provided a bittersweet feel, the sweetness was so very sweet that I must rate this region with top marks.

After the British Virgin Islands, we stopped briefly in the US Virgin Islands to pick up a new guest, Kyle, who offered to help us sail to Puerto Rico, Grand Turks, Caicos, Hogsty Reef, eventually arriving in Fort Lauderdale, Florida.

[See Appendix A, 'V19. British Virgin Islands' for a link to the video]

Chapter 54: Hurricane season – a return to the States

Our insurance provider requires us to find a hurricane hole in the Caribbean or move north or south out of the region.

Many full time cruisers drop down to Grenada, an island still in the Caribbean above South America that is deemed safe. There are many other places called hurricane holes that provide boaters a safe haven from June to November. Other boaters have their boat pulled out and stored on the hard, taking a few months off to travel home to see friends and family.

We've decided to head north to the States. Considering our plans to head into the Pacific next year or the following year, now is the time to visit with our family and friends in America.

The plan is to stop in Florida first, meeting up with my father and his wife Suzi. I haven't seen him in a very long time (perhaps seven or eight years) and Sienna (age 6 now) has never met him.

After Florida, we'll head to North Carolina, staying in Wilmington to get boat work done. Within a couple hours from the marina are my brother and his family and my mom and stepfather. And then we may or may not sail up to New York and take a flight up to my hometown of Rochester to visit my grandparents, aunt, uncle and friends. Either way, we'll get to Rochester; it's just a matter of where we'll leave the boat.

For five months we'll spend time getting the boat serviced, visit with family and friends and do a bit of sightseeing.

So why my inner turmoil?

On one hand I'm super excited to see my family. I can't wait to get a hug from my dad and have him take a look at his amazing granddaughter. I can't wait to lounge out on my mom's sofa and get home cooking fed to me on request (mom spoils me when I come home). I'm excited to see my brother and sister-in-law – we always have a blast whether we're sitting in front of the television, doing a Segway tour of a city or hiking a mountain. And having plans to see all my family up in New York is very exciting.

But, I'm scared and I'm not sure why.

Perhaps I don't want to leave the freedom of being at anchor and not having anything planned out. Maybe I'm afraid that returning to land will make me feel constricted.

I'm scared that I'll go shopping and see amazingly lovely things that I know I can't buy because I don't have a house to store them in. I'm worried that Sienna will be affected by all the commercialism and develop an "I want" list a mile long.

I'm also afraid that perhaps I'll like being "home" so much I won't want to leave.

Some days I look out at the beautiful sea, the tropical beaches and open sky thinking I'll never want to leave this lifestyle.

Other days I want to curl up on a sofa in a large house with air conditioning, eat chili and have a shopping spree on Amazon.com for next day delivery. The old Kim loved to shop...Often it wasn't so much about actually buying things, it was more about window shopping – online or in person.

My old daily routine was to walk into town (in Aylesbury or Gosport, England) get a coffee at the coffee shop while doing work. I'd then wander for an hour or two looking in shops. If I entered a bookshop I'd be an extra hour – I LOVE REAL BOOKS and I love taking hours to read the back of books, smell the bookstore smells and get lost in fact and fiction. For two years I've had to get lost on Kindle, and let me say, it's not the same!

So...perhaps I'm scared that our five-month stay in and around North Carolina might demonstrate what I no longer have.

It's been 20 years since I've stayed in the States for longer than a vacation. Not only am I going "home" I'm taking my home with me. Will I want to keep both homes in one place? Will I want to get a real home on land and be close to my family so that I can go to my nephew's soccer games, help my mom with her garden and provide my daughter with the kind of upbringing I experienced?

Some days it's hard being abnormal. Some days it's difficult being the person who goes against the grain and says "I'm going to do it my way…"

I suppose it's time, or the season, for me to bring my home "home" and I'll just have to wait and see what that means for me.

[See Appendix A, 'V20. USVI to USA Voyage' for several video links]

Chapter 55: Arriving in America

We arrived in Fort Lauderdale, mooring up at the Hyatt Regency Pier 66 Marina. When we first entered the marina we didn't know how long we'd stay. A tropical storm was gaining strength. It would be a waiting game.

Since arriving I've been experiencing massive highs.

I've binged on American food and my belly is reflecting my overconsumption. I wouldn't be surprised if someone asks how many weeks pregnant I am. So far I've had pizza, chicken wings, hamburgers, clam chowder, grilled cheese and bacon, potato skins, nachos and on the higher end, Oysters Rockefeller, macadamia encrusted sea bass, prime rib and rib-eye steak. And those are just the lunch and dinners... For breakfast I've sampled the entire selection of bagel and egg sandwiches at the chain Eisenstein Bros Bagels.

Aside from the food selection my head has been spinning at all the shops. Just going into Walgreens caused a massive overload. With so many things to see, I spent an hour just walking along the aisles.

Simon found me on the floor grabbing as many hair dye kits as I could pull out. I'm so accustomed to making multi-purchases of the same things because I often can't ever find them again! Simon reminded me that I don't need to buy out the store anymore – I can get hair dye anywhere and everywhere. Heck, here in America I can probably have it delivered by a drone within 15 minutes.

We visited Sawgrass Mills Mall, and I'm not kidding when I thought about calling a taxi to get back to our car. Apparently it's Florida's second largest attraction behind Disney World!

From one end to the other it took us over 40 minutes to walk it. The stores, the sales, the little shops in the walk way offering new hair straighteners, miracle moisturizers, teeth whitening, and on and on made my head spin. I felt almost numb. Part of me was excited, part of me wanted to go crazy and buy things and then part of me felt lost.

Added to that my father and his wife drove from the west coast of Florida to meet us at the marina.

Considering that I haven't seen my dad in about 10 years and haven't really spoken to him in over two years, it was an emotional time.

I had emailed him to ask if he wanted to meet his 6-year-old granddaughter. The minute I told my dad where we were, they booked a room at our hotel and drove from Sarasota the very next day.

Our reunion couldn't have been more enjoyable. Sienna was adorable, giving hugs to both of them, and the conversation flowed.

There's no definite reason why my father and I didn't talk or see each other. Perhaps we were both scarred by life's experiences and needed time to heal ourselves. Being with my dad was like meeting up with an old friend from school. I didn't feel like time had passed without him.

So…food, shops, seeing my dad and what else could I compact into the first four days in my home country?

Simon and I took Sienna to the hotel pool each day. Every three hours she would come up to us and say that her new-found friends are leaving and hang her head. Usually, within five minutes, she would have a new set of friends…but for all of us I think it's getting annoying to say goodbye to people so often.

We sailed non-stop for three days to North Carolina where we had the boat hauled out.

While the boat was being worked on we stayed with my brother and then moved *Britican* to Charleston, South Carolina, so we could have Sienna spend some time in a real school.

Part of me wants Sienna to understand what a full day of school is like. I think that time at a real school will help her.

Over the course of the last couple of years we've had some serious lows, like being laid up for a month longer than expected. We've had some serious highs, like meeting friends who are so amazing that they've become family. Simon, Sienna and I have enjoyed nature at its best – hiking through rainforests, swimming with whales, watching volcanoes erupt, eating fruit right from the trees, and having the sea dance for us every day.

We've also experienced nature in bad times. In fact, the most scared I've ever been is when sailing our boat through gusts of 50 mph winds, massive 30 foot waves, lightning and thunder in the pitch black off the coast of Morocco.

For the most part, I loved moving from one place to the next, always seeing new sights or meeting new people. Every once in a while I'd get a bit down, usually when stuck in a marina for longer than expected.

Looking back, and although we took various courses and had our own smaller sailboat to practice with, nothing could have prepared us for buying a larger boat and taking on the world.

In the beginning, money flew out of our bank account and the results were mediocre at best. I learned never to use a marine service provider unless I could come up with a handful of previous happy customers. Over 75 percent of the work we had done had to be done again.

Eventually, however, we did meet some exceptional engineers, technicians and marine service companies that became our life line. It took a while to find the good providers, but when we did we were ever so grateful.

Interestingly, I also discovered that a boat is not like a house from a servicing and repairs perspective.

With a house, you can do your best to keep the lawn and house looking good; perhaps a lick of paint now and again in addition to routine lawn and garden maintenance. From time to time the boiler or heating system might break, but after a professional comes out, it will be good to go for a while.

Sure…the fridge or the washing machine might give up the ghost, but a replacement is "only" $800. And repairs are a walk in the park. Something breaks, you get in the car, drive to the store, easily find what you need and return home to have it fixed the same day.

When living on a boat (used or new), servicing and repairs are a way of life. It's not something that happens every now and again. Every single day there's a list of things that need fixing. Usually the problem is intermittent and no amount of testing various scenarios provides a quick diagnosis as to what the actual problem really is. For two years we've had an issue with our AIS, a positioning signal that tells us what boats are in the area and lets other boats know where we are. Sometimes it works for weeks and other times it comes and goes every five minutes. We've had over 10 experts look at it and it's never changed. A few times it's gone down for a week or so and then miraculously it comes back to life.

And when something "easy" breaks it's not a matter of going to the store, finding a replacement and then fixing it. Usually, it's a matter of rummaging through your spare parts box and praying that if you don't have the exact part you need, you have something similar that might work. Failing that, it's a dinghy ride to shore, miles of walking around asking for help, usually in a foreign language, and after a couple days the best-case scenario is to order a part from USA or the UK that might arrive in a week.

The part usually takes a month to arrive and in some cases you have to bribe the local post office to release it to you. (As a side note, if you need a part and you're not in a First World country, your best bet is to pay for a friend to fly with it out to you. In the end, that is usually the least expensive option.)

In two years we've only ever had to wait a couple extra weeks waiting for a part. We have, however, had work schedules increase from one month to two (and even longer). It's no one's fault either – if you combine sun, salt water and stuff that shouldn't be in sun or salt water you're asking for problems! Heck, even fresh water can do a doozy on a boat if it's not where it's supposed to be.

And interestingly it's not the extended stays that really upset me. When we thought our stay in Antigua (Caribbean Island) was going to be three weeks and it turned into six weeks, I really couldn't complain about my surroundings. The island is beautiful, the food is amazing and everyone was super helpful.

Rather, my issue is with the cost of the extended stays. A repair that's going to cost $2,000 can quickly turn to $5,000 due to more parts needed, an increase in labor, marina fees (when you would have otherwise been at anchor), having to pay for high priced food and so forth.

The other things that can catch a full time sailor out are the weather and inexperience.

Once you're on the sea for a year or so you'll come to the conclusion that the generalized weather report has no reflection on what is actually happening in your local area.

More times than not we've headed out thinking we'd have 20 knots of wind heading from the east, and it's been 40 knots coming from the west.

What we've realized is that weather reports, GRIBS and forecasts are a very loose guide. They'll generally give you an idea as to what might be happening, give or take a very wide berth.

I've met so many newbie sailors who say, "Don't worry, if we think there's any chance of a storm, we won't sail." Well…that won't work. No matter what, you will get caught in a storm or squall. And on the flip side, no matter what, you'll find yourself in situations where there's no wind.

And this leads me to inexperience. Heck, even the most experienced sailors in the world get into trouble often. It's easy to get the tides wrong, especially if you're distracted or sleep deprived after a long journey. It's easy to think you'll be able to outrun a storm. It's easy to think Google will have the answer to your latest catastrophe! It's easy to think you'll actually have access to Google!

The Catch 22 is that you have to get out there to become experienced. The key, however, is that no matter how much experience you have, you're still vulnerable. The sailors who think they know everything are probably just as dangerous as the sailor who's new to the game.

Looking back, I wouldn't be where I am today if I didn't sell up and sail away. I wouldn't know how to fix refrigeration systems, pumps, diesel engines or know how to set our sails in the multitude of various configurations. I wouldn't know what it's like to be scared out of my pants.

I also wouldn't know what it's like to have the majority of my nights filled with family memories, beautiful sunsets, amazing fresh local food, peace and freedom.

Is it bad that we've paid a lot of money out? Is it bad that we've been forced to become electricians, plumbers, carpenters, engineers, (not to mention homeschoolers)?!

Not at all. It's amazing.

The crappy stuff has helped us to learn, grow and live life. It wasn't necessarily fun to live through, but the part of the whole experience that isn't that great is far smaller than the part that's truly amazing.

Reflecting back, I think I spent quite a bit of time worrying about doing something wrong in the past or speculating about my future. To just enjoy life as it's playing out is amazing. It's so refreshing. It's so different. It feels right, that's for sure.

As I close this chapter of my life, we are located in South Carolina where Sienna will be attending school during the 2016 hurricane season. We will be visiting friends and family, and then planning the next phase of our life. While I plan a sequel to this book, I invite you to follow our adventures on my blog at https://sailingbritican.com/blog/, and feel free to contact me via email, Twitter and Facebook with your thoughts.

And please, don't be afraid to step out of your comfort zone and try something different. It might be sailing, as it was for our family, or something for which you have a real passion. Don't let an opportunity to truly live your life pass you by.

Appendix A – Links to Videos

A note about videos: When first starting our journey I had no intention on developing an on-going video diary. The very first videos are not good but hopefully you'll notice an improvement in my skills over time.

Not all videos have been included from my channel. If you want to check out the full collection, visit the YouTube Sailing Britican channel.

A note about links: I've done my best to put working links below but things break. If you're having trouble finding a particular video search for it, by name, in the YouTube search area.

Main video links

- Link to my YouTube SailingBritican Channel:
  https://www.youtube.com/c/Sailingbritican

- Link to my YouTube Britican Galley recipes:
  https://www.youtube.com/channel/UC629tnYwtbKXZMduPAD
  n0sA

Links in reference to the chronology of the book

V1. Buying the boat
- Video 1: Sell Up & Sail Away – Step 1 (Video 1):

  https://youtu.be/Epdpqn8aQSU?list=PLIdscMcv4lOu0xAg7s6C
  bPaX8M3bSosdu

- Video 2: Sell Up & Sail Away – Step 2 (Video 2):

  https://youtu.be/F_cQmnAvobU?list=PLIdscMcv4lOu0xAg7s6C
  bPaX8M3bSosdu

- Video 3: Sell Up & Sail Away – Step 3 (Video 5):

  https://youtu.be/1lmmkpVGUNw?list=PLIdscMcv4lOu0xAg7s6
  CbPaX8M3bSosdu

V2. Gibraltar to Malta
- The swell during the start of the storm Gibraltar to Malta (Video

  8): https://youtu.be/Z9p7KbA4SzM

- Manoel Island, Malta – Our Mooring (Video 9):

  https://youtu.be/fA7PIe90NRg

- Leaving Gibraltar heading towards Malta (Video 10):

  https://youtu.be/8_nThpHy1ew

V3. Sailing from Malta to Sicily
- Sailing from Malta to Sicily (Video 11): https://youtu.be/u-Xq-
  IGi1i0

V4. Corinth Canal
- Sailing through the Corinth Canal (Video 16):

  https://youtu.be/gJUVzD9J_CU

V5. Preveza Refit

- Preveza Greece refit of our Oyster 56' (Video 25): https://youtu.be/-pFxke3jTEg

V6. A child living on a boat

- What's it like to be a 5 year old living on a sailboat (Video 28): https://youtu.be/35oIBINLykI

V7. Port Kastos

- Port Kastos Greek Ionian – A 360 View (Video 29): https://youtu.be/6JXtxt7-gTI

V8. Riposto Marina

- Sailing into an Italian Marina – Riposto Marina, Sicily (Video 30): https://youtu.be/YKdr0MuLbnU

V9. Southwest coast of Italy

- Sailing up the southwest coast of Italy – Part 1 (Video 32): https://youtu.be/z9jCz9ScAlU

- Sailing up the southwest coast of Italy – Part 2 (Video 33): https://youtu.be/B_GxFaXor84

V10. Bonifacio

- Sailing into Bonafacio on the French Island of Corsica (Video 34): https://youtu.be/u-wA1QQP7dM

V11. Crossing the Atlantic Ocean

- Part 1: Atlantic Crossing with the Atlantic Rally for Cruisers ARC (Video 36): https://youtu.be/WJJcbj3-ZrE

- Part 2: Atlantic Crossing with the Atlantic Rally for Cruisers ARC (Video 37): https://youtu.be/hm5XBELhYBw

- Part 3: Atlantic Crossing with the Atlantic Rally for Cruisers ARC (Video 38): https://youtu.be/M4YRw86V2tk

V12. Discovering Bequia

- Discover Bequia Island, St Vincent and the Grenadines (Video 39): https://youtu.be/R6iyNm9IUBI

V13. Mustique

- Sailing to Mustique, St Vincent and the Grenadines (Video 40): https://youtu.be/uuq7Anpl9E0

V14. Tobago Cays

- Tobago Cays, St Vincent and the Grenadines (Video 41): https://youtu.be/5tu9xRdUHwU

V15. What to do during marina visits

- 12 Things to do to make the most of a marina visit (Video 43): https://youtu.be/YFGFsckRemk

V16. Martinique

- Sailing around Martinique in the Caribbean (Video 44): https://youtu.be/EkIdjIjzjFI

V17. Dominica

- Part 1 of 2: The Caribbean's largest secret – Dominica (Video 47): https://youtu.be/Iaan14v0eKc

- Part 2 of 2: The Caribbean's largest secret – Dominica (Video 48): https://youtu.be/pqHCYRzkLsw

V18. Racing in the Oyster Regatta

- Does Britican win the Oyster Regatta Part 1 (Video 51): https://youtu.be/OLXzkojGfFs

- Does Britican win the Oyster Regatta Part 2 (Video 52): https://youtu.be/kgWlta9MaSE

V19. British Virgin Islands

- Sailing around the British Virgin Islands (Video: 54): https://youtu.be/On3Bnwdi12Y

V20. USVI to USA Voyage

- Part 1: Sailing from USVI to North Carolina: Puerto Rico (Video 57): https://youtu.be/uwlu5YZ0xkg

- Part 2: Sailing from USVI to North Carolina: Grand Turk (Video 58): https://youtu.be/G3B5X9bsSAg

- Part 3: Sailing from USVI to North Carolina: Provo, Caicos (Video 60): https://youtu.be/b3QsdnP1ZHA

- Part 4: Sailing from USVI to North Carolina: Hogsty Reef (Video 61): https://youtu.be/eyYsIOWW38E

- Part 5: Sailing from USVI to North Carolina: Fort Lauderdale (Video 62): https://youtu.be/pI6qsFbJqk0

- Part 6: Sailing from USVI to North Carolina: North Carolina (Video 63): https://youtu.be/z5gHdjKS5lw

Visit the Sailing Britican YouTube channel to catch up on what's happened since arriving in North Carolina. Visit the channel here: https://www.youtube.com/c/Sailingbritican

Make sure to hit the 'subscribe' button and you'll then be notified every time I upload a new video.

Appendix B – Other Publications by Kimberly Brown

Find out more information about these guides on offer at: https://sailingbritican.com/shop/

Boat Buying: Boat Ownership Costs

Have you been trying to get an answer to the question, "How much does it cost to buy, own and maintain a boat?" Once and for all you can finally discover an honest answer by using these budgeting and forecasting checklists.

- Avoid missing key costs that have the potential to make or break your budget (and the fulfillment of your dream)
- Discover all the costs you didn't know you needed to know about
- Remove uncertainty
- Live the dream

Boat Buying: How To Live The Dream

This 'Boat Buying: How To Live The Dream' workbook offers a variety of exercises to help the reader set goals while removing limiting beliefs about what is and is not possible. These are the methods my husband and I used to go from living in the rat race to sailing around the world. If used properly, this workbook has the potential to help you get your boat and live your dream soon...very soon!

Boat Buying: Pre-Viewing Questions

The questions enclosed within this guide have been created to help you to initiate the boat buying process. Once you find a boat that seems to fit most of your requirements the next step is to call or email the owner/broker to request more information. The 'Boat Buying: Pre-Viewing Questions' will help you to:

- Save time: quickly weed out unacceptable boats and reduce the likelihood for disappointment
- Save money: avoid unnecessary travel costs looking at boats that don't meet your requirements

Boat Buying: Viewing Boats to Buy

Congratulations on your decision to start viewing boats to buy! Out of all the guides I create this one will potentially save you the most...and this is the one that boat sellers and boat brokers don't want you to see.

- Save money - avoid overlooking potentially disastrous issues, or worse, buying the wrong boat for you
- Save time - you don't have to research what to look for - it's all laid out in one consist action-oriented guide
- Prevent your dream from becoming a nightmare - take responsibility for your decision and buy wisely

Boat Safety: Hurricane Preparedness

Living in an area that has the potential for hurricanes or typhoons can be nerve wrecking, unsettling and down right horrifying. This 'Boat Safety: Hurricane Preparedness' guide was created so to help you:

- Save time researching how to best prepare your boat for an imminent hurricane
- Save money knowing what to do, when to do it and how to do it
- Reduce the anxiety and stress associated with hurricane planning

Boat Safety: VHF Radio Broadcasts

'Boat Safety: VHF Radio Broadcasts' is a boaters must-have VHF Radio broadcast reference guide. When using the VHF to call another boat, marina or send a broadcast to all boats (MAYDAY, etc.) there are set steps to take and very specific words to use. This guide will help the user to:

- reduce mistakes
- lessen anxiety
- make speaking over the radio easier

Boat Safety: Preparing for Seasickness

Seasickness sucks! I know first hand because I'm a massive sufferer. Even after three years of living full time on a boat I have problems. There are ways, however, for preparing for seasickness. Some people can avoid it, others can mitigate its affects and many are afflicted only mildly. This guide is for anyone afraid of getting seasick or having to deal with someone who is sick. It's fast, hard-hitting and full of potential solutions.

Boat Owners: Choosing A Dinghy

Choosing the right dinghy depends on a wide range of factors. I've you've had a large amount of experience with dinghies you'll know what you like versus what you don't like. But what if you haven't had much experience?

- Save money by getting what you want rather than what a sales professional tells you what you want
- Save time trying to figure out what's best for you and your travel plans
- Avoid getting a dinghy that doesn't do what you need it to do

Boat Owners: Choosing A Marina

Whether you're looking for a long-term home for your boat or in the process of finding a seasonal berth for safe keeping, this checklist will help you to get answer for over 60 questions - many of which you probably didn't know you needed to ask.

- Save time: choose the right marina for you and your boat
- Save money: understand the extra costs at each marina to determine what's best for your budget
- Remove unknowns: determine if your expectations will be met or not

Boat Owners: Selecting Insurance

When looking for the best value for money it's important to call around and compare and contrast a few insurance providers. It's also imperative to know that the cheapest deal isn't always the best. Use the 'Boat Owners: Selecting Insurance' guide to ask the questions necessary to make a final decision.

Boat Basics: Mooring Balls Explained

Entering a mooring ball field can be intimidating at first. And in busy areas like the Caribbean and around several Mediterranean countries mooring fields can be jam-packed. Avoid getting laughed at by missing the mark. This 'Boat Basics: Mooring Balls Explained' guide will help you to:

- Properly prepare to moor safely and securely
- Set up good lines of communication
- Understand how best to secure the mooring
- Avoid making common mistakes

More guides coming soon. Visit my shop to see the full collection here: https://sailingbritican.com/shop/

Made in the USA
Columbia,
30 July 20